This is all about my dissertation

I BN

1 1 0282229 7

LORD HAW HAW

LORD HAW HAW

The English Voice of Nazi Germany

Peter Martland

THE NATIONAL ARCHIVES

First published in 2003 by

The National Archives
Kew
Richmond
Surrey
TW9 4DU
UK

www.nationalarchives.gov.uk

The National Archives was formed when the Public Record Office and
Historical Manuscripts Commission combined in April 2003

ISBN 1 903365 17 1

All images from The National Archives, UK.
Front of jacket: William Joyce photograph found at the Joyces' Apen residence
(KV 2/346); newspaper image from the William L. Shirer article in the
Sunday Chronicle, 14 September 1941 (KV 2/245/274); Nazi emblem from Joyce's
certificate of war merit (KV 2/250/2). Back of jacket: William Joyce photograph
from the MI5 files (KV 2/246).

Typeset by Textype, Cambridge
Printed in UK by Biddles, Guildford, Surrey

Contents

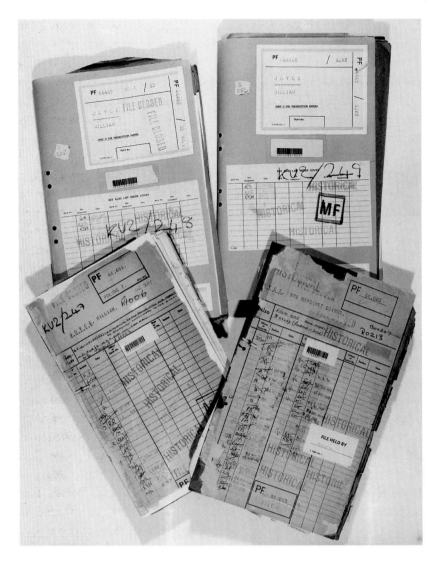

A selection of the MI5 files on William and Margaret Joyce.

Preface

In January 1946, eight months after the Second World War ended in Europe, the American-born Nazi propaganda broadcaster William Joyce, popularly known as Lord Haw Haw, had the unwelcome distinction of being the last person in Britain ever to be hanged for high treason. His three-day Old Bailey trial held in September 1945 ended with his conviction not for espionage offences or other acts of treachery, but rather for giving aid and comfort to Britain's enemies. This, the court decided, he gave through the hundreds of radio broadcasts he made from Germany during the first year of the war. Because he held a British passport during this critical period, obtained through a criminal deception, the court decided he owed allegiance to the British Crown. However, as far as the British public was concerned, Joyce was the propaganda broadcaster whose activities had first amused then angered them from the earliest days of the war till his final drunken microphone appearance a few days before the German capitulation.

Although there have been many books concerning William Joyce, this work is different, examining the story from a fresh angle: through the eyes of those in the British intelligence services who pursued him from his teenage dalliance with British fascism in the 1920s to his execution in 1946. Until the late 1990s it would have been impossible to write a book from this perspective, because until that time the British intelligence services had no policy of document release. However the early 1990s saw not only the end of the Cold War but also, for the first time in their history, the placing of Britain's intelligence agencies on a statutory footing. Before that seminal change, the British government had always refused to discuss the activities of its intelligence services or even acknowledge their existence. In those circumstances, access to files held by the Security Service, popularly known as MI5, was out of the question. However, in this new climate of openness, MI5 instituted a programme to release many of its historic files into the public domain by means of deposits at The National Archives (then the

Public Record Office), at Kew, near London. In the year 2000, as part of this policy, MI5 deposited a large number of files relating to the Second World War. Among these were twelve bulky volumes and other bundles of papers and artefacts relating to the case of William Joyce. This unique collection contains many new and important documents, including a detailed journal Joyce kept between 27 February and 1 May 1945, which provides remarkable insights into his thinking during this critical period of his life and career. In addition to the paper files, the collection contains a number of personal artefacts, such as his gold cuff links, signet ring, watch, together with photographs and the war merit cross, first class, and an accompanying certificate signed by Adolf Hitler. A few months later, MI5 released files concerning Joyce's second wife, the British-born Margaret Joyce (née White). She accompanied her husband to Germany in late August 1939, and was a regular broadcaster. Known as Lady Haw Haw, she specialized in broadcasts to the women of Britain. Her file includes a previously unknown, but as it turns out vitally important, diary she kept during the war years.

Between them these extraordinary files contain a mass of previously unseen evidence, from which it has been possible to construct a fresh picture of the man who was William Joyce and the motives that drove him to eventual destruction. This book has been written in order to make this material more readily available to those not in a position to visit The National Archives and is divided into two parts. The first tells the story of William and Margaret Joyce through the medium of the documents that make up their MI5 files, and the second takes the form of an annotated selection of the most important documents in the collection. It is from these unique sources, and therefore through the eyes of his MI5 pursuers, that this story of William Joyce, Lord Haw Haw, is told.

Peter Martland
Cambridge, England

Acknowledgements

This book appears as part of The National Archives' 'Secret History Files' series of publications. It is therefore to my editor, Sheila Knight, who asked me to write this book, that my thanks must first go. Her patience, encouragement and understanding made a real difference to the finished work. Many others helped me get my ideas into shape, including Christopher Andrew and Kurt Lipstein, both of Cambridge University. They, together with Bruce Phillips of Scarecrow Press, our American distributor, have my grateful thanks, though any mistakes are mine and not theirs.

I also thank Michael and Doreen Forman of Historia Publishing – The Forman Archive for their kind permission to reproduce from the Joyces' personal correspondence and journal

William Joyce as a young man. This photograph was found amongst other belongings at the Joyces'. deserted residence in Apen in May 1945. (KV 2/346/6)

Chapter 1

British Empire Loyalist

The strange and still controversial case of William Joyce is unique in the annals of high treason. Its controversy arises from two important facts: first that Joyce was hanged for what he said in a foreign country rather than what he did in Britain, and second because he was not a British subject, for although he had been a pre-war British resident and fascist activist, he was in fact born in New York, the son of naturalized American citizens. His conviction for high treason was based on a single and as it proved fatal error he made in the mid-1930s, when he obtained a British passport by falsely claiming to be a British subject born in Ireland. At his 1945 trial, prosecutors contended that as a British passport holder Joyce, notwithstanding the criminal deception, enjoyed the protection of the British Crown. Therefore, they argued, he owed allegiance to the Crown; the passport expired in July 1940 nearly a year after he began his broadcasts, and that was sufficient to hang him. The issues raised by the trial conviction and execution continue to excite criticism, not least among many Irish people who erroneously believe he was an Irishman, but also among lawyers, many of whom regard the prosecution arguments as tendentious, bringing the law of treason into disrepute.

At the time of his trial and execution there was little sympathy for William Joyce, for by the end of the Second World War he was, after Adolf Hitler, by far the most detested man in Britain. It was his sinister, sneering, fake upper-class accent that did it (and got him the name Lord Haw Haw), together with the boastful, vile and vindictive broadcasts he made over the radio. Joyce's notoriety was earned during the early years of the war, especially between 1939 and 1941, specifically in 1940 when, to many, Britain appeared defeated and facing imminent invasion by the German army and the destruction of its cities by German bombers. Certainly those broadcasts sealed his reputation, and, as it turned out, his fate as the most recognizable English-speaking voice over the wartime radio; that is, after Winston Churchill. Yet even today and despite many biographies, the man behind the voice of Lord Haw Haw, the individual that was William Joyce, remains something of an enigma. This work seeks to break through that enigma and shed new light on the life of this remarkable man. It does this by examining his life, career, trial and execution through a unique source and one that has only recently been made available: the eyes of those who relentlessly pursued him, the agents of the British Security Service (MI5).

American beginnings

One of the main points of contention at William Joyce's trial was the location of his birth and critically his nationality. As this issue reaches into the heart of this strange man's life, the relevant MI5 papers provide a useful starting point for the Joyce story. The files contain many hundreds of documents relating to his parents, his birth and his claim to American nationality. Curiously, they appear in the later stages of the files, when the assertions he was a US citizen were brought to the attention of the British authorities. At the time they were reviewing the evidence against him with a view to a post-war prosecution for treason, as until that point the British had always assumed Joyce was a British subject born in Ireland, and as such regarded him as a British renegade working for the Nazis. However this assertion was challenged in June 1945 during a court appearance prior to his trial when his lawyer argued Joyce was in fact a native-born American whose parents were both naturalized US citizens. The lawyer also contended that in 1940, at a time when Germany and the United States were still at peace, Joyce had taken German citizenship – in these circumstances, the lawyer's argument went, Joyce had no obligations to the British Crown. The Joyce MI5 files note in meticulous detail this key point of the defence case, making it evident that the agency was fearful that this central issue might bring about the collapse of the Crown case. To prevent this, MI5 and the US Federal Bureau of Investigation (FBI) mobilized their considerable resources and spent enormous amounts of time and effort to determine Joyce's true status. As a consequence, there emerges from the files a wealth of detailed information, which taken together builds up a vivid picture of William Joyce's family background.

Gathering the necessary information was not at all plain sailing for the FBI, who had the unenviable task of trying to locate the US naturalization papers relating to Joyce's father, a man with the not uncommon name of Michael Francis Joyce. Unfortunately, Michael Joyce died in February 1941 some months after enemy bombing destroyed the family house in Dulwich, South London, which caused the loss of practically all the Joyce family papers. MI5 did obtain, via the British embassy in Dublin, a copy of Michael Francis Joyce's Irish birth certificate, which now forms part of the Joyce files. This shows he was born in Ballinrobe, County Mayo, Ireland on 9 December 1866. His father (William's grandfather), Martin Joyce, was an illiterate farmer (he was unable to sign his name as the informant of the birth) from Killour, and his mother was Mary Joyce née Naughton.[1] (**document 7**) The FBI, shadowed by British consular officials in New York who were under pressure from MI5 and the Foreign Office, itself reacting to pressure from Joyce's lawyers, set about locating Michael Joyce's naturalization papers. The fragmented nature of the naturalization process in the years prior to 1895, when Joyce senior became a US citizen, compounded their difficulties. Before that date responsibility for naturalization and granting of citizenship lay not with the Federal government but with individual states, and the process was administered through the district court system. This meant that prior to 1895 the United States had no central record of naturalization applications or grants of citizenship. During the early summer of 1945, FBI agents checked the records of several district jurisdictions in and around New York and came up with a total of 21 men with the name Michael Joyce who had been naturalized within the relevant time frame. They had all been born in Ireland, all were of about the right age, but unfortunately none was the right man. (**document 1**) However, on 18 August, J. Edgar Hoover, the director of the FBI, despatched information to London proving Joyce's assertion that his father was a naturalized US citizen. FBI agents discovered his US naturalization had taken place in the New Jersey district court at

---

[1] Entry of a birth relating to Michael Francis Joyce. William Joyce files, The National Archives, Kew (hereafter Joyce files) KV 2/246/409.

Hudson County on 25 October 1894. The documentation forwarded to London included a photostat of the original 1892 application made by Michael Joyce seeking US citizenship, which noted the date of his arrival in the USA as May 1888 and his age as being 25. The final petition to court requesting the granting of US citizenship, dated October 1894, was also photostatted and fully confirmed Joyce's new status.[2] (**document 2**)

The FBI also located and photostatted a US immigration record dated 30 April 1905 relating to the arrival in the United States of William Joyce's mother. Known to friends and family as 'Queenie', Gertrude Emily Brooke was a native of Shaw, near Oldham in Lancashire, and was 25 years old when she landed in New York, accompanied by her brother Edgar Brooke.[3] The purpose of their visit was to effect Michael and Gertrude's marriage. (**document 3**) The couple had first met in the town of Galway, Ireland, where the Brooke family spent holidays; Gertrude's father Dr William Brooke was a respected physician and a medical officer of health in Lancashire. It appears Michael Joyce returned to Ireland on a number of occasions and also stayed in Galway. It was during the course of these visits the couple met.[4] They married on 2 May 1905 in All Saints Roman Catholic Church at 47 East 129 Street, New York. The church and New York city records indicate Michael Joyce's occupation as a building contractor (though he was later described by his son as an architect), but no occupation was placed against Gertrude's name. On 24 April 1906 their first child was born, a boy they called William.[5] (**document 6**)

Taken together, the information gathered by the FBI in 1945 made it clear to both US and British authorities that William Joyce was correct in asserting he was born an American citizen to parents who had acquired US citizenship either by naturalization or by marriage. Despite this setback, the prosecution believed they still had a case that would hang Joyce, and clearly Joyce and his lawyers believed they had the perfect defence to the charge of treason.

[2] FBI documents. Joyce files KV 2/246.
[3] US immigration record for Gertrude and Edgar Brooke. Joyce files KV 2/245/337a.
[4] Interview statement of Gilbert Brooke, Derbyshire County Police, 6 August 1945. Joyce files KV 2/246/477.
[5] Entry of a birth relating to William Joyce. Joyce files KV 2/250/1.

Irish upbringing

The Joyce family left the United States in the autumn of 1909, when William was 3½ years old. (**document 4**) Even then it appears he was showing signs of a precocious intellect. In a Special Branch interview, John Macnab, a former fascist intimate, related how Joyce told him he had learned the German language as a small child in the United States, through a friendship with a German-speaking family.[6] No official record survives to indicate precisely when the Joyce family left the United States, though surviving evidence suggests Michael Joyce left New York for Ballinrobe, County Mayo in October 1909, with Gertrude and William following the next month.[7] In the course of an article published in the German newspaper *Hamburger Fremdenblatt* on 6 October 1944, William Joyce explained why the family left New York. He wrote:

> I inherited the unambiguous dislike of my mother for the Americans. And I remember how once when I was already old enough to understand the sense of what she was saying, she said to me 'I shall never in my life forget how lonely I have felt in America. Even before you were born you were the only comfort in this atmosphere of strangeness, lack of understanding, and hostility'.[8]

All that survives is the tendentious statement Michael Joyce made to his children, in which he claimed to have lost his American citizenship because of some kind of failure to renew it. The Joyce MI5 files contain a series of helpful reports of interviews conducted by Derbyshire County Police with Gilbert Brooke, Joyce's uncle, during and shortly after the Second World War. (**document 24**) These, together with a transcript of evidence given by Frank and Quentin Joyce, William's younger brothers, to the wartime Home

---

[6] Advisory Committee's examination of John Macnab. Undated. Joyce files KV 2/248.

[7] See trial evidence of Detective Superintendent John Woodmansey, Lancashire County Constabulary, trial transcript, p. 76. Joyce files KV 2/250/2.

[8] English translation of part of an article written by William Joyce, 6 October 1944. Joyce files KV 2/245/354a.

Office Advisory Committee and at the Old Bailey trial, help build a picture of the Joyce family. The move back to Ireland evidently proved critical in forming William Joyce's own warped outlook on life. In his police statement, Gilbert Brooke claimed the Joyce marriage was unhappy, a fact he ascribed to religious differences: Michael Joyce was a Roman Catholic and Gertrude a Protestant. William's younger brother Frank Joyce was born in 1912 at Westport in the West of Ireland. After his birth the family moved to Galway, where his father became manager of the Galway Bus Company.[9] At that stage in his life Michael Joyce was evidently a man of some substance and owned a row of houses at Rutledge Terrace, Rockbarton, Salthill, a Galway suburb; the family lived at 1 Rutledge Terrace, deriving rental income from the rest of the block. Politically they were all staunch British Empire Loyalists; unfortunately the area in which they had chosen to live was staunchly nationalist. This was at a time when the country was slipping into anarchy and revolution as a result of sectarian divisions over the issue of Home Rule, the First World War and, in 1916, the Easter Rising.

The 3½-year-old William Joyce was educated first at the Catholic Convent of Mercy School, then, between 1915 and 1921, at a Jesuit-run secondary school, St Ignatius College, Galway.[10] Already a precocious child, his opinions even as a schoolboy were, according to Gilbert Brooke's account, well-formed and extreme. This was something the school authorities failed to appreciate, and, as a consequence, during the later phases of the 'Troubles' he was either removed or left St Ignatius College.[11] Further evidence from this period of his life appeared during the Second World War. A letter in the *News Review* on 4 April 1940 from a Galway contemporary, responding to an earlier article about Joyce, observed:

> Ever since those broadcasts started I was struck by the familiarity of that voice. I often mentioned that I had heard that voice before but could not place it, but the

---

[9] 1945 police interview with Gilbert Brooke. Joyce files KV 2/246/477.
[10] K. N. Egan, principal's secretary, University of London, Senate House. Joyce files KV 2/246/466a.
[11] Statement by Gilbert Brooke, 18 March 1940. Joyce files KV 2/245/230b.

minute I saw your photograph and read the paragraph,
I knew at once it was Willie. Even as a small precocious
child he had the same sneering venom when speaking of
anything Irish or pertaining to Galway. He has not lost
this 'accomplishment' – rather it is much more
pronounced when criticising Mr Churchill. I have shown
News Review to some of Willie's schoolmates. Each had
the same story of recognising 'Lord Haw Haw's' voice
but were puzzled by its familiarity.[12]

Further evidence from his childhood in Ireland appeared in a July
1940 GPO mail intercept of a letter from another Galway resident,
this time writing to a friend in England. In it the writer claimed to
recognize Joyce's voice from his radio broadcasts, noting: 'I get
tickled to death when I hear his marvellous accent. One of the Jesuit
priests recognised his voice. He happened to be at their day school
for a bit until they cleared him [sic]'.[13]

William Joyce always maintained he was a member of the
infamous 'Black and Tans'. Made up largely of First World War
veterans, this force of British irregulars was drafted into Ireland to
quell the Irish revolution, and between 1919 and 1921 operated a
reign of terror. Their violent and murderous methods prefigured the
methodology favoured by German fascists, though in the end they
failed to quell the revolution. Some historians have doubted William
Joyce's claims that he had been a member of the Black and Tans,
citing his extreme youth and inexperience – during these years he
was aged between thirteen and sixteen. It was therefore interesting
to see a number of documents in the MI5 files giving credence to at
least some of his assertions. One takes the form of a letter written by
a childhood contemporary, A.W. Miles Webb, to the Wiltshire police
in 1945 and later passed to MI5. In it Webb claimed he had been an
English boy living in Galway during these years and to have been
one of Joyce's school friends: they were about the same age.
Although MI5 dismissed the letter as an irrelevance adding little
to the agency's own knowledge, the letter contains a number of

[12] Press cutting: *News Review,* 4 April 1940. Joyce files KV 2/245/234b.
[13] Terminal Mails report, 15 July 1940. Joyce files KV 2/245/247a.

fascinating insights into the personality of the young Joyce. For example, Webb described him as being 'very pro-British', a fact Joyce perversely claimed to the end of his life. Webb also described him as speaking in 'an exaggerated fashion and bubbled over with self-importance', again a feature of his interwar public speaking and wartime broadcasts. The letter relates how Joyce spent considerable amounts of time at the 'Black and Tans' local barracks and at Lenaboy Castle, then the headquarters of the Royal Irish Constabulary Auxiliary Cadets. Webb confessed to liking the young Willie Joyce, though he noted that the townspeople, particularly those who were anti-British, believed he was a police spy engaged in betraying Irishmen to the Crown forces. Webb also observed Joyce's fanaticism, stating:

> Certainly he reviled everyone who held anti-British views. There is no one more pro-British than your extreme Irish loyalist, he is almost as fanatic as Joyce certainly was and he was heartily detested by, not only the ordinary local Irish townspeople but even by the average loyalist too.[14]

Webb said he liked and respected his young firebrand friend, and on one occasion visited Lenaboy Castle with him. In his letter Webb asserted: 'I doubt if Joyce was "officially" a police spy but I have no doubt on the other hand that he interested the Auxiliaries and they made use of him'.[15] He recalled one particular event and in retelling it unintentionally provides an insight into William Joyce's mindset. It concerned the funeral in Galway of two murdered British officers, one a soldier, the other a policeman. Joyce and Webb positioned themselves at the front of the crowd to watch the procession. As the military cortège passed, the troops marching with arms reversed and the band playing: 'Joyce sprang to attention and, although dressed in ordinary clothes like myself gave a most elaborate salute, holding it with a grim set face for two or three minutes with everyone gaping as much at him as at the cortège.' Webb praised

---

[14] A.W. Miles Webb to Wiltshire Constabulary, 26 June 1945. Joyce files KV 2/249/54b.
[15] Ibid.

him for his courage and said he had never forgotten the incident.[16] (**document 9**)

One of the most important, detailed and instructive documents to survive on Joyce's MI5 files is dated 21 September 1934, which is a report concerning Joyce prepared by an agent known simply as 'M'. This was Charles Henry Maxwell Knight, who had been involved with the British fascist movement from the early 1920s. This double agent proved the major source of information both to Special Branch and to MI5. Maxwell Knight's report suggests he knew William Joyce and his family intimately, whilst the detailed knowledge of his political activities confirms he was an insider, not just at the British Union of Fascists but also with predecessor organizations. The 1934 report takes the form of a personal and political appraisal of Joyce, and provides much helpful information concerning his early life in Ireland. Maxwell Knight begins by asserting that William Joyce 'is certainly a very complex character'. He then goes on to suggest his birth, upbringing and early life contributed to this, before observing: 'He is the son of Irish loyalists and was born and brought up in a very political atmosphere'. Regarding his assertions about joining the Black and Tans, Maxwell Knight reported:

> He left school at about the age of fourteen or fifteen [around 1920] and more or less ran away from home to join the Black and Tans during the Irish troubles. He was with them some time until he was sent home as being too young, and he saw battle, murder and sudden death at a very tender age.

Impressed with the young man's courage and daring, he observed: 'He was brought face to face with desperate situations and happenings even younger than the average junior officer in the war period'.[17] The information Maxwell Knight and the other sources provide suggests Joyce was a foolhardy, brave and fanatical young man. He was also something of an adventurer and a nonconformist, someone unconstrained by a conventional view of society or of established political institutions, an individual who was, even as a

---

[16] Ibid.
[17] Report, agent 'M', 21 September 1934. Joyce files KV 2/245/1b.

teenager, something of a loose cannon. His youthful experiences in the Black and Tans also suggest he was a young man who enjoyed violence – another feature of this complex personality, and something that stayed with him for the rest of his life. (**document 8**)

British fascist hero

In the years following the birth of Frank Joyce in 1912, Michael and Gertrude Joyce had three more children, remaining in Ireland until the end of the 'Troubles'. According to Frank, following the formation of the Free State in December 1921, they were, as British loyalists and having lost the protection of the British Crown (ironic in view of what he later argued at his trial), forced to leave Ireland. Whether the forced move was a consequence of William Joyce's youthful dalliance with the 'Black and Tans' or the activities of other family members remains unclear. However, Frank Joyce said of this episode: 'my people being loyalists to this country, were given a week's notice to clear out of the country or be shot. At the time my mother was nursing a child aged about two days'.[18] Although Frank claimed the forced move cost the family its wealth and property, after some moving around they were able to settle in 1923 at 3 Allison Grove, Dulwich, in South London, where they remained until the house was destroyed by enemy action during the Second World War.

Whatever the family circumstances, the eldest son William Joyce, then aged 16, began his personal quest for an education and for opportunities to make his mark either as an army officer or politically. After an unsuccessful attempt to enlist in the British Army, this quest eventually took him to London University, whose records were later used by MI5 to complete a picture of the years between his arrival as a teenager in 1922 and his departure for Nazi Germany in August 1939. After checking the university records the secretary to the principal wrote to the agency on 19 July 1945:

---

[18] This was Robert Patrick, who was born in Galway on 12 February 1922. Evidence of Frank Joyce to the Advisory Committee, 1940. Joyce files KV 2/249/61b.

> He [William Joyce] entered for the Matriculation Examination in September 1922 . . . He passed the examination in the 2nd division. In October 1922 he registered as an internal student of the University in the Faculty of Science at Battersea Polytechnic . . . He entered for the General Intermediate Examination in Science in July 1923 but failed in two of his subjects. In October 1923 he registered as an internal student of the University in the Faculty of Arts at Birkbeck College . . . He took his final examination for the B.A. Honours Degree in English (Subsidiary Modern History) in 1927, obtaining I Cl. Hons [First Class Honours].[19] (**document 14**)

In his 1934 report MI5 agent Maxwell Knight observed the cost Joyce was prepared to pay for this extraordinary record of academic achievement. It also helps place this remarkable man in perspective and highlights characteristics that remained to the fore for the rest of his life. He wrote:

> When he returned to England after the Irish trouble he commenced to educate himself and achieved comparatively brilliant success. He was as fanatical in his studies as he is in other directions, and several times during his scholastic career he reduced himself to the verge of a nervous breakdown.[20] (**document 8**)

If signs of wild fanaticism were present in Joyce's approach to education, they were also present in other spheres of his life. Each MI5 file is divided into two parts. On the right-hand side are original documents and reports, whilst on the left are minute sheets for case officer commentaries, notes and other data. These notes provide some additional information about these early London years. In fact, the first minute entry in the Joyce files is by Maxwell Knight and dated 18 January 1924. In it he claimed Joyce to be a member of the

---

[19] K. N. Egan, principal's secretary, University of London to MI5, 19 July 1945. Joyce files KV 2/246/466a.
[20] Report, agent 'M'. 21 September 1934. Joyce files KV 2/245/1b.

so-called 'K' society, also known as the 'Inner Organisation', a shadowy group of fascist thugs responsible for the breaking up of communist meetings. Maxwell Knight later claimed that in 1923, the same year as Hitler's failed Munich *putsch*, the 17-year-old Joyce had joined another shadowy group established by the highly eccentric Rotha Linton-Orman and known as the British Fascisti Ltd (later renamed the British Fascists). This group of far-right British extremists modelled themselves on Mussolini's Italian fascist movement. According to a Maxwell Knight report, Joyce was put in charge of a district in Battersea, where he 'was untiring in his efforts and made himself so obnoxious to the Communist Party that during the election of 1924 he was "razored" at a conservative [party election] meeting' in Lambeth's Bath House which had been stewarded by eleven fascists, including Joyce. In a later note Maxwell Knight observed at the end of the meeting there was the usual mêlée as known communists rushed the platform to try and seize the Union flag (**document 16**). In the ensuing confusion William Joyce was slashed across the face with a razor. He continued:

> The writer actually saw this take place. There is little doubt but that the attack on Joyce was a serious assault little short of attempted murder. His life was only saved by the action of a police officer who ran with Joyce in his arms the whole way to the nearest police station.[21]

Maxwell Knight also noted that a fascist named Webb 'marked down his assailant and felled him with a spanner'.[22] Joyce nearly bled to death and would evidently have done so but for the police officer's prompt action. This attack and Joyce's hospitalization were widely reported in the press. As a result, Joyce became a youthful hero of the embryonic British fascist movement, and for the rest of his life bore a livid scar stretching across the right-hand side of his face from ear to mouth. Joyce appears to have parted company with the British Fascists in 1925, though his commitment to fascist ideology and far-right politics remained undimmed.

---

[21] Notes, agent 'M', 'Communist disorders at political meetings', 15 June 1944. Joyce files KV 2/245/331b.
[22] Minute, 18 January 1924. Joyce files KV 2/245/1a.

During his years at London University, when he was not engaged in fascist activities, William Joyce was a member of the university Officer Training Corps (OTC). During the Second World War his application to join the OTC together with other correspondence was found preserved in the London University OTC records. The file was sent to MI5 and its contents used to build the prosecution case for his treason trial. This file of documents contained an important and insightful letter written by Joyce to the OTC adjutant. Dated 9 August 1922, just before his matriculation, Joyce asserted in this letter his ambition to seek a commission in the British army, adding:

> I have served, with the irregular forces of the Crown, in an intelligence capacity, against the Irish guerrillas. In command of a squad of subagents I was subordinate to the Late Capn. [sic] P. W. Keating, 2nd R.U.R. . . . I have a knowledge of the rudiments of musketry, bayonet fighting and squad drill.[23]

In the same letter Joyce also acknowledged his American citizenship, expressing the hope that this would not prove an impediment to his undertaking military service in the OTC or eventually becoming a British officer. This letter also contains an assertion of his absolute loyalty to Britain, pointing out that he left the United States as an infant and had no intention of ever returning to that country. (document 15) In sharp contrast, during the course of a broadcast he made in Germany in August 1944, he reviewed these youthful aspirations by observing:

> In my youth I at one time aspired to hold the King's commission [become a British army officer], but – and I say in full consciousness of the impression it will create upon my listeners – if I held the King's commission today I would desert rather than be a party to the creation of a Bolshevik hegemony in Europe.[24]

---

[23] Joyce–London University OTC correspondence, 1922 to 1925. Joyce files KV 2/245/301a.

[24] 'Views on the News'. Transcript of a William Joyce broadcast, 28 August 1944. Joyce files KV 2/245/340b.

Taken together, the words he wrote in 1922 and those he spoke in 1944 proved fateful, and they were used against him at his Old Bailey treason trial in September 1945.

In 1927 William Joyce, then aged 21, graduated from London University with a good first-class honours degree. However, according to Maxwell Knight, his earlier plans to become an officer in the British army had changed and he now looked to become a teacher with the intention of breaking into politics. To provide for his present needs, his excellent degree enabled him to gain employment as a private teacher. It appears that at this stage of his life he was able to make a reasonable living as a language teacher, as he spoke four languages, including French and German fluently, and could teach other subjects.[25] Other changes soon followed. In the year of his graduation he married his first wife Hazel Kathleen Barr, whom he had met during his time with the old British Fascists. During their marriage, which lasted eight years, the couple had two daughters, born in 1928 and 1930. When he was unmasked as Lord Haw Haw his first wife said of him: 'His friends prophesied a great career for him, but I am afraid he had a queer streak in him'.[26] In order to pursue his political ambitions Joyce joined the Junior Imperial League, then the Conservative Party's youth wing. According to Maxwell Knight, he threw himself wholeheartedly into the League and became one of its principal speakers in South London. Maxwell Knight also identified the emergence at this time of some of Joyce's more disagreeable traits, including a natural aptitude for intrigue and an abhorrence of compromise. Other traits were however more worrying and included the crude, extreme opinions of an anti-Communist, an anti-Semite and an anti-Catholic, which he articulated to anyone who would listen to them, and which later became the hallmark of his speeches, writings and broadcasts. Taken with his predisposition to and enjoyment of violence, particularly street violence, he made little progress in the Junior Imperial League. In fact he appears to have alienated his more peaceful, mainstream League colleagues. After much strife he resigned, turning his back once and for all on mainstream political

---

[25] Statement of Gilbert Brooke, 18 March 1940. Joyce files KV 2/245/230b.
[26] *Sunday Pictorial*, 17 December 1939. Joyce files KV 2/245/208a.

parties. From that point on he realized his own increasingly radical opinions could not be accommodated anywhere but within a fascist party. However his period in the Junior Imperial League was not a complete waste of time. For example, it helped him recognize, in himself, a natural talent as a public speaker, a talent he developed to good effect in the decade or so before his abandonment of Britain for Nazi Germany.

Sir Oswald Mosley and the British Union of Fascists

In 1931 the British intelligence agency popularly known as MI5 underwent a significant reorganization. Founded in 1909 as the Secret Service Bureau and headed by an army officer, Sir Vernon Kell, MI5 had many successes, particularly in its early years and during the First World War. At its peak in 1918, MI5 employed around 850 agents and held a substantial budget. Following the Bolshevik revolution in 1917 and the defeat of Germany the following year, MI5's primary role changed to one of countering Bolshevik and communist subversion in Britain, specifically in the armed forces. In 1931 War Office oversight of MI5's work ended and was replaced by the Home Office, which retains control of the renamed Security Service to the present day. At the same time the agency experienced a significant victory in the never-ending 'turf war' with the police Special Branch. On this occasion the Security Service took over responsibility for civilian subversion, acquiring oversight of all communist, fascist and other extremist subversive organizations. With these new tasks MI5 acquired and shared Special Branch agents, such as Maxwell Knight, known on the Joyce files as agent 'M'. As a consequence of all this, important individuals on the extreme right, such as William Joyce, now came within MI5's purview, although it continued to rely on Special Branch and other police reports in the tracking of Joyce's activities. Throughout the 1930s, despite these and other new burdens, the agency, in common with other branches of government, experienced severe funding problems, which seriously inhibited its work. Furthermore, until the mid-1930s, other considerations clouded close scrutiny of individuals like Joyce and fascist groups, not least the long-standing view that communist rather than fascist groups posed the main danger to Britain. Nonetheless, as the bulky William Joyce files for this period show, the Security Service was not idle in its attempts to keep track of fascist subversion.[27]

In May 1932, the 26-year-old father-of-two William Joyce registered as a PhD student in psychology at King's College, University of London, under the supervision of Professor Francis Aveling. However, the agency's wartime correspondence with London University tells of his leaving during the academic year 1933–1934,[28] the reason for leaving being the offer of a full-time job with Sir Oswald Mosley's British Union of Fascists (BUF). Formed in October 1932, Mosley based the BUF on Mussolini's Italian fascist movement; during the 1930s it was the most important and best-known fascist movement active in Britain. A baronet, Oswald Mosley was a wounded war veteran and failed mainstream politician, who entered the House of Commons in 1918 as a Conservative, but soon fell out with his party. He was subsequently re-elected as a Labour MP and served as a cabinet minister in Ramsay MacDonald's 1929 Labour government. However, that too ended with his resignation and he subsequently formed the 'New Party'. In the wake of the New Party's utter failure in the 1931 general election, Mosley began his journey to the far right of British politics. Encouraged by Mussolini's success in Italy he formed the British Union of Fascists, and William Joyce became one of its earliest recruits. Mosley's BUF specifically appealed to the patriotism of war veterans and the young, his declared intention of reversing Britain's decline attracting Joyce, who threw himself wholeheartedly into the movement – at last he had found a political home, or so it appeared.

On 4 July 1933 William Joyce applied for a British passport, in doing so falsely describing himself as a British subject by birth, asserting he had been born in Galway, Ireland. In those days additional means of proving identity, citizenship or place of birth

---

[27] For further information relating to these changes and the problems faced by the Service during the 1930s see David Curry, *A History of the Security Service: 1909 to 1945* (London, 1998).

[28] K. N. Egan, principal's secretary, University of London to MI5, 19 July 1945. Joyce files KV 2/246/466a.

were not required and no check was ever made as to the veracity of his statements. A passport was issued to him for use, as he stated on the application, in connection with business travel and for holiday purposes. Joyce renewed his passport on 24 September 1938, a further renewal being made on 24 August 1939. Two days later he used it to make good his escape from Britain. This passport expired on 1 July 1940 and it was this albeit false declaration that, five years later, brought about his conviction for treason and subsequent execution.

By 1934 William Joyce was working full time for the British Union of Fascists, with the title of Director of Research, also being described as the BUF's Director of Propaganda. Attracted by the BUF's blackshirt uniform and military-style discipline, Joyce quickly emerged as one of the movement's principal speakers, as such spending much of his time addressing political meetings up and down the country. There are many accounts of Joyce's spellbinding, tub-thumping oratory and of his ability to sway audiences – a skill that paralleled the 1920s political development of his new idol, Adolf Hitler. The William Joyce MI5 files contain minute sheets for the years 1934 and 1935 filled with information derived from Special Branch and other sources, which provide clear insights into Joyce's activities at the BUF. Earning around £300 per year ($1,200), Joyce was evidently a high flyer as a speaker and Director of Propaganda. In May 1934, for example, it was noted that Joyce had emerged as a mature public speaker. Recording an account of a BUF meeting in Surrey the minute observed: 'Joyce showed himself to be a very able speaker. Some of his remarks were rather insulting and provocative, but he managed to transform the subsequent heckling of his opponents into support for his own proposals'.[29] Yet even at this stage of his BUF career, he was fermenting trouble within the organization. MI5 minutes suggest he was trying to supplant the BUF's Chief of Staff and his being made Officer Commanding Home Counties, assisted by a secretary and receiving expenses on top of his salary.[30] Joyce was also producing pamphlets and organizing teaching groups covering a variety of

---

[29] Minute, May 1934. Joyce files KV 2/245/1a.
[30] Ibid.

subjects ranging from economics to India. Another figure active in the
BUF at this time was the MI5 double agent Charles Henry Maxwell
Knight, who held the post of BUF Director of Intelligence. His
continued reports to MI5 and Special Branch ensured that rarely a
week went by without fresh information being added to Joyce's file.
Maxwell Knight saw Joyce as 'a born leader of men, and . . . very loyal
and sincere in his ideals. . . He is a rare combination of a dreamer and
a man of action'.[31] He noted that Mosley recognized Joyce as probably
the most skilful and efficient officer that he had at BUF
headquarters.[32] As far as Joyce was concerned, Maxwell Knight noted
the following disturbing assessment:

> [Joyce] does not model himself on the lines of the ascetic
> Hitler. He drinks, plays about with women and plans. It
> is easy to see that he is an expert at intrigue but
> temperament does not allow him to seek popularity. He
> is pleasant to those who do not oppose him but never
> what I would call friendly. I have been acutely conscious
> that he is irritated sometimes to the point of insanity
> by the men above him, especially the old men.[33]
> (**document 18**)

At this stage Mosley's BUF was receiving financial support from
major industrialists such as Lord Nuffield, Lord Austin and Lord
Rothermere, the proprietor of the *Daily Mail*. Rothermere even went
so far as to bankroll the BUF Olympia rally in London, offering
tickets to readers who could write the best article entitled 'Why I am
a blackshirt'. In 1935 the general election provided the BUF with its
greatest opportunity to break into national politics. However,
despite fielding a large number of candidates, it failed to win a single
seat and its share of the poll proved disappointingly small. That year
also saw the BUF move sharply away from constitutional politics
towards the violence and street-fighting that had been the hallmark
of Hitler's Nazi party. As Joyce, the man who claimed absolute

---

[31] Minute, 28 January 1935. Joyce files KV 2/245/1a.
[32] Extracts, Special Branch reports, 24 January 1937. Joyce files
KV 2/245/24a.
[33] Ibid.

loyalty to Britain and its empire, embraced Nazi ideology and tactics, Adolf Hitler became his new hero and thereafter was the model for all his ideas. Joyce's speeches to meetings and rallies became increasingly peppered with virulent anti-Semitic rhetoric. It was at this time that Mosley's BUF, ably supported by Joyce, started organizing marches and rallies in the East End of London in its attempts to galvanize poor working- and lower middle-class residents into a defence of 'British values' from attacks by so-called 'Jewish communists'. This move culminated in the infamous 'battle of Cable Street', when the Metropolitan Police tried to separate fighting between Mosley's BUF and East End communist and Jewish activists. (**document 17**) After these disturbances, the government acted decisively and quickly passed the Public Order Act, which banned uniformed marches. As a consequence, the BUF lost its distinctive blackshirt uniform and Joyce was outraged, as Maxwell Knight observed:

> Joyce is apparently fed up about the loss of the uniform. From what I was told, I feel certain that Joyce had turned from the Napoleonic pose to a copy of a Prussian officer. I hear that his manner had steadily been becoming more parade ground like and that his head was cropped closer than ever before.[34]

In the midst of the upheavals in the movement he had done so much to create, William Joyce found himself the centre of other changes. In 1936 his marriage to Hazel ended in divorce. She had been subjected to regular physical abuse at the hands of Joyce, who had had many affairs during the course of their eight-year marriage. The two children of this marriage remained with their mother, who remarried, her second husband being Eric Herbert Hamilton Piercy, another member of the British fascist movement.[35] Free from the confines of his first marriage, he met and eventually married a fellow BUF activist, Margaret Cairns White, who became the second

---

[34] Extracts, Special Branch reports, 24 January 1937. Joyce files KV 2/245/24a.
[35] Cross-reference in Joyce files, 2 October 1940. Joyce files KV 2/245/250b.

Mrs William Joyce and later notoriously Lady Haw Haw,[36] although this did not prevent Joyce continuing a long series of liaisons with a variety of women. Towards the end of the Second World War he recalled this aspect of his life, a 20 March 1945 journal entry observing: 'Think much of Mary and 15 years ago – that magic evening at Prince's Risboro! Ah! Well. I am cut off from that life anyhow'.[37]

The MI5 file relating to Margaret Cairns Joyce was released to the PRO (now The National Archives) in 2000, several months after William Joyce's own file.[38] Opened in 1941, it contains important biographical and other details of her life and career with her husband until his execution in 1946. Margaret was born in Old Trafford, Manchester on 14 July 1911. Her father was Ernest Robert White, a factory manager who later became a postman. He was of Irish descent, though he and her mother, Mabel Evelyn White, were both born in London.[39] The girl was known as Margot to the family and fellow workers, being brought up mainly in Carlisle, an English town near the Scottish borders, where she met William Joyce in about 1936. At the time she lived with her parents and was, with her father, an enthusiastic member of the British Union of Fascists. Educated at Carlisle's Girls' County High School, Margaret obtained employment as a typist at a local textile factory. The report said Margaret's father was made redundant at the end of 1937 and he and his wife left Carlisle for Manchester soon after.[40] On 27 September 1945 Carlisle police took a statement from one of her former employers, Donald Howard Nicholson, in which Nicholson, who had recognized Margaret's distinctive voice over the radio early on in the war, said Margot had been employed as his typist between 1934 and 1937. He described her as a 'capable girl, with plenty of

---

[36] Joyce evidently had a complex attitude towards women. He married twice and had many mistresses, but he could be coarse and extreme about women. A journal entry for 16 March 1945 (KV 2/250/2) notes his wife's monthly period in the following terms: 'M[argaret], of course, has Mrs. Thing. It seems that I have become a human contraceptive. Well, for the present, so much the better.'

[37] William Joyce journal entry, 20 March 1945 (KV 2/250/2).

[38] Margaret Cairns Joyce née White files, KV 2/253.

[39] 'MI5 Report and documents re Margaret Joyce submitted to DPP'. Statement of Margaret Cairns Joyce, 30 May 1945. Margaret Joyce files KV 2/253.

[40] Police report by William Carruthers, 17 February 1941. Margaret Joyce files KV 2/253/22z.

The young Margaret Joyce who was later to become
'Lady Haw Haw'. (KV 2/346/2)

initiative'. A dedicated blackshirt, he said she spoke at meetings and
sold the BUF newspaper in Carlisle.[41] Margaret White was clearly
besotted by William Joyce and they became engaged, being married
on 13 February 1937 at the Kensington Registry Office in London.
Together, Margaret and William Joyce made an excellent,
ideologically committed team. She acted as his secretary and typed
his speeches, as well as her own, and they often travelled together to
meetings around the country. They both enjoyed the thrill of packed
meetings and gained strength from William's provocative,
haranguing style of oratory as he took on hecklers and poured scorn
on his favourite enemy, the 'Jewish communist'.

---

[41] MI5 Report and documents re Margaret Joyce submitted to DPP. Police
statement by Donald Howard Beatie Nicholson, 27 September 1945.
Margaret Joyce files KV 2/253.

National Socialist League: 1937–1939

By early 1937, MI5 agent reports noted serious organizational and financial problems within the British Union of Fascists. (**document 18**) An 8 February 1937 Special Branch report passed to MI5 highlighted growing differences between competing factions within the organization, revealing William Joyce at the heart of this in-fighting. The financial problems were due largely to successful pressure applied by the government and other sources to prominent wealthy BUF backers.[42] Also the BUF's increasing use of violence cost it dearly, and such political support it had acquired began to melt away. The crisis was mitigated to a small degree through the continued receipt of funds from Mussolini's Italian fascist movement and from Nazi sources, though these were not sufficient to stave off the coming crisis. A Special Branch note on Joyce's MI5 file stated that on 11 March Oswald Mosley met with senior BUF officials. At the end of the meeting, most people were handed envelopes containing money and a letter giving them a week's notice and instructions not to turn up for work again. Among those given notice was William Joyce.[43] A report Special Branch received from the Liverpool police suggested that the services of a total of 104 salaried members at the national headquarters had been dispensed with, the report also noting that many of the people dismissed had agreed to continue their work for the BUF on a voluntary basis.[44] Joyce's reaction to his dismissal was typical – he simply cut himself off from them, refusing to speak or write for the BUF or to give voluntary service; he even cancelled his subscription to the BUF newspaper *Action*.[45] Although Joyce had a face-to-face confrontation with Mosley it did no good and he was, for his pains, expelled from the movement, although he always claimed he had resigned. Joyce later sued Mosley and the BUF for wrongful dismissal and won an out-of-court settlement.[46] Ten years later William Joyce confided to his journal his thoughts on all of this:

---

[42] Special Branch report, 8 February 1937 and David Kimpton to K. B. Stamp, 5 March 1941. Joyce files KV 2/245/30a and 266b.

[43] Special Branch report, 12 March 1937. Joyce files KV 2/245/29a.

[44] Special Branch report, 10 April 1937. Joyce files KV 2/245/36b.

[45] Ibid.

[46] David Kimpton to K. B. Stamp, 5 March 1941. Joyce files KV 2/245/266b.

> 11th March 1945: Eight years ago today [I left] the
> B.U.F. . . . Recall the scenes from 11th March 1937.
> How [John] Beckett and I suspected what was afoot and
> held [a] council of war – the 'leaders'' tragedy parade,
> the envelopes . . . in or out? The sherry bar . . . and the
> sense of relief.[47]

Rumours concerning the collapse of the BUF abounded in extreme right-wing circles. One suggested the financial crisis had merely provided the pretext for those who hated Joyce to persuade Mosley to get rid of him. Another suggested Joyce was guilty of conspiracy and treason against the BUF. In a 26 August 1937 Special Branch report the attitude of BUF headquarters staff towards Joyce's departure is recorded: 'the general feeling was one of relief that the brilliant but warped brain had gone'.[48]

There was something of the inevitable about the parting of the ways between the pure ideologue that was William Joyce and Sir Oswald Mosley, the figure from the political establishment. Since their first meeting in 1933 the relationship between the two had steadily deteriorated. Mosley had come to regard Joyce as an increasingly unstable liability, a threat to his own respectability as a politician and, most importantly, to his leadership of the BUF. If Maxwell Knight was correct, then by 1937 Joyce was already harbouring ideas that 'Mosley was little more than a conceited popinjay'.[49] Whatever the reasons, by 1937 the heady days of 1934 and 1935 were little more than a distant memory – the time had already entered the fascist folklore memory of men like William Joyce and others on the extreme right. For them it was a golden age, when the British Union of Fascists appeared an unstoppable force, with Joyce tipped as a possible successor to Mosley and a future Viceroy of India in a BUF-headed government. Despite the bitter parting of the ways, Maxwell Knight still considered Joyce 'one of the most fascinating character studies in the movement'. In his January 1937 report he speculated:

---

[47] Joyce journal entry, 11 March 1945 (KV 2/250/2).
[48] Special Branch report, 26 August 1937. Joyce files KV 2/245/60a.
[49] Special Branch report 24 January 1937. Joyce files KV 2/245/24a.

> If this movement does collapse, it will not mean the last
> of Joyce. If on the other hand the movement succeeds in
> coming to power, I fancy that one of the first things
> Joyce will try to do is bring about a purge of the party.[50]

Maxwell Knight concluded his important January 1937 eve-of-crisis report with a prophetic assessment of Joyce:

> Joyce knows what he wants in life, and is out to get it. I feel
> somehow, despite the fact I dislike the man intensely, that
> in him there is someone who might one day make history.
> With all his faults he remains in my mind one of the most
> compelling personalities of the whole movement.[51]

Instead of making history, William and Margaret Joyce found themselves after his 1937 dismissal without either a political base or an income, as a consequence of which they quickly descended into a kind of genteel poverty. However all was not lost, for when he and Mosley parted company, Joyce took with him a small band of like-minded hard-line, pro-Nazi fascists and together they formed the British National Socialist League, with a newspaper called *The Helmsman,* a steering wheel as its insignia and the motto 'steer straight'.[52] This time William Joyce was the undisputed leader and a former BUF associate John Angus Macnab became his deputy.[53] In all there were probably no more than twenty members of this splinter group, who all professed to believe in the principles of the BUF but rejected Mosley's methods. More importantly, they were without exception true believers in Adolf Hitler's Third Reich and

---

[50] Ibid.

[51] Ibid.

[52] *Sunday Pictorial*, 17 December 1939. Joyce files KV 2/245/208a.

[53] Note on John Angus Macnab, 18 June 1945. Joyce files KV 2/248. John Angus Macnab was born in 1896 and educated at Rugby School and Oxford University. In 1932 he became a classics master at a private school and met Joyce through their joint interest in the BUF. When the NSL was established the two established a tutorial business, which did not flourish. Although Macnab visited Germany just before the outbreak of war in 1939, he returned to Britain claiming he would never help Britain's enemies. However, at the start of the war, he was interned for a period under Defence Regulations.

unashamedly pro-Nazi, at a time when Britain was in the final countdown to the Second World War.

Between its formation in 1937 and the outbreak of war in 1939 Joyce's National Socialist League made repeated overtures to other extreme right-wing groups in Britain to gain both support and money. He contacted Lord Lymington, leader of the self-styled 'British Array', and in September 1938, during the Munich crisis, the two organizations created the British Council Against European Commitments. Maxwell Knight tracked some of these moves and wrote an MI5 report, also in September 1938, which suggested that because of increased tension Joyce had become much more hysterical and militantly pro-German. He is alleged to have kept in 'constant touch with the N.S.D.A.P. (German Nazis) during the last week or so'. This self-proclaimed 'British patriot' is said to have told a German he met whilst attending one of the British Council Against European Commitments meetings that: 'If there is war with Germany I will be shot rather than take any part in it on behalf of Britain'. (**document 19**) Maxwell Knight concluded his report by noting his informant had seen Joyce with tears streaming down his face, adding: 'But I am convinced that we shall one day see Germany the master of Europe'. Predictably, once the Council had served its purpose, Joyce fell out with it and after attacking it at a public meeting stormed off the platform. (**document 21**) Photographs of Joyce from this period were found amongst his possessions in 1945, one of which shows him dressed in Nazi uniform complete with a Hitler-style toothbrush moustache. The pose he strikes in the photograph shows his shirt and tie in disarray, creating an image that is more Charlie Chaplin than the Führer. Maxwell Knight also told his MI5 masters that if it came to a war with Germany, then Joyce's loyalty could not be relied on.[54]

To earn money during this difficult phase in his life, Joyce and John Angus Macnab established a small teaching business at 83 Onslow Gardens, South Kensington, London. Macnab and Joyce coached language students and had one single rule – they would not teach Jews. The business failed to flourish and both Margaret and William Joyce found it hard to make ends meet. Nonetheless they

---

[54] Report concerning William Joyce, agent 'M', 27 September 1938. Joyce files KV 2/245/62x.

continued their political campaigning, publishing pamphlets and addressing street-corner and other meetings which invariably led to clashes, often involving the police. On one occasion Joyce and Macnab were both charged with riotous assembly, though later acquitted. On another, in November 1938, after a public meeting Joyce was addressing had to be closed by the police who feared violence, Joyce and Macnab were both prosecuted. The surviving police Special Branch reports suggest an episode straight out of a French farce, with Joyce, against whom there appeared little evidence, being acquitted of a charge of assault, whilst Macnab was fined one pound for obstruction.[55] After the court success Joyce, Macnab and their supporters went to the nearby Rochester Row police station and sang *God Save the King* at the police.[56]

This final period before the Joyces' fateful 26 August 1939 departure for Nazi Germany was not simply a time of evaporating political aspirations: it was also a period when he became increasingly involved in subversive activities with known German intelligence agents active in Britain. Given this and his existing profile, he was inevitably, in the eyes of Britain's Security Service, the focus of increased attention. William Joyce's MI5 files indicate that in September 1938, during the Munich crisis, the agency obtained a Home Office warrant (HOW) permitting his telephone to be tapped and the interception of his mail. There were good reasons for this increased activity – for some time MI5 had been aware of the association between William and his younger brother Quentin, and a known Nazi agent called Christian Harri Bauer. In his report, Maxwell Knight told how he had known Quentin and Frank Joyce since childhood, adding that Quentin was enjoying his work at the Air Ministry, whilst Frank, employed as an engineer at the BBC, 'worships at the feet of Sir John Reith', the Director-General. Maxwell Knight also noted his own reluctance to do anything that might prejudice their careers.[57]

Posing as a German journalist resident in Britain, Bauer was believed to have been engaged in espionage and deported in November 1937. (**document 20**) A copy of a 1938 Secret Intelligence

---

[55] Report, Special Branch 'Police court proceedings 15th November 1938'. Joyce files KV 2/245/96a.

[56] Kimpton to Stamp, 5 March 1941. Joyce files KV 2/245/266b.

[57] Report, agent 'M', 26 May 1937. Joyce files KV 2/245/40a.

Service (MI6) report held on Joyce's MI5 file provides ample evidence as to the importance of the Bauer-Joyce connections, describing a meeting in Belgium between 'a casual MI6 informant' and Joyce's business partner, John Macnab, who was staying there *en route* to Germany. When they met, Macnab was described as being quite drunk and told the informant he was going to Cologne to meet a man called Bauer who was an important Nazi. He also said he was carrying secret messages to Bauer. The following day, before he left for Germany, a rather more sober Macnab begged the informant to forget he had ever mentioned the man or his name.[58]

However, the intercepts of mail to and from Bauer continued, and included correspondence with the Joyce brothers. To make matters even more serious, Quentin Joyce was at the time employed in the Directorate of Signals at the Air Ministry, and was in a position to obtain information of a highly confidential nature. Surviving examples of this correspondence in photostat form include letters from Bauer to William Joyce, together with his replies. (**document 22**) To show where his true feelings now lay, Joyce always concluded these letters with the appellation 'Heil Hitler'. A review of the correspondence, with the benefit of hindsight, doesn't reveal anything of significance, but from time to time there appear cryptic comments that self-evidently addressed the minds of MI5 officers.[59] Action was not taken on the basis of this surveillance – for example, Quentin Joyce remained in his post – but the material was retained in case it was needed as evidence to support wartime detention orders.

During the spring and summer of 1939 the MI5 minute sheets in the William Joyce series of files show the agency's continued interest in him and his activities. The entries also show the extent of his correspondence with Bauer and others in Germany, and there are notes on meetings held by his National Socialist League at locations in London which were addressed by him. The pace of events quickened as the international crisis mounted and in July 1939 MI5 recommended

---

[58] SIS report, 17 November 1938. Joyce files KV 2/245/96b.
[59] Photostats of correspondence between William Joyce and Christian Harri Bauer 1936–39, and MI5 report of suspicious remarks in the correspondence between the Joyce brothers and Bauer. Joyce files KV 2/245.

to the Home Office that in the event of a war with Nazi Germany, William Joyce should be detained. In its memorandum recommending this action, the agency noted his formation of the National Socialist League as a 'more violently anti-semitic and pro-German body than the BUF'. The memorandum continued:

> He has identified himself unreservedly with the Nazi cause, maintains close contact with Nazi officials and has shown that he would be quite willing to take action inimical to this country in order to further the campaign against the supposed 'world Jewish conspiracy'. He is also on intimate terms with a German who is strongly suspected of having carried on espionage in this country. He has on several occasions shown that he favours violent methods and through his whole career has shown himself to be a man of unbridled fanaticism.[60]
> (document 23)

The Joyces defect to Nazi Germany

On 24 August 1939, Joyce renewed his British passport for a further year, and two days later left for the continent accompanied by his wife. On 2 September, acting on a Home Office warrant, the police attempted to locate and detain him. They searched his basement flat in the Fulham district of London but found nothing except old National Socialist League propaganda and evidence testifying to the couple's abject poverty. On 5 November 1939 Special Branch interviewed his friend and colleague John Macnab, who had been detained under defence regulations and who in better days shared the flat with the Joyces. He spoke of the failure of the tutorial business and of their joint despair at the lack of funds and a future. Unemployed, Macnab had visited Germany between 14 and 23 August 1939, staying with Bauer who he told of Joyce's predicament. Using Macnab as a courier, Bauer sent a message to Joyce offering him work in Germany and assuring him he would be able to take

---

[60] Memorandum to the Home Office, 18 August 1939. Joyce files KV 2/245/160a.

German citizenship if he threw in his lot with the Nazi state. The die was cast. According to Macnab, on 25 August Joyce attended the regular Friday night gathering at the National Socialist League, during the course of which he announced his and Margaret's intention of leaving for Germany the following day. The next morning Macnab, members of the Joyce family and a few other die-hard NSL friends witnessed their departure from Victoria station. According to his testimony, Joyce prophetically told him:

> I am determined to throw in my lot with Germany and become a German and if I do return to England, it will simply be for the purpose of putting my affairs in order and then returning to the land I have chosen. [61]

However, there remains one unanswered question: was he tipped off about his impending detention or was he simply ahead of his pursuers? Maxwell Knight was the man most likely to tip Joyce off, though, as his reports indicate, he had come to detest him and was therefore an unlikely informant. In sharp contrast, Maxwell Knight knew and was very fond of Joyce's two brothers, Frank and Quentin. When war broke out, Frank Joyce was interned and despite Maxwell Knight's efforts he was unable to secure his release.

After bidding farewell to Macnab and the others, William and Margaret Joyce headed for Germany. Once in Berlin they sent a postcard to their friend telling of their safe arrival. Macnab later showed the postcard to Special Branch officers as proof that the couple had slipped away. The Joyces were joined by a handful of other British fascists, but the bulk remained at home. Macnab's explanation for this is instructive – he always argued he supported German fascism, not Britain's enemies. In the end it is impossible to judge whether it was the push of the near certainty of war or the pull of Bauer's offer of work for the multilingual Joyce. All Joyce's life to this point suggests he was not a coward fearing detention, rather he

---

[61] By the time of this interview the National Socialist League had been dissolved and, as Macnab claimed, he and many other members were involved in national service. Extract from Advisory Committee examination of John Macnab. Joyce files KV 2/248.

was vain and self-important, and Bauer knew this and played on it. The Joyces' MI5 files contain their justifications made in their own words. William Joyce's testimony was best articulated in a broadcast he made to Britain on 28 August 1944 which was transcribed by the BBC monitoring service. It marked the fifth anniversary of his arrival in Berlin and is a clever though self-pitying statement, made in almost sacrificial terms. He said:

> Five years ago today I arrived in Berlin having, on the previous day, left London and severed associations which, in their general pattern, had made up most of my life . . . Those who have never felt for England as I was taught to feel, those who had never suffered for England as I was made to suffer during long years, will not know or understand what that decision meant. In the lives of most people there remain, fixed upon the memory, certain indelible pictures, few in number but so clear that nothing will erase them, and one of these rare but life-long visions is that of the last few moments in which I beheld the land to which I had devoted myself until I saw that it had, in essence, become a colony of Palestine. With my wife, whom I came to know and married in the struggle to save England from the fate which befell her in September 1939, I stood on the upper deck of the mail packet from Dover to Ostend on Saturday, 26th August, five years ago. It was one of those beautiful later summer days on which the sun, to have full meaning, must pierce the mists hanging over the azure sea. We kept our eyes fixed on the Dover cliffs until the haze drew over them that impenetrable veil which, for us, was the end of the old life and the beginning of the new. When we could see no more of the land which we loved and tried to serve, I said to my wife, curtly enough, 'Let's go to lunch', and so we did.[62]

On 30 May 1945, the day of her arrest in Germany, Margaret Joyce wrote a statement, which she gave to an MI5 officer. In it she said:

---

[62] 'Views on the News' broadcast transcript, 28 August 1944. Joyce files KV 2/245/340b.

I came to Germany on 26th August 1939 having left England because I felt that as I was morally unable to assist in Britain's war effort it would be unfair to remain in the country. Having observed England's attitude since Munich in 1938, I regarded the outbreak of war as inevitable. It was my opinion that a war between Britain and Germany would be a national tragedy for both countries but I did not regard it so much a war between nations as a war between opposing political faiths.[63]

Whatever the reasons, William Joyce, this complex man of contradictions, capable of being both a British Empire loyalist and a loyal supporter of Hitler's Third Reich, quietly slipped out of Britain on a cross-channel ferry. It proved the end of one stage of his eventful life and the start of another. He left Britain a largely unknown figure, outside those politically active in the fascist movement and those who pursued him. Turning his back on the country he claimed to love, he decided instead to throw in his lot with Britain's enemies. When he returned to Britain in the early summer of 1945 it was in quite different circumstances, for although few people could recognize his face, just about everyone in Britain knew the voice of the infamous propaganda broadcaster, Lord Haw Haw.

---

[63] Statement, Margaret Cairns Joyce, 30 May 1945. Margaret Joyce files KV 2/253.

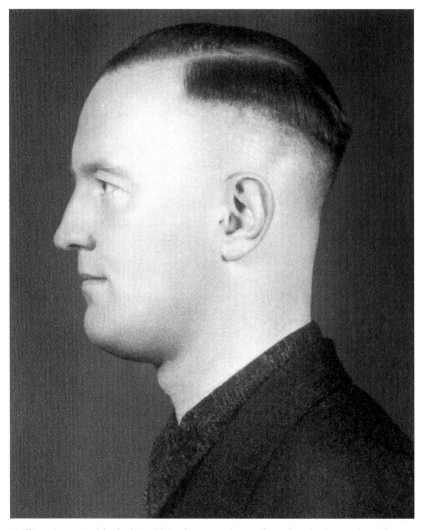

William Joyce in black shirt. This photograph was found at the Joyces' residence in Apen in May 1945. (KV 2/346/6)

Chapter 2

'Germany Calling, Germany Calling . . .'

By the time Britain went to war with Germany on Sunday, 3 September 1939, MI5 and Special Branch had discovered, to their intense embarrassment, that William and Margaret Joyce had disappeared, the couple's abrupt departure for Germany the previous week having pre-empted their detention under wartime defence regulations. This turn of events poses difficulties for anyone attempting to track the couple's subsequent wartime activities from the perspective of MI5 files. Quite simply, until their arrest on the German–Danish border in May 1945, no one at MI5 had any means of directly monitoring their activities. In fact the intelligence reports of MI5 stalkers like Maxwell Knight simply vanish from the later volumes of the files. What remains is made up of broadcast transcripts, newspaper articles, notes and reports, together with secondary material relating to Joyce's activities in Germany, assessments as to his nationality and the potential for using this material as evidence in a post-war prosecution for treason.

As for William and Margaret Joyce, by leaving Britain when they did, they had cut their links with everything and everyone connected with their former lives. Within a few days of their arrival in Germany, Adolf Hitler launched his long-expected attack on Poland and war broke out between Germany, France and Britain. In Berlin, the Joyces were greeted by their friend Christian Harri Bauer. In the event he proved less helpful than his promises had indicated. However, the couple found somewhere to live and, capitalizing on his skills as a German-speaker, translator and fascist propagandist, found ways of introducing Joyce to Goebbels' German propaganda ministry and the Reichs Rundfunk, the Nazi-controlled German radio service. He was immediately offered a job as an announcer in its Deutsche Europasender, specifically to its British broadcast section.

Though Joyce quickly became the best known of the German propaganda broadcasters, his recruitment was by no means the only British appointment during these opening days of the war. In fact, by the time he made his first broadcasts other so-called British renegades were already plying their trade over the airwaves. Among them was a former British army officer, Norman Baillie-Stewart, who had served a five-year term of imprisonment in the Tower of London following a conviction for treachery in the mid-1930s. Another was John Amery, a known British fascist and son of former conservative cabinet minister Leopold Amery. According to statements made at the end of the war by German nationals employed in the broadcasting of propaganda to Britain, these early days of the war were characterized by the same kind of improvization and chaotic conditions as occurred in Britain, for in early September 1939, and for some time after, arrangements for propaganda broadcasts to Britain were disorganized and badly managed by the German Foreign Ministry. They remained so until 1940, when the star of propaganda minister Josef Goebbels gained the ascendancy in the eyes of his boss Adolf Hitler. Until that time, Ribbentrop's foreign ministry officials wrote most of the material broadcast to Britain and simply used British personnel to deliver it over the air. These broadcasts took the same form, starting with short news bulletins and ending with a commentary on the news. As the foreign ministry officials had little understanding of Britain and the British way of life, the material they wrote and the resultant broadcasts were often ludicrous and came to be regarded with derision by listeners, though they did have the effect of providing the hard-pressed British public with much unintended amusement.[1]

The development of radio

Radio turned William Joyce from what might have been no more than a mere irritant into a uniquely powerful, though despised and hated, figure. This transformation was possible because of the manner in which radio broadcasting developed in the decade or so before he began his new career. During the 1920s radio technology and its range advanced at a rapid pace, to the point that, by the end

---

[1] For an account of the wartime development of the German radio propaganda machine see 'Statement of Dr Friedrich Wilhelm Schoeberth', 28 May 1945. Joyce files KV 2/246/387b.

of the decade, the creation of high-powered, medium-wave wireless transmitters and affordable receivers became possible. In the 1930s developments in short-wave transmitters and receiver technology extended this range even further. In order to accommodate these rapid changes and avoid transmission overlaps a European conference was called in 1929 at Prague, Czechoslovakia, which successfully divided the available medium- and short-wave bands up between the different states.[2] This allowed Europe's broadcasters to create national networks: for example, in Britain by 1930, the British Broadcasting Corporation (BBC), largely operating from London, was broadcasting nationally through a network of medium-wave transmitters. The system worked well, though because the BBC was a monopoly broadcaster its programming was notoriously dull. However, as the corporation's charter gave it the duty to 'educate, inform and entertain' so the BBC's values were expressed via a middle-class metropolitan culture mediated from London. For many listeners, the BBC's Sunday broadcast schedule proved a particular burden, its programmes consisting of church services, readings from the Bible and other worthy books and the playing of solemn music. They may have reflected the belief system of John Reith, a son of the manse and the BBC's founding Director-General, but they did not play well with the mass of listeners.

Although the BBC had a monopoly on broadcasting and therefore programming within Britain, owners of the new medium- and short-wave radio sets discovered that a simple turn of the tuning knob gave them access to a wide range of alternative European-sourced, English-language programming. This became possible because the take-up of radio in continental Europe lagged significantly behind that of Britain where, by the outbreak of war in 1939, around 80 per cent of households had a radio receiving licence. This low continental take-up resulted in valuable spare airwave capacity – by renting this out to commercial programme-makers, many cash-strapped countries gained significant windfall incomes. These commercial radio programme-makers in turn used the spare wavelengths to broadcast a daily diet of commercially sponsored programming directly into Britain, the format used being quite

[2] For a contemporary account of the conference and a listing of the new division of wavebands see *The BBC Year-Book, 1930* (London, 1930), pp. 357–70.

simple – wall-to-wall popular music sourced either from commercial gramophone records or via transcription discs made by popular dance bands, usually in London; programmes were sponsored by British business anxious to sell its products to the masses. As a consequence, British broadcasting, as it developed in the decade before the outbreak of war in 1939, was quite different to the perceived view of a country settled with comforting sounds emanating from an all-wise and all-knowing BBC. In fact British broadcasting developed much more in line with the experience of the United States, with a rich variety of radio stations to choose from, offering what listeners wanted to hear combined with advertising for the kind of lifestyle products they aspired to own. The British market for this kind of commercial radio proved insatiable, and during the 1930s dozens of these English-language stations appeared from what seemed to British listeners exotic locations such as Paris, Luxembourg, Berlin, Hamburg and Bremen. The BBC board of governors responded to this effective breaking of its monopoly by making a concerted attempt to win back audiences through a modification of its austere programming. By any measure they failed miserably, and the habit of listening to English-language continental radio stations stuck.

English-language transmissions from continental Europe continued into the Second World War and gave William Joyce his nightly audience and his infamy. However, there was a downside to listening in to these broadcasts, for until the introduction of high-powered transmitters capable of beaming signals across Britain, radio reception deteriorated the further listeners lived from the broadcast station. However, once the Germans occupied north-western Europe, they were able to take over a range of existing broadcasting stations, including one in Calais, which took feeds from Joyce's Berlin studio before transmitting to nearby Britain. None the less, such deterioration of sound quality appears not to have deterred listeners, although, as will be seen, it caused serious problems to those attempting to obtain broadcast evidence of William Joyce's treachery.[3]

---

[3] According to a 1945 pre-trial statement by BBC engineer Thomas Cecil Burningham: 'Throughout the period of the war and prior thereto the BBC has had a wireless broadcasting receiving station at Tatsfield in Surrey at which broadcasts from broadcasting stations overseas are picked up'. He also explained how in 1943 this receiving station was connected by land line to the BBC recording premises in Maida Vale, London, from where most of Joyce's later broadcasts were recorded and transcribed. Joyce files KV 2/250/1.

As far as the public was concerned, the BBC's war started very badly. The corporation activated a set of contingency plans which caused a widespread dispersal of BBC staff and performing artists away from London to a number of pre-arranged locations. As a result of all this, a sudden windfall of talent arrived at BBC regional stations and other facilities; unfortunately, it was never used. Instead those same war contingency plans ensured that the British public lost its regular programmes and was forced instead to endure wall-to-wall broadcasts of light organ music played by Sandy Macpherson or programmes of gramophone records. These stultifying substitutes for regular programming were interspersed with news bulletins and announcements of various government edicts.[4] After radio, cinema provided the masses with its other main pre-war leisure activity, with about half the population visiting cinemas at least once a week. An important feature of cinema was the weekly newsreels, which provided, with radio, one of the main sources of news and news commentary. Therefore, when on the outbreak of war the government closed all places of entertainment, including cinemas, theatres, concert and dance halls, the population became even more dependent on radio. The logic for all this government activity was irrefutable. They had been panicked into believing that the outbreak of hostilities would precipitate an immediate and intense aerial bombing campaign of Britain's towns and cities. As well as high-explosive bombs and incendiaries, this destructive campaign, it convinced itself, would also include the dropping of poison gas bombs and involve massive casualties. In the circumstances large gatherings of people seemed highly risky, and so they were banned. In fact events proved them wrong, for, during the eight months immediately after the declaration of war, Britain experienced little fighting. It was an eerie and as it proved a wholly untypical portent of what was to come. In the event, Poland fell to German forces within three weeks and then, until the spring of 1940, and apart from the unrelenting war at sea, there was little or no military activity and certainly no air raids over Britain. American reporters resident in Britain at the time dubbed it 'the Phoney War'.

---

[4] The best contemporary critique of this policy is Compton Mackenzie's editorial in *The Gramophone*, p. 183, October 1939. Volume XVII, Number 197.

The making of Lord Haw Haw

It was in these 'Alice in Wonderland' circumstances that William Joyce's voice came into its own. For, scheming, ambitious and ruthless, he designed his broadcasts to please his German masters. Armed with a reputation, he soon elbowed other renegades out of the way to emerge as the main British broadcaster, crucially producing his own material.

From the start of the war the British government and its intelligence service knew all about German propaganda broadcasts by people purporting to be British. It also knew from 'Mass Observation' reports and the activities of British journalists that large numbers of British people were listening to and being influenced by these broadcasts – in other words they were proving a highly successful propaganda tool. To find out just how bad the problem was, the British Ministry of Information asked the BBC in December 1939 to find out the size of Joyce's listening audience. The results proved startling. Using data collected at the end of January 1940, the report established that one-sixth of the adult population or 6,000,000 people were regular listeners, half or 18,000,000 people were occasional listeners and only one-third or 11,000,000 never listened; this compared to 23,000,000 regular listeners to the BBC's own news programmes.[5] With the propaganda initiative in German hands the British government faced a perplexing problem. Since the start of the war all news had been subject to strict government censorship; however, because of radio, German news reports and propaganda entered Britain uncensored and there was no apparent means available to the British government to prevent it. In fact these broadcasts were the only messages the government was unable to censor, and therefore in its eyes were potentially dangerous, particularly as far as morale was concerned – in fact, very dangerous. In many ways it was a spectacular own goal. Had the government and the BBC not panicked at the start of the war, then the potential for Joyce and his friends to make mischief would have been that much reduced. However the damage was done, Joyce

---

[5] Cited in E. S. Turner, *The Phoney War on the Home Front* (London, 1961), p. 110.

had an audience and it seemed nothing could be done to prevent people listening to him.

The opinion of the British government and the press appeared to be that if Joyce could not be controlled, then other means would have to be found to neutralize him. To this end the first attempts were made during the early weeks of the war, a period when censorship restrictions meant that little by way of active news reporting of the conflict itself was reaching the press. In these conditions journalists found themselves scratching around for stories and they unwittingly provided the German radio propagandists with the necessary publicity they needed to grow and gain strength. The story first broke in the *Daily Express*, Lord Beaverbrook's mid-market, best-selling newspaper. On 14 September 1939 a journalist writing the 'Jonah Barrington' column made a series of withering comments about German propaganda broadcasts to Britain, focusing on one particularly offensive though anonymous broadcaster: 'He speaks English of the haw, haw, damit-get-out-of-my-way variety, and his strong suit is gentlemanly indignation'. Four days later 'Jonah Barrington' used the expression Lord Haw Haw for the first time; it was, coincidently, 18 September, the day of Joyce's first broadcast. The journalist intended to ridicule the individual, remarking on his irritating upper-class accent, which he compared to the braying of a donkey. This prompted him to name the individual 'Lord Haw Haw'.[6] In fact the subject of the attentions of the 'Jonah Barrington' column was not William Joyce but probably the former British army officer Norman Baillie-Stewart. Ironically, soon after the title was bestowed on him he disappeared from the airwaves, apparently fed up with the rubbish the German Foreign Ministry made him read on air, but the title struck a chord with the British public, and was soon applied to Baillie-Stewart's microphone successor, William Joyce. However, during this phase of the war the name Lord Haw Haw was not universally applied to William Joyce. For instance, as long as the German broadcasters remained anonymous, monitors at the BBC responsible for taking transcripts of these broadcasts made up their own names for the various speakers. One of these monitors was Doreen Fattah who in September 1945 described the development of the various Joyce nomenclatures used by German radio and others:

---

[6] *Daily Express*, 14 September 1939.

> In the monitoring service of the Corporation [BBC],
> there was a great deal of speculation as to the identity of
> the various speakers. One of the speakers, who spoke
> with a cultured accent was to my knowledge dubbed by
> the British press as 'Lord Haw-Haw'. There was,
> however, another speaker with an equally distinctive
> voice to whom the Press gave no appellation. I myself
> christened him Sinister Sam to distinguish him from
> the then Lord Haw-Haw.[7]

This, she explained, was William Joyce. She went on to show how,
during the summer of 1940, she listened to the first announcement
of Lord Haw Haw by German radio, and how in 1941 William Joyce
announced his real name to the listening audience.[8] (**document 52**)

Soon after Joyce began his broadcasting career, reports claiming
to identify him arrived at MI5 positively identifying him as one of
the mystery announcers.[9] The relative ease with which he was
identified was prompted by the number of giveaway commentaries
he made, for Joyce, unlike Norman Baillie-Stewart, was able to
rework and broadcast some of his old trademark speeches. The
relevant evidence is contained in a September 1945 MI5 pre-trial memorandum which helpfully details the evidence that led to Joyce's
positive identification. For example, among the informants cited was
an ex-colonial policeman who had been a former British Union of
Fascists officer. In a 6 October 1939 statement, he identified Joyce
from the subjects mentioned in his broadcast commentaries, which
he described as being:

---

[7] Doreen Constance Abdel Fattah, statement, 8 September 1945. Joyce files
KV 2/249/87a. An MI5 pre-trial memorandum dated 8 September 1945
suggests the title 'Sinister Sam' was first applied by BBC monitoring staff
in January 1940. Joyce files KV 2/247/497a.
[8] This was the date given in his German *wehrpass* (work-book) (**document
34**).
[9] See memorandum 'Evolution of William Joyce', 10 September 1939. Joyce
files KV 2/249/89a. See also undated unsigned memorandum 'William
Joyce early broadcasts'. This document suggests that during the first
broadcast he made Joyce introduced himself as 'William Joyce of the
National Socialist League speaking to his English friends'. There has been
no confirmation one way or the other that this revelation ever took place.
Joyce files KV 2/247.

practically identical with his old speeches, including one on October 1st about the 'power' of International Finance behind the British press which the informant described as 'practically unaltered in form from the form it took when he delivered the speech so often in England.' He also quotes a phrase used by Joyce 'The General Manager of the *Daily Express*, Mr R. D. Blumenfeld, whose Chinese name sufficiently denotes his racial origin'.[10] (**document 13**)

Ex-wife identified him

Further evidence as to Joyce's identity was found in a *Sunday Pictorial* article, preserved in the Joyce files. Dated 17 December 1939 and entitled 'Lord Haw-Haw's ex-wife tells: he's an Englishman!' The article takes the form of an interview with Hazel Kathleen Piercy, the first Mrs William Joyce. In it she claimed: 'I am positive he is the man. He even tells the same stories that he used to tell me'. To back up her assertion she cited letters written by her mother and sister identifying Joyce as Lord Haw Haw; she also said the two children she had by Joyce recognized him from the broadcasts, adding:

> One night I turned on the wireless while they were in the room. Joyce was speaking. My eldest daughter turned pale, and when I asked her what was the matter, she said, 'That's W. J. isn't it?' – she always called her father W. J.[11]

Whatever name he was known by, in the months leading up to Hitler's May 1940 spring offensive William Joyce's broadcasts made the name Lord Haw Haw known throughout Britain. His signature call sign 'Germany Calling, Germany Calling' delivered in pinched, rasping, nasal tones that made Germany sound like 'Gairminy' (said by some to be the result of a badly healed broken nose gained from childhood fighting) became a byword. The rest of the trademark call

---

[10] Memorandum 'Evolution of William Joyce', 10 September 1939. Joyce files KV 2/249/89a. Also in KV 2/247.

[11] 'Lord Haw-Haw's ex-wife tells: he's an Englishman', *Sunday Pictorial*, 17 December 1939. Joyce files KV 2/245/208a.

sign was: 'Here is the news and a talk [this was later changed to 'the news and views on the news'] in English broadcast from stations in Hamburg, Bremen, Essen on the medium wave and station DXQ on the short wave'. In contrast to accounts of his speaking voice at pre-war public meetings, his fake, upper-class accent came across far more strongly to the hidden radio audience. To many people his voice sounded odd, undoubtedly due, at least in part, to the fact that individuals with voices like Joyce would never have been employed as pre-war broadcasters, as all BBC announcers spoke in an authoritative and authentic English upper-class accent.

William Joyce became so well known that the German black propaganda radio stations, such as the New British Broadcasting station, cited Lord Haw Haw's remarks as evidence of the truth. For example on 6 May 1940 it broadcast: 'And now we are told by Haw Haw that Norwegian soldiers, who have laid down their arms, express the bitterest resentment against the British Expeditionary Force'. However, many NBBS broadcasts were conducted by 'the professor', which had been Joyce's nickname in the early BUF days. On 3 August 1940 the German Overseas Service first announced Joyce as Lord Haw Haw, then on 2 April 1941[12] at the conclusion of a talk in which he attacked the London newspaper the *Evening Standard* for publishing an article in which he was accused of being a pre-war spy, he revealed himself as William Joyce.[13] (**document 25**) In this later guise his broadcasts were announced, or he announced himself, as 'You are about to hear "Views on the News" by William Joyce', which ensured his listeners knew how to maintain their link with him.[14]

The sources used for these talks by Joyce and foreign ministry officials appear to have been censored German news reports, feeds from neutral news agencies and British newspapers and magazines, obtained from the passenger flights still operating between London and Lisbon in neutral Portugal. If these sources provided the essence of the talks, Joyce himself supplied the substance. Shortly after the

[12] 'References to talks on Military operations by William Joyce (Haw Haw) during May/June 1940', 7 March 1945. Joyce files KV 2/246/372a.
[13] Ibid.
[14] As the German army over-ran western Europe other radio stations like Luxembourg, Calais, Hilvershum and Paris were added.

end of the war Dr Friedrich Wilhelm Schoeberth, who was Joyce's colleague during these years, gave an insight as to how he worked:

> Joyce, who was only received by Goebbels during the last six months of the war, came in in the afternoon and went through the news from the monitoring service and wrote his 'Views on the News', which was broadcast uncensored (the censor responsible found it easier to listen to it while it was being broadcast).[15]

In every broadcast his vindictive, never-ending hatred of Jews, communists, the British press, international capitalism and British political and other public figures was stirred to provide a potent witches' brew. Furthermore, in an attempt to ferment dissention and panic in Britain, he resorted to blatant falsehoods or a blind acceptance as truth of the lies spewing forth from Goebbels' Propaganda Ministry. In his broadcasts, these usually took the form of an expounding on the failures of British military, naval and RAF operations and the lies British politicians were spreading – which led to some ludicrous claims. For example, on a number of different occasions he triumphantly claimed the German navy's success in sinking the British aircraft carrier HMS *Ark Royal*; he also claimed that British towns on the south coast had been destroyed by the German air force, months before the start of the Blitz. These falsehoods were so obvious that people came to regard all the blustering sneering claims he made as one big joke. It was in these circumstances that Lord Haw Haw entered the public imagination, specifically during that first bleak winter of the war when he provided many opportunities for innocent fun and became the butt of endless jokes and send-ups. Except for a few people who knew him, his face was unknown, although in sharp contrast, the character of Lord Haw Haw began to appear in various forms, mainly in cartoons, often in the guise of a braying donkey. Popular entertainers like the Western Brothers created sketches using both Haw Haw and Hitler, and even made a popular gramophone record

---

[15] Statement of Dr Friedrich Wilhelm Schoeberth, 28 May 1945. Joyce files KV 2/246/387b.

called 'Lord Haw Haw of Zessen'.[16] Lord Haw Haw became the source of comic material used in countless routines in the reopened theatres and on the radio. However, all this did not reduce his radio audience, for publicity from whatever source proved in the end good publicity. His high profile in Britain also suggests that at this stage of the war Joyce and the German propaganda machine were experiencing great success in getting their message across.

No longer a laughing matter

The 'Lord Haw Haw' jokes, like Neville Chamberlain's lame-duck government, quickly wore thin, though in the spring of 1940 a disastrous turn of events transformed Joyce's broadcasts and they took on a more sinister and menacing guise. This stemmed from a whole catalogue of British military disasters and defeats during that spring and early summer. They started in April, when the German army began to move, first occupying neutral Denmark, then Norway. With a German land border there was little either the British or the French could do about Denmark; however, Norway was quite different. In the event a hastily put-together Allied army was landed in Norway only to be rebuffed by the German occupiers, suffering heavy losses during the course of a humiliating withdrawal. At this point the British House of Commons turned on the hapless Chamberlain government, and on 10 May 1940 a new government was formed – this time an all-party coalition led by a new prime minister Winston Churchill. That very same day Hitler launched his long-awaited offensive in the West. First neutral Holland and Belgium were attacked and overrun, then, by the middle of June, France was defeated and occupied. In the midst of all this the British Expeditionary Force in France retreated to the English Channel at Dunkirk, from where most of it was rescued and returned to the relative safety of Britain.

The British army had survived Dunkirk but at a very high cost, with most of its stores and equipment left behind and in German hands. To many, including William Joyce, Britain appeared close to

---

[16] Released as a 10-inch Columbia record DB1883 in December 1939.

defeat. However, the new prime minister would have none of it, and in those terrible days he went on the radio and did something no other politician had ever dared do: he took the British people into his confidence. He told them of the misfortune into which they had fallen and explained with disarming frankness that he had nothing to offer but 'blood, toil, sweat and tears'. He also told them that the Battle of France was over and the Battle of Britain was about to begin. He said that on the outcome of this battle rested the whole future of Christian civilization and the long continuity of British institutions. He went on to explain that Britain could win this battle and if it did then in years to come men would look back and say this was Britain's finest hour. It took Churchill's breathtaking honesty, directness and oratory to make him not just the great war leader that he was but also the master of the medium of radio. He succeeded in gaining the confidence of the hidden radio audience and at a stroke transformed the battle of the airwaves for the hearts and minds of the British people – at last William Joyce had an opponent who could take him on and beat him at his own game.

During that Battle of Britain summer of 1940 the British waited for the German invasion to come, although the main drama was not played out on the coast but in the skies above southern England. It was in these circumstances that Royal Air Force fighter pilots engaged their German counterparts in a life-and-death struggle, with the fate of Britain as the prize. During that summer Churchill warned of the dangers posed by so-called fifth-column infiltrators, who, he argued, had been critical in the defeat of France and other European states. Although cartoons appeared showing German paratroops descending over Britain disguised as nuns, there was a serious side to all this. Though, in truth, the fifth column was little more than justified paranoia and hysteria, in fact all the German spies landed in Britain were quickly captured. One consequence of these fears was the round-up of many pre-war British fascists, including Oswald Mosley. Somehow Lord Haw Haw became involved in all this paranoia, with many people coming to believe he controlled a vast army of fifth-column agents operating from inside Britain – listening to his broadcasts, these agents were simply waiting to carry out his orders. Rumours circulated and eventually entered folklore to the effect that during the months of the Blitz

Lord Haw Haw broadcast the names of buildings he wanted destroyed and they always were. He was said to disclose an intimate and detailed knowledge of public life that could only be supplied to him by a massive agent network – for example, when public clocks were running slow. It was as if Lord Haw Haw knew everything about daily life in Britain and was using agents to disrupt it. A thorough review of the Joyce series of MI5 files and the transcripts of his broadcasts for this period indicate there was no truth in any of this. In fact there are no references to detailed plans of bombing in either MI5 agent reports or in the minutes sheets. This mythical aspect to Joyce's career as a propaganda broadcaster reflected more the heightened awareness of him and the extraordinary impact he had made on the British people.

Today, a reading of surviving written transcripts of Joyce's broadcasts rarely provides an insight into the fear engendered by the cold menace in his voice. Clearly a part of his success was an extraordinary ability to use the power of his voice to infuse ordinary words with threat and intimidation. A rare example of a written transcript that does betray the reality behind the voice is found in the broadcast for 22 June 1940, the day France and Germany concluded an armistice. On that occasion Doreen Fattah was on duty as BBC transcript monitor. During the course of his concluding remarks, she took it on herself to insert the various emphases Joyce gave to his words and, at the end, commented on the tenor of his delivery. He said and she wrote:

> In this matter [of RAF bombing raids on Germany], as in all others, [the] Fuehrer has been very patient. But it would be absurd to assume that nothing would be done to protect ordinary non-combatant people of Germany. **All resources of warning have now been exhausted.** (These last eight words heavily stressed). You will agree that these warnings have been numerous and now (sinister pause), unfortunately (this word was laughed), you will see the result of disregarding them. The British people have taken no action to restrain their government from attacking our non-combatants, and **deeply as we regret the necessity** (heavily stressed)

from departing from principle which we honoured long after England had abandoned it, it will be shown once again that Germany of today **cannot be provoked with impunity** (heavily stressed). Her women and children are entitled to be protected in [the] **most effective fashion** (heavily stressed). We wanted, and tried, to keep the war as clean as possible. Churchill wanted to make it dirty, and he has succeeded. To [the] British people we would say: Do not waste your time abusing us for **repaying like with like** (heavily stressed). Take your complaints to Churchill, who must bear full responsibility for this terrible development in war that we tried to wage against combatants only. **He is the culprit** (heavily stressed).

(N.B. The whole talk was read in the most dramatic fashion).[17]

Lord Haw Haw's radio broadcasts continued unabated throughout the Blitz by German bombers of the autumn, winter and spring of 1940 and 1941, revealing his contempt for a Britain then experiencing death and injuries on a nightly basis. He crowed at the suffering endured and wallowed in delight at the destruction of towns and cities, prompting many to despise and even hate the man, while he continued to sneer at the suffering they endured and promised much more to come. His bile for Churchill, who he dismissed as the great demonic cause of the war, remained undimmed, as did his belief in and worship of Hitler, who, he kept emphasizing, was the sole defender of civilization and light from the barbarians. Curiously, as the Blitz ended in May 1941, the impact of Lord Haw Haw's broadcasts seemed to diminish – the Nazi state had done its worst, yet the British had survived against all the odds. As far as most people were concerned, Joyce was no longer regarded as a joke, nor even as a figure to be feared; instead he became what he had been in 1930s Britain, a fascist speaker whose views most people despised. Yet curiously he seemed to relish this. At this time

---

[17] BBC transcription of Joyce's news report 'News and talk in English from Bremen', 22 June 1940, 10.15 pm. Joyce files KV 2/249/88a.

he believed he had cut his ties with Britain forever, and in September 1940, as his friend Christian Bauer had promised, he and Margaret took German nationality. From this time on, within Germany, the couple also used the alias Froelich, which means 'joyful' in German. All this was highly symbolic to William Joyce, for not only did he believe himself to be in the land of his dreams, he had also been accepted as one of the elect.

During the months leading up to the entry of America into the war in December 1941, US journalists such as William L. Shirer saw him regularly. This distinguished American correspondent remained in Germany until the summer of 1941 and on his return to the United States wrote an article, which was later published in the British press. It was entitled 'I meet Haw-Haw' and appeared in the *Sunday Chronicle* of 14 September 1941. The article, preserved in the Joyce MI5 files, informs of Joyce's attitudes at this point in the war. Over a blackshirt image of facially scarred William Joyce, Shirer recalled his encounter with the couple during an RAF air raid over Berlin. He explained how in the air-raid shelter they drank a bottle of schnapps, remarking: 'Haw-Haw can drink as straight as any man, and if you can get over your initial revulsion at his being a traitor, you find him an amusing and even intelligent figure'. Shirer continued:

> He argues that he renounced his British nationality and became a German citizen and that he is no more a traitor than the thousands of British and Americans who renounce their citizenship to become comrades in the Soviet Union, or than those Germans who gave up their nationality after 1848 and fled to the United States.

In a shrewd assessment of his man, Shirer summed up the basic ideas that drove William Joyce throughout his adult life. Of these he said:

> I should say he has two complexes which have landed him in his present notorious position. He has a titanic hatred for Jews and an equally titanic one for cap-italists. These two hatreds have been the mainsprings of

I MEET HAW-HAW

by
William L. Shirer

Famous neutral journalist.

I HAD just finished my broadcast in Berlin. It was one o'clock in the morning and the British bombers were over us again. The Nazi air-wardens forced me into the air-raid cellar. I tried to read Carl Crow's excellent book "Four Hundred Million Customers," but the light was poor.

Finally, " Lord " Haw-Haw and his wife suggested we steal out. We d past the guards and found nfrequented underground tun , where we proceeded to dispose of a bottle of schnapps which " Lady " Haw-Haw had brought.

Haw-Haw can drink as straight as any man, and if you can get over your initial revulsion at his being a traitor, you find him an amusing and even intelligent fellow.

When the bottle was finished we felt too free to go back to the cellar. Haw-Haw found a secret stairway and we went up to his room, opened the blinds, and watched the fireworks.

To the south of the city the guns were hammering away, lighting up the sky. Sitting there in the black of the room, I had a long talk with the man.

Haw-Haw, whose real name is William Joyce, but who in Germany goes by the name of Froehlich (which in German means "Joyful "), denies that he is a traitor.

He s es that he has re nou his British nationality and ome a German citizen, he is no more a traitor that ousands of British and Americans who renounce their citizenship to become comrades in the Soviet Union, or than those Germans who gave up their nationality after 1848 and fled to the United States.

Joyce's complexes

THIS doesn't satisfy me, but it does him. He kept talking about " we " and " us," and I asked him which people he meant.

" We Germans, of course," he snapped.

He's a heavily built man of about five feet nine inches, with Irish eyes that twinkle and a face scarred not by duelling in a German university but in Fascist brawls on the pavements of British towns. He speaks fair German.

I should say he has two complexes which have landed him in his present notorious position. He has a titanic hatred for Jews and an equally titanic one for capitalists.

These two hatreds have been the mainsprings of his adult life. Had it not been for his ysteria about Jews, he ight easily have become a ccessful Communist agitator. Strange as it may seem, he

thinks the Nazi movement is a proletarian one which will free the world from the bonds of the " plutocratic capitalists."

He sees himself primarily as a liberator of the working class.

Haw-Haw's story, as I've pieced it together from our conversations and from his little booklet, " Twilight over England," is this:

He was born in New York in 1906 of Irish parents who, he says, lost what money they had in Ireland " by reason of their devotion to the British crown."

He studied literature, history and psychology at the University of London, and in 1923, the year of Hitler's ill-fated Munich " Putsch," joined the British Fascists. He says he earned his living thereafter as a tutor.

In 1933 he entered Sir Oswald Mosley's British Union of Fascists and became one of its chief speakers and writers. For three years he was Mosley's propaganda chief. He claims he left Mosley's movement in 1937 " owing to differences on matters pertaining to organisation."

He teamed up with a former Socialist M.P., and started the National Socialist League, but within a few months the ex-M.P. left it because he thought Joyce's methods " too extreme."

Of these days Joyce writes: " We lived Nation Socialism. . . . We were all enough to know the horror cedom in Democracy. it on world was dr

eighteen months of unemployment and starvation. I lived for months with real friends who loved Britain and could not get enough to eat from her."

Twice during the year that preceded the war he was arrested on charges of assault and disturbing the peace. Then came the war clouds.

" For me," he writes, " the decision was easy to make. To me it was clear on the morning of Aug. 25 that the greatest struggle in history was doomed to take place.

" It might have been a very worthy course to stay in Britain and incessantly work for peace. But I had one traditionally acquired or inherited prejudice. . . . Britain was going to war.

" I felt that if, for perfect reasons of conscience, I could not fight for her, I must give her up for ever."

He did. On Aug. 25 he and his wife, " who had to leave without even being able to say farewell to her parents," set out for Germany to take part in what he calls the " sacred struggle to free the world."

Any mind which sees Hitler's cold-blooded trampling down of the free peoples of Europe as a sacred struggle to free the world speaks for itself.

Haw-Haw's book is a hodgepodge of Nazi nonsense about Britain, studded with obvious truths about its blacker and meaner side which the whol world knows.

Haw-Haw's extremely voice was at first consider opaganda Ministry offic

at the inane things Goebbels makes him say

There is another Brit aitor to note here in Be He is Baillie Stewart for O. of the Seaforth H landers, who a few years was sentenced to impri ment in the Tower for bei ing military secrets to a f Power.

The girl who led him was a German siren, an his release he followed here.

He did some broadcas first, but his Scottish na was too unbending for Nazi officials of the Propaga Ministry and the Ger Broadcasting Company.

He is now off the working as a translator in Foreign Office.

The " gate-crash

WHILE o mi

Am N C Io the Natio cere f fight when him.

He is I avoid a Kaltenba was at Com having one of with the Nazi radio

They gave orders that he not to be taken from Par Compiègne, but he stole a with some army officers " gate-crashed " the cerem He was continually being rested by the military ejected from the grounds, he came back each time. Most Nazis find him " too American " for their

JOYCE. They call him Froehlich—" Joyful ! "

The William L. Shirer article on William Joyce published in the *Sunday Chronicle*, 14 September 1941. (KV 2/245/274)

his adult life. Had it not been for his hysteria about Jews he might easily have become a Communist agitator. Strange as it may seem he thinks the Nazi movement is a proletarian one which will free the world from the bonds of 'plutocratic capitalists.' He sees himself primarily as a liberator of the working class.

Concluding his article Shirer observed: 'Any mind which sees Hitler's cold blooded trampling down of the free peoples of Europe as a sacred struggle speaks for itself'.[18]

Life in wartime Germany

William Joyce was not simply the master propaganda broadcaster to Britain, for throughout the war he took part in a variety of other activities for the Nazi regime, including direct short-wave propaganda broadcasts to pre-Pearl Harbor America and to other, usually neutral, countries; in early 1940 he even found the time to write a book entitled *Twilight over England*.[19] In his 1941 article about Joyce, William L. Shirer described it as 'a hodge-podge of Nazi nonsense about England, studded with obvious truths about its blacker and meaner side'.[20] A review of the text confirms this; however, the book does place Joyce's ideas in perspective. *Twilight over England* was little more than a synthesis of his pre-war speeches and earlier publications complete with the usual ranting and tirade against Jews, communists and Churchill. Interestingly, in the preface to the book, Joyce, with evident relish, described himself as 'a daily perpetrator of High Treason'.[21] Five years later this claim returned to haunt him. The book does have a somewhat

[18] William L. Shirer, 'I meet Haw-Haw', *Sunday Chronicle*, 14 September 1941. Joyce files KV 2/245/274.
[19] *Twilight Over England* (Berlin, 1940), republished by the Imperial War Museum with an introduction by Terry Charman. Facsimile reprint series number 5. See also the account of MI5's search for the publisher in 'William Joyce – International Verlag', 12 September 1945. Joyce files KV 2/247/500z.
[20] Shirer, *Sunday Chronicle*.
[21] Author's preface, *Twilight Over England*.

macabre side to it, for at one point Joyce makes an eerie if ironic prophesy, speculating of a time in the future when, presumably after the Nazi victory over Britain, Winston Churchill would be led out to be executed, with these words: 'Before the Governor of a British prison accompanies Mr Churchill on that last cheerless walk on a cold grey morning just before eight . . .' However, the fates had it differently and in 1946 it was William Joyce not Winston Churchill who made that last cheerless walk.[22] Although not a great work of literature or even good history, MI5 considered it sufficiently important to spend a great deal of time and effort trying to obtain a copy, but even by the time of the Joyce treason trial in September 1945 it had been unable to locate one, although it was said 100,000 copies had been printed for distribution to British prisoner-of-war camps.

In a broadcast he made on 2 April 1941 William Joyce announced his real name for the first time over the air, stung into this action by a virulent attack on him in an article contained in the 21 March 1941 edition of the *Evening Standard*. The article followed an interview with a dubious woman named Mary Marovna, who had evidently visited Joyce on a couple of occasions. Under banner headlines 'Girl tells of Haw-Haw as spy in London', the article claimed that Joyce was, during his final years in Britain, a German spymaster supposedly controlling 300 spies. It was a ludicrous interview, which owed everything to the fantasies of the interviewee, but it clearly annoyed Joyce to the point that he ended his broadcast by naming himself and making an apologia for his work in Germany:

> I, William Joyce, will merely say that I left England because I would not fight for Jewry against the Fuehrer and National Socialism, and because I believe most ardently, as I do today, that victory with a perpetuation of the old system would be an incomparably greater evil for England than defeat coupled with a possibility of building something new, something really nationalist, something truly socialist.[23] (**document 25**)

---

[22] *Twilight Over England*, p. 57.
[23] Transcript of a broadcast by William Joyce, 2 April 1941. Joyce files KV 2/245/285.

Thereafter all pretence of anonymity or hiding behind the 'Lord Haw Haw' tag was dropped and until his final broadcast in April 1945 he was announced as William Joyce.

The Joyce MI5 files contain a series of documents found in William and Margaret Joyce's possession at the time of their arrest. Among them was a series in German. These were later translated and include correspondence concerning his contract with German radio, the Reichs Rundfunk. One letter, written on 26 June 1942 by the foreign director, Dr Winkelnkemper, contains details relating to his promotion from announcer to chief English-language commentator for the 'English service', and highlighted Joyce's 'many years of efficiency as an announcer and commentator'.[24] His surviving 1942 contract shows he earned 1,200 Reichmarks (the equivalent of £60 or $240.00 at 1942 valuations) per month.

In addition to his heavy broadcasting schedule William Joyce undertook other duties for his German masters, including visits to British prisoner of war and civilian detainee camps with the intention of discovering individuals who might collaborate and make propaganda broadcasts. Sowing the seeds of defeatism among those he saw, he used his visits to attack morale among the prisoners and civilian detainees. The Joyce MI5 files contain a number of statements made by individuals, mainly written after the war, in which they tell of their meetings with Joyce.[25] (**documents 40** and **42**) As well as undermining morale, these statements suggest Joyce used such interviews to gain insights into life in wartime Britain and the dramatic changes that had taken place in the years since his departure. They clearly provided unwelcome and wounding criticism of him and his broadcasts. The statement of quartermaster sergeant John Henry Owen Brown, who later broadcast Nazi propaganda for Joyce, tells of his first meeting with him. He described how, under escort, he went to Berlin where, after about two weeks, two men wearing civilian clothing interviewed him, one of whom he recognized as William Joyce. Of his interview Brown said:

---

[24] Winkelnkemper to Joyce, 26 June 1942. Joyce files KV 2/250/2.
[25] See for example statement, Henry Mollison, 5 June 1945. Joyce files KV 2/246/400a. Henry Mollison was an actor interned as a civilian detainee. His statement concerned his interview with William Joyce and is of particular interest. It shows the extent Joyce was prepared to go in order to sow seeds of defeatism in POW camps (**document 42**).

Joyce did all the talking. The other man said nothing. Joyce questioned me closely on the camp welfare and entertainment facilities, also illegal supplies at Blechammer and then turned to the question of wireless. I told him that as no wireless was supplied to us by the Germans, I could not listen in (this of course was untrue, but I felt it was a catch question). Joyce then asked me if I had ever heard 'Lord Haw Haw' and I told him I had in England. He asked me 'Why?' and I told him that lots of people listened as they found it very amusing. He appeared surprised and annoyed. The interview terminated by his saying that he would see me again. Throughout this interview he did not disclose his identity to me.[26] (**document 36**)

In addition to his duties as a writer and broadcaster for the Reichs Rundfunk English-language service (Deutsche Europasender), William Joyce was also involved with Josef Goebbels' Ministry of Propaganda's secret propaganda radio, the so-called 'Bureau Concordia'. Based at Berlin's Reichsportsfeld, the whole operation was run by an SS officer, Dr Erich Hetzler, with transmissions taking the form of Nazi black propaganda. Bureau Concordia operated a number of these secret stations, whose programming was written in such a way as to make them appear to emanate from clandestine radio stations operating in Britain and run secretly by British opponents of the war. Dr Friedrich Wilhelm Schoebeth, a Reichs Rundfunk colleague of Joyce, told MI5 at the end of the war that Joyce worked for Concordia in the mornings and the rest of the day for the Reichs Rundfunk, a fact confirmed by Lance-Corporal Ronald Spillman, another former prisoner of war and British renegade broadcaster.[27] From these and other statements it transpired that William and Margaret Joyce wrote much of the programme content for these stations and also

---

[26] Statement, John Henry Owen Brown, 23 May 1945. Joyce files KV 2/246/384b.
[27] Statement, Ronald Spillman, 18 May 1945. Joyce files KV 2/246/382b. 'William Joyce used to come to Concordia in the mornings and dictate N.B.B.S. [New British Broadcasting Service] talks to one of the secretaries.'

participated in the actual broadcasts, sometimes anonymously and sometimes announced.[28] Joyce established a Bureau Concordia station known as 'Workers' Challenge', for which he wrote most of the broadcast material; ironically, it was a supposed secret communist station. Bureau Concordia was also responsible for a range of virulent anti-Semitic broadcasts, mainly written by Joyce, together with forces' programming such as 'Jerry calling', which started in June 1944 soon after the D-Day landings. The purpose of these broadcasts was to undermine morale and cause divisions between the Allies, especially between British and US forces fighting in the Normandy beachhead. Bureau Concordia also ran a station called 'Radio National', which was designed for Britain's civilian population and used British renegades like John Amery, together with William and Margaret Joyce.

A personal nirvana

When William and Margaret Joyce arrived in Germany at the end of August 1939 it must have been something of a mystical experience. After years of fighting, at times literally, for the fascist cause in Britain they had finally made it to what they believed was their personal nirvana. In sharp contrast to the hostility of London, in Berlin they were treated as honoured guests, being provided with decent accommodation and well-paid employment, thus leaving behind them the days of utter penury. On their own modest scale of achievement they had everything they desired and were able to serve the cause and the leader of their dreams, while September 1940 saw the culmination of this idyll with their achievement of German citizenship. In 1944 this was capped with an award to mark the anniversary of their fifth year in Germany as William Joyce gained what he believed to be the ultimate accolade, the war merit cross first class, together with a certificate signed by his hero, Adolf Hitler. (**document 29**) Such was his devotion that on his arrest at the end of May 1945 both the medal and certificate were found

---

[28] Statement, Dr Friedrich Wilhelm Schoeberth, 28 May 1945. Joyce files KV 2/246/387b.

among his meagre possessions. Somehow these artefacts, but not the naturalization papers, found their way to the MI5 files and are now preserved at The National Archives, Kew.[29]

In these circumstances the Joyces' personal fate during the war years seemed assured, although a reading of the MI5 files reveals otherwise. Captured documents and statements from those Britons and Germans who knew them in Germany tell part of the story, but the main story is told through a series of small pocket diaries and memorandum books kept by Margaret Joyce during the period 1940 to 1945, and supplemented by the journal Joyce kept between February and May 1945. The problem was simple. William Joyce had always lived life at the very edge, and from his earliest days fighting the Irish with the Black and Tans through to the London street-fighting with Jews, communists and others, he had demonstrated not just physical courage, but also pleasure from fighting and violence in general. The livid disfiguring scar he carried across his right cheek, a memento of a teenage brawl with communists in London, bore witness to that part of his personality and what proved the dominant element in his make-up. Of course all this went hand-in-hand with his hatred of the British press and politicians, international capitalism, the communists and the Jews, all of whom he blamed for the downfall of the British Empire and the war. This complex amalgam of a warped yet intellectually brilliant individual came together in the person of William Joyce, and it did not change simply because he and Margaret had moved to Nazi Germany.

From 1941 his boss at the Reichs Rundfunk was Eduard Roderick Dietze, said to be British-educated and a former BBC commentator. He first met Joyce in 1940 and initially, he told MI5 after the war, didn't like the man. None the less, 'Joyce is a man of great ability and great gifts and . . . I felt at the end that he was definitely a personality. He did nothing for personal ambition but always because of inner convictions'.[30] There was however one feature of Joyce's life Dietze and everyone who knew him came to notice and comment on – his heavy drinking. He had always been a chain

---

[29] War merit cross, first class: certificate in the name of chief commentator William Joyce. Dated 1 September 1944, signed Adolf Hitler. Joyce files KV 2/250/2.

[30] Statement, E. R. A. Dietze, 29 May 1945. Joyce files KV 2/246/388z.

smoker and a heavy drinker, but from the time he and Margaret moved to Germany his drinking got progressively worse and made its mark on his career. If a July 1944 British intelligence agent report from Stockholm is to be believed:

> William Joyce . . . is now almost permanently in a state of intoxication and [he] has adopted the system of writing out his scripts wherever possible two days in advance, so that they should be available for reading should he himself be incapable of coherent thought at the time of the broadcast.[31]

Corporal Francis Paul Maton, who knew Joyce well during these late war years, talked to the British authorities after the war. Maton was one of a number of prisoners of war who made propaganda broadcasts to Britain, for which he earned 300 Reichmarks per month (£15.00 or $60.00). He worked for the Bureau Concordia and used his Concordia pass to gain access to the Reichs Rundfunk, where he got to know William Joyce well. In his statement Maton provides a vivid description of Joyce:

> I think the most outstanding person of them all [the British renegades] is surely William Joyce. Joyce is a man who many people have tried to describe, and by reason of the fact that he is both universally known and hated over here, they have been inclined I am afraid to let their pens run away with them and I don't think that anyone has given an honest description of Joyce. William Joyce is a man who, as we all know, has many faults, but Joyce is an idealist and it is quite possible that as an idealist he is second only to Hitler himself.[32]

After describing Joyce's fearlessness in the midst of the RAF's nightly air raids over Berlin, Maton got to the nub of his assessment:

[31] 'Extract from L.271 (100) – Dietze, Eduard Roderick'. Joyce files KV 2/245/336b.
[32] Statement, Francis Paul Maton, 8/9 September 1944. Joyce files KV 2/245/342aa.

No doubt most people will have noticed that during five years of war Joyce's sarcasm has somewhat toned down, but I personally feel that this is not due to any fear on his part but due to the fact that I am told that in the early days of his career all his manuscripts were written for him, and were just plain German propaganda, cleverly interwoven with hate against our own country. However, now Joyce has risen into the position where he is king pin of the whole show and I don't believe he ever uses manuscripts now. I have myself seen him sit down in front of a radio, listen to the BBC news, walk straight over to a microphone and broadcast his well known 'Views on the News'.[33]

Corporal Maton described the Joyce he knew as being 'rather moody and at times is nervous'. He told how 'He also beats his wife, who is rather a fast woman, and has had affairs in Berlin with a large number of men'.[34] (**document 30**) Another account supported this view of the Joyce marriage, although this one took the form of a rather gossipy report, which said:

Mrs Joyce had an affair with a German which caused Joyce to divorce her, but within a year they had re-married. They had both begun to drink heavily, and people who had seen them described Joyce as having descended in appearance to that of an Apache. Their hang-out appeared to be a café in the Adolf Hitler Platz near the German propaganda station. They were said to have an expensive flat in the Kaiserdam nearby.[35]

The failure of his second marriage and Margaret's behaviour brought into focus the basic unhappiness and instability at the heart of William Joyce's existence from his birth in 1906 to his death on the scaffold 40 years later. What Margaret's cuckolding did for his

---

[33] Ibid.
[34] Ibid.
[35] Extract, typescript by Henry William Wicks, 16 February 1945. Joyce files KV 2/246/370b.

brittle self-esteem is difficult to assess, though her diary entries give some indication and they do make it relatively easy to reconstruct key events. Her 18 January 1941 entry read:

> Talk 8.30. Dinner Rund-Eck [bar]. Gilbert came in. He took me home. Nick [Margaret's lover] came in for a drink. He stopped rather late and as he went W[illiam] came in. I was frightened because I thought he would be angry – he was.

The entry for 23 January was equally stark:

> Left town to be out for W[illiam]. Lunch at Wilhelmshaven then home. He slept and I sorted out stuff. Then he beat me because of Saturday until I could hardly stand and then we went to dinner at the Int[ernational] Club. Gilbert came in and came back with us for a drink.

At this point Margaret left William Joyce and thereafter some of her diary entries become terse in the extreme. For example:

> **13 February 1941**: '4th anniv[ersary] of our wedding.'
> **24 February 1941**: 'Had a foreign press report that W[illiam]'s father died [on 19 February 1941] as a result of a heart attack after the Dulwich [family house in London] was hit [by a German bomb].'
> **12 April 1941**: 'Nasty letter from W[illiam].'

Given the poverty of their lives in London, the entry for **26 April 1941** is somewhat ironic: 'W[illiam] sent some money and two rather queer letters – we have to pay an awful lot of income tax.'

> **2 May 1941**: 'Lunch with Will[iam] – he wants us to live apart, although he is still fond of me. Home for some things.'
> **7 May 1941**: 'Drink with Will[iam]. Said he would never trust a woman again.'
> **12 May 1941**: 'We heard that Hess had pinched a plane and gone to England. He's gone mad. Got tight.'

4 June 1941: 'W[illiam] wants me back.'

5 June 1941: 'Lunch with Nick at H St. He is worried – wants to keep me but thinks I ought to go back to W[illiam]. Dinner with W[illiam] at Irish Exch. – we talked about things and I really decided to go back but broke down at thought of losing Nick.'

6 June 1941: 'Lunch at Gerald – Sany and Will[iam] there. W[illiam] forced it out of me that I'd stayed with Nick after getting his letter – left the restaurant in a passion. I had dinner at the Runk Eck and he was there so we sat together – he told me what he thought of me and then said "goodbye".'

13 June 1941: 'I went Rund-Eck for dinner and met Will[iam] coming out – he cut me.'

16 June 1941: 'Nick came to Rundfunk to see me – he says his business is all arranged – we can get married. Completely flattered. Will asked me to go back to him again.'

25 June 1941: 'W[illiam] saw me and apologised for his behaviour and said whole thing his fault.'[36]

The couple divorced in 1941, but found they could not live without each other; there was a reconciliation, and in 1943 they remarried.[37] Thereafter they stuck with each other until their arrest in May 1945. William and Margaret Joyce were clearly an odd couple, each fiercely independent, but equally utterly dependent on each other. In his statement to MI5 in May 1945 Joyce's colleague Edwin Schneider told of their professional relationship:

> During the time I was in Hamburg Joyce used to prepare his own scripts, sometimes assisted by his wife. I saw him on several occasions in his office typing his

[36] Margaret Joyce diary series, 1941. Margaret Joyce files KV 2/346/8.

[37] The relationship remained strange, if this extract from a statement by an unnamed Concordia employee is to be believed: 'He [Joyce] refused to allow her [Margaret] to communicate with his cousin Michael Joyce in a prisoner of war camp (Dulag Luft), because he had served in the RAF against Germany'. Joyce files KV 2/246.

own script. I also saw his wife type some of it. They had
two small typewriters which had been sent from Berlin,
and Joyce had a small portable one of his own which he
took away with him. Mr and Mrs Joyce also used one of
the studios in the 'bunker' (air raid shelter) as an office
and they had a typewriter there too.[38]

If evidence were needed this shows Margaret was anything but a
simple helpmate to Joyce. She began her own broadcasting career early
in the war and wrote scripts for use in both the Reichs Rundfunk and
Bureau Concordia stations. Initially her broadcasts were anonymous,
but once her husband began to be announced as 'Lord Haw Haw, she
was announced as 'Lady Haw Haw'. However, after 1941, when
William revealed his identity, she was announced as Margaret Joyce.

Joyce's wartime pursuers

By the mid-years of the war, and unbeknown to William and
Margaret Joyce, MI5 and others in London were making their
dispositions and collecting evidence for use in any post-war treason
trial of William, and possibly Margaret, Joyce. To this end, in the
early months of 1943, BBC engineers collaborated with Special
Branch officers to make a series of transcription discs and written
notes of several William Joyce broadcasts, the venue for this activity
being the BBC's Maida Vale studio and office complex, the first
taking place on 30 January 1943. In a statement, Special Branch
officer Inspector A. Hunt told how he and another officer, Sergeant
Buswell, had known Joyce during his pre-war BUF and National
Socialist League days, and were, crucially, familiar with his voice.
Hunt explained how he and Buswell attended the Maida Vale
studios and listened to the transmission, taking shorthand notes of
what was being said; both claimed to have recognized one of the
voices they had listened to as belonging to William Joyce. In addition
to the taking of shorthand notes, BBC engineers made a recording
of the transmission, copying it onto four transcription discs, each of

---

[38] Statement, Edwin Schneider, 21 May 1945. Joyce files KV 2/246/384z.

which the officers and engineers signed. They also replayed part of the final record containing the final moments of Joyce's speaking voice. The transcript of that broadcast reveals it as a paean of praise to National Socialism and Adolf Hitler, then celebrating the tenth anniversary of his coming to power.[39] On 8 April 1943 senior MI5 officers joined Special Branch and BBC engineers to supervise the recording and shorthand note-taking of a second Joyce broadcast. In his note of the proceedings, MI5 officer T. M. Shelford told of his walking between the locations where the recording was being made and the Special Branch officers listening to the broadcast and taking the shorthand notes. At the end of the broadcast the transcription discs were marked, placed in a container and sealed with wax marked with Shelford's signet ring.[40] These broadcasts contained the standard Joyce fare and are filled with the usual hate and self-justifying boastfulness. Joyce always used the word 'we' when referring to the German people – if the MI5 pursuers were seeking self-incriminating evidence to hang a British renegade then these and the evidence derived from other broadcasts taken at this time were perfect. In the end, however, factors that no one could have anticipated prevented the use of this and other evidence in Joyce's trial. (document 27)

The net closed in on the Joyces in other ways. For example, the minute sheets of the William Joyce MI5 files reveal an important note by T. M. Shelford dated 31 August 1943. It reads:

> I do not suppose that either William Joyce or his wife will return from Germany before the end of the war but they may do so then: alternatively they may seek to escape from Allied justice by fleeing from Germany to some other part of the world and pass through British or British-controlled territory on the way. It would seem prudent to have their names on the Black List. In case this should happen, and I suppose the Black List will not come to an end with the cessation of hostilities, I am

[39] Statement, Inspector A. Hunt, Special Branch, 19 February 1943. 'A transcript of shorthand notes taken by Inspector Hunt on 30 January 1943'. Joyce files KV 2/245/287a.

[40] Note, T. M. Shelford, 9 April 1943. Joyce files KV 2/245/288a.

sending you Mrs W. Joyce's file at the same time for similar action.[41] (see also **document 28**)

The acquisition of the London University Officer Training Corps (OTC) files relating to Joyce during his time as an undergraduate during the1920s provided MI5 with startling new evidence that cast the whole case against Joyce in a fresh light. As discussed in Chapter 1, these files reveal Joyce's American origins. From this point onwards officers at MI5 began to seriously doubt the viability of the case, arguing that if Joyce was a citizen of the United States, then how could he be charged with committing treason against the British Crown? G. E. Wakefield, a senior MI5 officer, made the point: 'If he is in fact only an American citizen, and he became a naturalized German before the outbreak of war between [the] USA and Germany, he is not presumably a traitor?'[42] These fears troubled the agency right down to the start of William Joyce's treason trial at the Old Bailey in September 1945.

Götterdämmerung: twilight of the Gods

During the course of 1942 the war turned decisively against Germany and its allies. The German armies that had appeared invincible in 1940 and 1941 were defeated first by the Red Army at Stalingrad in Russia and then by the British Eighth Army at the Battle of El Alamein in Africa. That same year also saw the United States Navy inflict a crippling defeat on the Japanese navy in the Pacific at Midway, and the Anglo-American naval and intelligence offensive against the U-boat menace in the Atlantic was also bearing fruit. Thereafter, on every front, the Allies moved decisively onto the offensive. In Germany itself, the towns and cities of the Third Reich became the target for round-the-clock bombing raids by the RAF and USAAF; by the start of 1943 it was clear to anyone with eyes to see

[41] Minute, T. M. Shelford, 18 September 1943. Joyce files KV 2/245. The names of William and Margaret Joyce were added to the Foreign Office Black List and in September 1944 to the SHAEF list of people to be detained. J. Nunn to T. M. Shelford, 11 September 1944. Joyce files KV 2/245/342b.
[42] Note, G. E. Wakefield, 7 March 1944. Joyce files KV 2/245.

that the war was moving towards a new and final phase. In these circumstances, William and Margaret Joyce were forced to face the inevitability of the utter annihilation of their beloved Nazi state and its final defeat at the hands of those on whom, in their broadcasts, they had heaped so much scorn and venom. In these circumstances the couple began to make their own contingency plans.

When the British detained the couple at the end of the war, William Joyce's German military passport together with other identity documents were discovered and now form a part of the Joyce MI5 collection; in contrast, his British passport was never located. (**documents 32 and 34**) The German documents show that from the earliest days of the war William Joyce had, as a precaution against his notoriety, used the name Wilhelm Froehlich. However, his military passport was made out in his real name, giving New York as his place of birth. Similarly his December 1944 Deutscher Volkssturm (Home Guard) pass also uses his real name and place of birth.[43] (**document 31**) However, Joyce was taking no chances, and according to his boss at the Rundfunk, the Gestapo issued him with a set of papers made out in the name of Wilhelm Hansen, in which he is described as a teacher and his place of birth is given as Galway, Ireland.[44]

Joyce needed these papers as from 1943 he was on the move. By that year the constant bombing of Berlin had steadily reduced the city to rubble and as a consequence it became a dangerous place to live and work. As a precaution, the Joyces were moved west to the relative safety of Luxembourg. From there the couple were accommodated in the Hotel Alfa and made their nightly broadcasts using the facilities of the Radio Luxembourg studios. The broadcasts were not simply made and transmitted from Luxembourg; they were also sent via landlines to those transmitter stations controlled by the Germans. However in the autumn of 1944, as the Allied armies closed in, the Joyces were forced to evacuate from their Luxembourg base.

When the British took Luxembourg, Captain William James Skardon, the MI5 officer assigned to collect information and if possible capture Joyce and other British renegades, combed the

---

[43] Joyce could never resist embellishing the facts, and he described his father as an architect in his 1941 military passport. Joyce files KV 2/250/1.

[44] Statement, E. R. A. Deitze, 29 May 1945. Joyce files KV 2/246/388z.

Radio Luxembourg premises for signs of the Joyces' occupancy, and a great deal of evidence was found among the material left behind by the couple during their hurried evacuation.[45] It included scripts, research notes, evidence of payments and a large collection of radio transcription discs of their broadcasts.[46]

After the withdrawal from Luxembourg, the Joyces returned to Berlin for a while and it was during this period that William enrolled in the Deutscher Volkssturm (Home Guard), wanting to do his bit in the defence of Berlin, where conditions were deteriorating daily. Fortunately, during this period of their lives, both William and Margaret Joyce kept diaries. In the case of William Joyce, it was more a detailed journal of happenings supplemented with often ironic comments as to his feelings.[47] These accounts provide detailed insights into their lives, experiences and their state of mind; in fact the first entries in William Joyce's journal are a chronicle of the worsening situation in Berlin. In early March he noted: 'Cold at Funkhaus. No enemy raid. But, if you please, between 3 & 4 in the morning. Probably the silly British think that the nightly raid is intolerable. It is not. It is just a nuisance'.[48] The following day he added: 'As I told M[argaret] I am not in the least perturbed, quite calm and whereas I might well expect the worst, I have an unbounded trust in God. And He alone can provide a way out. So why worry?'[49] However, Joyce's working conditions deteriorated with each passing day. As he noted on 6 March: 'Few of my listeners would believe how little is done to facilitate my work'. He used this opportunity to blame everybody else for his misfortune, observing: 'If I were a quarter Yid, like [John] Amery, I should be rolling in luxury: but I made the mistake of

---

[45] Memorandum, Captain W. J. Skardon, 21 October 1944. Joyce files KV 2/245/353a. Memorandum Captain W. J. Skardon, 11 June 1945. KV 2/246.

[46] These are now held at the National Sound Archive in the British Library, London.

[47] This was the only journal found among Joyce's possessions. It is therefore difficult to ascertain for certain whether or not it was anything more than a personal apologia. A 13 March 1945 entry tends to support this view. On that day he wrote: 'I find it hard to write with complete frankness, for, if I did, the diary would not be very helpful if it fell into the wrong hands.' All journal entries KV 2/250/2.

[48] William Joyce journal entry (hereafter journal), 4 March 1945.

[49] Journal, 5 March 1945.

beginning as a National-Socialist. The Germans are a funny people.'[50]

William Joyce had always been a very heavy drinker and smoker, however, during this final phase of the war, the pressures under which he was living took their toll and he became even more reliant on alcohol and tobacco. On 3 March 1945 he wrote: 'I wonder why I can drink so little without becoming violent and subsequently showing symptoms of amnesia?'[51] On 8 March 1945 Joyce noted: 'Went with Margaret to Club. Walked from Nollendorf Platz. Lunch at Club. Chateau Neuf du Pape. Marvellous, RM.6 per glass, but worth far more at present rates'.[52] (**journal**, see p. 259) Shortly before the couple's final departure from Berlin Joyce was involved in another bout of drunkenness. Of the episode he wrote:

> I believe a bomb fell quite near, but I was indifferent to it, was really drunk. Margaret left me, nearly had a scene. . . Thank heavens I did not. Bashed myself badly coming home.
>
> Woke up feeling sorry for myself. Left leg badly hurt and face a mess. I regret my exit from Berlin should be so undignified. Naturally the reasons for my scars is obvious to anyone who knows my little habits.[53]

By mid-March 1945 it was clear that if the couple's broadcasts were to continue they would have to leave Berlin immediately. When they learned of this, William and Margaret confided their feelings in their respective journals. Angry and frustrated at the hand he had been dealt, William Joyce blamed the Germans for his ills. As to their inefficiency he commented:

> The Germans simply do not know what time means. I believe that the Indians are more time conscious. Oh! Lord! I pity them in the awakening that is coming. Trouble is that so many decent and innocent people have to suffer.[54]

---

[50] Journal, 6 March 1945.
[51] Journal, 3 March 1945.
[52] Journal, 8 March 1945.
[53] Journal, 13–14 March 1945.
[54] Ibid.

This growing anger and despair extended to those German colleagues running the propaganda machine:

> The Japanese and the Italian propagandists may be worse than the Germans, but otherwise no competition! Goebbels is a genius – brilliant beyond words – but his henchmen are putrid. They might be masons or in the enemy pay. Half of them look like Yids and the other like idiots. Perhaps they are not paid enough. I don't know, anyhow they let him down.[55]

With the world collapsing around her, Margaret Joyce noted in her diary on 13 March 1945: 'Packing. Imminent. Lunch at club said goodbye S.O.B. office . . . Last dinner at club . . . quarrelled with W[illiam] and came home alone. Miserable miserable'. The following day she noted: 'Packed office. Lunch at club . . . back to office – [with] W[illiam] to Potsdam – nearly missed train. Apen 12.33. Town crowded. So unhappy'.[56]

Ironically, as the couple were leaving, they unexpectedly bumped into their friend Christian Harri Bauer, who had met them on their arrival in August 1939.[57] The couple went to the small town of Apen, near Hamburg, the site of a radio amplifier station. The town had excellent landline links to the transmitters at Hamburg, Norden and Wilhelmshaven, then still in German hands. Makeshift broadcast studios were created, including magnetophone tape-recording facilities, at the town's main inn, the Hotel Bremers.[58]

At Apen, the Joyces were installed in lodgings next door to the studio. William described them as:

> 2 attic rooms with a puffing billy [stove]. Much trouble about the beds, which were given as a rare concession, and were hard and damp. Everything damp here: but I think it might be worse. How many people have tonight no roof over their heads at all?[59]

---

[55] Ibid.
[56] Margaret Joyce diary series, 1945. Margaret Joyce files KV 2/346.
[57] Journal, 14 March 1945. All journal entries KV 2/250/2.
[58] Statement, Guy Della-Cioppa, 23 May 1945. Joyce files KV 2/250/1.
[59] Journal, 15 March 1945.

In fact conditions in Apen proved better than Berlin where, Joyce noted, they were almost starving. Despite being able to continue the work he loved, Joyce noted on 16 March 1945: 'How long shall we be able to function at all under present testing conditions?'[60] William Joyce knew the war was lost. On 20 March 1945 he wrote in his usual blunt way: 'Today's news makes it clear that the bloody war is lost, unless a dozen miracles happen – which they won't, I fear. Sad, but, true – we had made a complete balls of it'.[61] (**journal**, see p. 270) In these circumstances he also started to ponder his own fate, a fate he now knew would overtake him once the war ended, writing pensively on 24 March 1945: 'Most people here are wondering what will happen to them. Perhaps I have the greatest cause: but I feel quite serene, not a bit worried'.[62] (**journal**, see p. 274) He returned to the subject of his own fate on 29 March:

> I still love England and hate to think that I am to be regarded as a traitor to her, which in my own opinion I am not. I am deeply sorry for Germany: but I can see how the whole ghastly situation has come about.[63] (**journal**, see p. 280)

He was clearly very frustrated by the drawn-out death agonies of his beloved Third Reich; he also wanted but knew he would not find a hero's death, confiding these thoughts to his journal: 'Damn it! I wish I could go out like a man – with plenty to drink and good cigars.' He was also concerned that as a thinking man he was finished and wrote: 'I regret that I have gone to seed. Otherwise I might have amounted to something. I fear that I am spent now'.[64]

The strange and contradictory relationship with Margaret remained one of the most important themes in William Joyce's journal. Of their turbulent past he wrote on 27 March 1945, when Margaret, worryingly for him, was away in Berlin:

---

[60] Journal, 16 March 1945.
[61] Journal, 20 March 1945.
[62] Journal, 24 March 1945.
[63] Journal, 29 March 1945.
[64] Journal, 27 and 26 March 1945.

It is 4 years today since we parted . . . Evil omen. May
God bring her safely back. If of course Apen is going to
be cut off it is very well that she is gone. Better that way
than the other. But I trust that God will rejoin us in
happiness. Well. This is life that one can and must
breathe in with both nostrils.[65]

His attitude seemed to vary with his mood. On the one hand he
became desperately worried when she was away, but on the other
was caustic about her poor attitude to work and other matters. As
late as 15 April 1945 this poisonous mood prevailed:

It is almost impossible to work with her. Not only does
she vastly overestimate her own abilities, but she
continually presumes on the fact that she is my wife to
contradict my orders and wastes my time. She has
become quite unreliable.[66]

Although much better food was provided, for much of their time in
Apen basic necessities like tobacco and alcohol were lacking. Joyce
felt this keenly, claiming it affected the quality of his work; however,
when supplies of these essentials arrived he indulged himself with
his usual excess.

The broadcasts from Apen continued until mid-April 1945, when
with the remaining English language broadcast team they moved to
Hamburg.[67] On 19 April Joyce noted the fall of the Bremen
transmitter, also noting that he and Margaret would soon be on the
move again. On 20 April, the couple went to the Hamburg
headquarters of the Gestapo to receive fresh papers complete with
new identities. Joyce observed on 28 April: 'The future does not look
promising. We have several plans, but I doubt if any of them will
work. However, I am not worried, if I cannot dodge the bill, I must
pay it'.[68] (**journal**, see p. 299) It was in Hamburg on 29 April that
William Joyce, angry and defiant to the end, made his last drunken

---

[65] Journal, 27 March 1945. All journal entries KV 2/250/2.
[66] Journal, 15 April 1945.
[67] Statement, Edwin Schneider, 21 May 1945. Joyce files KV 2/246/384z.
[68] Journal, 28 April 1945.

appearance before the microphone, concluding with a defence of his and Germany's position, asserting:

> Now, in this most serious time of our age, I beg you to realise that the fight is on. You have heard something about the Battle of Berlin. You know that there a tremendous world-shattering conflict is being waged. Good. I will only say that the men who have died in the Battle of Berlin have given their lives to show that whatever else happens, Germany will live. No coercion, no oppression, no measures of tyranny that any foreign foe can introduce will shatter Germany. Germany will live because the people of Germany have in them the secret of life, endurance and will of purpose. And therefore I ask you in these last words – you will not hear from me again for a few months, I say 'Es lebe Deutschland' Heil Hitler and farewell.[69]

final broadcast

On the day William Joyce made his final broadcast, an equally defiant Margaret noted in her diary: 'English crossed the Elbe at Luneberg. BBC confirmed Mussolini murdered and gave gloating description of how he was hung and then his body thrown in a Milan square and riddled with bullets – and the BBC calls these people patriots'. The following day, 30 April 1945, the day Hitler committed suicide, she noted: 'Grupe [the head of the Hamburg radio station] sent for us to have a huge lunch with him. Schnaping says he must go. Dinner at billet with Eddy [Edwin Schneider] and a woman. Drank with Grupe and Schnaping till 3.00 am'.[70] In his May 1945 statement Schneider said: 'On 30 April 1945, I dined with Joyce and his wife at the Vier Jahreszeiten Hotel. The same night, at about 3.00 am, Margaret and William Joyce were driven away by car for an unknown destination'.[71] (**document 35**) In these circumstances this strange couple, whose tryst with destiny began with their August 1939 flight to Berlin, began a second journey, during the course of which they reaped the bitter harvest of that fateful first journey.

---

[69] Transcript of a broadcast by William Joyce, 30 April 1945. KV 2/250/2.
[70] Margaret Joyce diary series, 1945. Margaret Joyce files KV 2/246.
[71] Statement, Edwin Schneider, 21 May 1945. Joyce files KV 2/246/384z.

Photograph of William Joyce from the MI5 files. (KV 2/246)

Chapter 3

Traitor

of meeting

In November 1944, some months before the final flight of William and Margaret Joyce from Hamburg, an important meeting was held in London to discuss the case of high treason against the couple and to prepare for a trial. The meeting was called by Director of Public Prosecutions, Theobald Mathew, who was responsible for all serious criminal prosecutions, and was attended by senior figures from the Security Service (MI5) together with Special Branch officers. Mathew told them: 'The case was one which would be a leading state trial; its importance could not be exaggerated'.[1] In these circumstances he asked both agencies to furnish him with relevant evidence, specifically details of early broadcast material: 'in particular any broadcast made by him in 1940, giving his predictions on the bombing of the main cities of England'.[2] This material, he said, was needed in readiness for any coming trial. From this point onwards the energies of MI5 and Special Branch were focused on creating what they hoped would prove a watertight case of high treason against William Joyce. Accounts of these agencies' activities, together with those of the director's office, are spread among the later volumes of the MI5 Joyce files. The files also disclose the extent to which MI5 officers were prepared to go to ensure Joyce's conviction, including the interception of family and defence correspondence and the collection of detailed information concerning Joyce's correspondence and the conversations with his lawyers, family and friends; information that continued to appear in the files until a few days before his execution on 3 January 1946.

---

[1] Note, W. E. Hinchley Cooke, 11 November 1944. Joyce files KV 2/245/355a.
[2] Ibid.

Capture and arrest

According to the statement Margaret Joyce made after her arrest, supported by the entries in her dairy, the Gestapo had provided her and William with false papers and the offer of assistance to get out of Germany. However, she said: 'I thought my chances of leaving the country were very small and therefore fully expected to be arrested by the British authorities'.[3] The couple left Hamburg for the last time in the early hours of 1 May 1945, driven by two SS officers who took them to the small German town of Flensburg on the German–Danish border. The plan was to spirit them across the frontier and then smuggle them to neutral Sweden. The couple did cross briefly into Denmark, but the chaos they found forced their immediate return to Germany. In the back of her diary Margaret had written a short list of names and addresses in Switzerland and Spain, presumably of sympathetic fascist friends and safe houses that might offer asylum. Her diary entry for 1 May 1945 summed up her despairing state of mind: 'Very tired, weak and then got a room. At 22.25 [hours] the BBC announced that Adolf Hitler had been killed in the afternoon'. William Joyce's own journal note for that date is laconic:

> On this tragic day, the death of Adolf Hitler was reported. Admiral Donitz [sic] takes over as his nominated successor. Reach Flensburg about 8. Have to drink wine for breakfast – as nothing else is available.[4] (**journal**, see p. 301)

The entry for that day explains the failure of the couple to make progress in their flight into Denmark quite simply because there were no trains to take them, and although Joyce noted the availability of food, he added: 'but too little to drink'. The strain was evident and uncharacteristically Joyce remarked: 'Feel lonely, though Margaret is splendid'. Trapped, Joyce concluded his last journal entry:

[3] Statement by Margaret Cairns Joyce, 30 May 1945. Margaret Joyce files KV 2/253.
[4] Journal, 1 May 1945. All journal entries KV 2/250/2.

| 147—150 | MAI | 1945 |

Sonntag *Nick's birthday*

27 ☿

Trinitatis *Collected wood in the afternoon*

•

Normalzeit: SA. 3.49 SU. 20. 6 — MA. 20.30 MU. 4.18

Montag *Quarrelled with Will & let him go out*
28 *alone & he was arrested & shot at.*
I was arrested with all the Commissars
but they let them go. Some of the officers
came & jeered at me but some were nicer.

1940 Kapitulation der belgischen Armee

Margaret Joyce's diary entry for 28 May 1945 describing her husband's capture.
(KV 2/346/8)

We get a German paper and read the news. I miss the
wireless very much indeed. This day of complete
idleness seems unnatural. Perhaps it is well for a
change: but I feel I cannot stand it long. Well – will see.
The more I reflect – the more I am inclined to go back to
Germany.'[5]

Germany capitulated on 7 May 1945 and the Allied world
celebrated VE Day the following day. Stranded in Flensburg, he must
have realized that with the protective power of fascist Germany gone
the game was up. He had already noted his willingness to face the
consequences of his wartime activities; now with that fatalism borne
of his strange experience of life, Joyce saw they were fugitives on the
run, with the British in hot pursuit and likely to catch them. On

---

[5] Journal, 2 May 1945.

arrival in Flensburg, the couple stayed at the Railway Hotel and maintained contact with the SS officers charged with getting them across the border. Then occupying British forces arrived and, failing to recognize them, the couple joined the other guests in being turned out of the hotel. They spent the rest of the month of May 1945 lying low in the town, having found lodgings with a family called Asmussen. William Joyce's journal entries for the early part of 1945 show how even at the best of times his relationship with Margaret was brittle, and at this point it was evidently under severe pressure. In the end Joyce reached breaking point and turned on his wife, whose last diary entry, dated 28 May 1945, read:

> Quarrelled with Will[iam] and let him go out alone and he was arrested and shot at. I was arrested with all the Asmussens, but they let them go. Some of the officers came and jeered at me but some were nice.[6]

William Joyce was not so lucky. The statement made by Captain Alexander Adrian Lickorish, the British officer who caught him, is clear and to the point:

> On 28 May 1945 at about 7.00 pm I was with another officer Lieutenant Perry in a wood, a mile from the Danish frontier near Flensburg gathering fuel. A little earlier we had seen an individual, a man who was also in the wood and as we were collecting logs at 7.00 pm he turned towards us and waving his stick indicated some wood in a ditch. Thereafter he remained near us and presently spoke to us in French but we ignored his remarks except to thank him in German. After a while he said in English 'Here are a few more pieces'. I immediately recognised his voice as that of a broadcaster on the German radio known as William Joyce. I desired to confirm my suspicions and had a discussion with Lieutenant Perry. We evolved a plan as a result of which when the man was placing the wood on

Lickorish Statement

---

[6] Margaret Joyce diary entry, 28 May 1945. Margaret Joyce files KV 2/346.

our truck Lieut[enant] Perry taxed him by saying 'You wouldn't happen to be William Joyce would you?' He put his hand to his pocket and Perry shot at his hand. Joyce fell to the ground saying 'My name is Hansen'. I rushed to him and searched him with a view to disarming him. Joyce said 'I am not armed'. Looking through his pockets I found in the inner jacket pocket a Reisepasse in the name of Wilhelm Hansen and a Wehrepasse in the name of William Joyce. We treated his wound by giving first aid, later handing him over to the appropriate military authorities.[7] (**document 38**)

MI5 evidently attached great importance to Lickorish's statement, and the original manuscript copy was retained. On his way to the Luneburg military hospital for treatment to a wound to his right thigh, Joyce is alleged to have remarked: 'I suppose that in view of recent suicides, you expect me to do the same. I am not that sort of person'.[8] Reports of Joyce's detention, together with the arrest and custody documents, were passed to MI5 and are retained in the Joyce files. They show the couple had in their possession quantities of German, Swiss, US, Danish and Russian currency; there also survives an inventory of possessions, though this failed to prevent the loss, probably to pilfering, of much of Margaret Joyce's personal property. (**document 39**)

Two days after his arrest Joyce was visited at his hospital bedside by Captain William James Skardon, the MI5 officer tasked with interrogating him and gathering evidence for a future treason trial. Still recovering from the gunshot wound to his leg, Skardon's visit proved to be the first of three lengthy interviews. Having told Joyce who he was and why he wanted to talk to him, Skardon asked if he wanted to make a statement. Joyce agreed. The original manuscript copy of the lengthy statement Joyce dictated to Skardon is retained among the papers in the Joyce files. In it he repeated earlier claims concerning his US birth and gave an account of his early life. He also

---

[7] Statement, Captain Alexander Adrian Lickorish, 23 June 1945. Joyce files KV 2/248/39a.

[8] Arrest report, William and Margaret Joyce, 12 June 1945. Joyce files KV 2/248/8a.

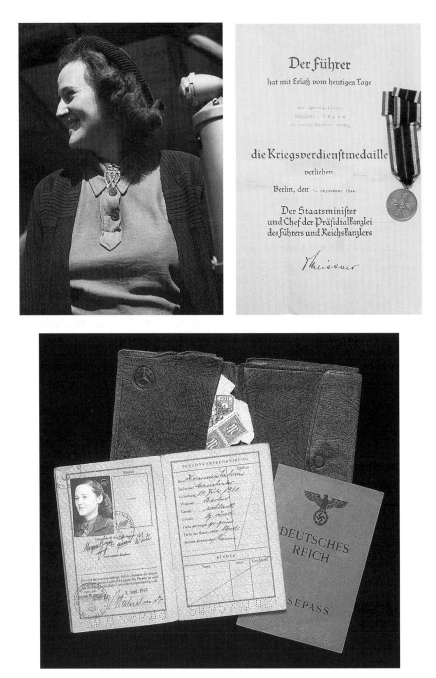

Belongings of Margaret Joyce found after the Joyces' arrest. They include a photograph of Margaret at the microphone, her wallet and German internal passport, and her civil war merit medal and certificate. (KV 2/346/6)

asserted his taking of German nationality in September 1940, though supporting documentation for this was never found. The core of the statement reads as a self-justifying apologia in which he said:

> When in August 1939 the final crisis emerged I felt that the question of Danzig offered no just cause for a world war. As by reasons of my opinions I was not conscientiously disposed to fight for Britain [against] Germany, I decided to leave the country since I did not wish to play the part of a conscientious objector and since I supposed that in Germany I should have the opportunity to express and propagate views the expression of which would be forbidden in Britain during time of war.

Joyce then explained how these opinions convinced him he had to go to Germany. He also remarked that he realized, once Russia and America entered the war, Germany might lose, concluding the statement:

> I know that I have been denounced as a traitor and I resent the accusation as I conceive myself to have been guilty of no underhand or deceitful act against Britain although I am also able to understand the resentment that my broadcasts have, in many quarters, aroused. Whatever opinion may be formed at the present time with regard to my conduct I submit that the final judgement cannot be properly passed until it is seen whether Britain can win the peace.

He ended with an assertion that Margaret went to Germany only because he did.[9] This statement is important as, in the event, it was to be the last the master propagandist William Joyce ever made. (**document 37**)

---

[9] Statement, William Joyce, 31 May 1945. Joyce files KV 2/246/390b.

The case for the prosecution

With Joyce in British hands, the Director of Public Prosecutions and L. A. Byrne, the treasury counsel who was due to take the Joyce case, called a meeting on 11 June 1945. Chief Inspector Bridges of Special Branch and senior representatives of MI5 attended and they discussed possible defence strategies in the forthcoming trial. Addressing the meeting, Byrne expressed the view that Joyce's likely defence was his claim to be an American citizen. According to the meeting notes, he argued:

> It was essential to prove that Joyce was not an American, and he accordingly asked for further enquiries to be made as to the possible naturalisation of Joyce's father, and that a witness who could speak as to the enquiries made should be available at the trial.[10] (document 43)

When the evidence of Joyce's assertion he was a British subject born in Ireland contained in the passport application was put to Byrne, he stated it was 'not necessarily conclusive, for which reason he was asking for this additional evidence'.[11] The fears of the prosecution team were clear: it might be possible for Joyce to defend himself against a charge of treason on the grounds he owed no allegiance to the British Crown. It was on the basis of this conference that the FBI and the British Consul in New York began their separate investigations described in Chapter 1 and police interviews were conducted with family members, particularly Joyce's uncle, Gilbert Brooke, in Derbyshire.

In the meantime, William and Margaret Joyce were moved to places of detention controlled by the British military in Brussels, where Margaret remained until a decision as to her future could be made. In the case of her husband, MI5 decided to move him to Britain as soon as his medical condition permitted. Joyce was

---

[10] 'Note of a conference' by D. H. Sinclair, 14 June 1945. Joyce files KV 2/246/411a.
[11] Ibid.

considered a very important catch and so, on 16 June 1945, an aircraft left Hendon airport in London for Brussels. On arrival at the Belgian capital, it collected William Joyce and his escort and flew them back to Hendon; it was Joyce's first sight of Britain since his departure in August 1939 – he had left for Germany an unknown and failed politician, but returned an infamous celebrity.

The Britain he returned to was a very different place to the one he left. On a personal level, his parents had died during the war: his father in February 1941 and his mother on 15 September 1944, some months before the end of the war in Europe. On disembarkation at Hendon he was met by Frank Bridges of Special Branch, arrested and taken to Bow Street police station where he was formally charged with high treason. The wording of the charge was significant, as it did not claim Joyce as a British subject. Rather, it read: 'he committed High Treason in that he . . . being a person owing allegiance to His Majesty The King adhered to the King's enemies elsewhere than in the King's realm, to wit, in the German realm.'[12] This ambiguous phrasing betrayed the deep unease felt by MI5 and the prosecuting authorities, who continued to fear if Joyce could prove his US citizenship, he might conceivably walk free. Whatever the legal niceties, if Joyce had any illusions as to his fate they were by now swept away, for the death penalty awaited anyone found guilty of high treason; he now knew he was fighting for his life. With Joyce came his belongings, which were all meticulously logged by the Metropolitan Police. Because of his medical condition the police surgeon saw him and after examining the gunshot wound together with the X-rays and medical report accompanying the prisoner, recommended periods of exercise. He also noted Joyce was being treated for what he described as seborrhoeic dermatitis.[13] (**document 44**)

The arrest of William Joyce and the charge of treason caused a sensation in Britain and in the British press. Every court appearance he made was characterized by packed courtrooms, with people and press vying with family and friends to get a glimpse of the man who had been such an important part of their lives for the

---

[12] Report, Chief Inspector Frank Bridges, Special Branch, 16 June 1945. Joyce files KV 2/246/418b.
[13] Ibid.

previous six years. The case coincided with the enactment of fresh legislation reforming Britain's antiquated treason laws which it was hoped would speed up the trial process. With this in mind, two days after William Joyce's dramatic arrival in Britain the wheels of justice ground into gear. On 18 June 1945 he made his first appearance at Bow Street Magistrate's Court before the chief magistrate, Sir Bertram Watson. He faced the single charge of high treason and was unrepresented at the hearing, the only lawyer present appearing for the Director of Public Prosecutions. Help was offered by his friend and former business partner John Macnab, who had spent much of the war in detention for his fascist activities. He went so far as to write a personal letter to the chief magistrate saying he wanted to give evidence on Joyce's behalf. The learned magistrate merely passed the letter to MI5 and it was retained on the Joyce files.[14] It was a preliminary hearing and Joyce was remanded into prison custody for a week and granted legal aid.[15] He was taken to Brixton prison in London.

The following week Joyce again appeared before Sir Bertram Watson for a second hearing. On this occasion he had a lawyer, C. B. V. Head of Ludlow and Co., solicitors. Three different accounts of the hearing survive in the Joyce files, from Special Branch and MI5 observers in court, suggesting the agency attached great importance to the arguments put forward by both sides. It was during the course of his prosecution outline that treasury counsel, L. A. Byrne, introduced the notion that: 'there was [legal] authority for saying that even an alien might in certain circumstances owe allegiance to His Majesty'.[16] The prosecution then put its evidence into court – from the passport office, then the police evidence regarding the broadcasts, Captain Skardon told of the statement Joyce had made, and finally evidence of German documents showing Joyce's employment contract with German radio and other material. At the conclusion of the prosecution outline, Byrne asked for the case to be committed for trial at the Old Bailey. In response, C. B. V. Head, Joyce's defence lawyer, argued there was no case to answer, saying:

[14] John Macnab to Sir Bertram Watson, 12 June 1945. Joyce files, KV 2/248.
[15] Note, 'Rex v. William Joyce', D. H. Sinclair, 18 June 1945. Joyce files KV 2/246/420a.
[16] Memorandum, 'Rex v. Joyce', D. H. Sinclair, 25 June 1945. Joyce files KV 2/246/435ab.

A Must Read

Joyce was not a British subject and that the onus was upon the prosecution to show Joyce was a British subject, as otherwise, if he were an alien, he could not be guilty of treason abroad; all the prosecution had shown was that he had been born in New York, and that on his passport application he had described himself as a British subject by birth.[17]

After considering the matter, the magistrate decided a prima-facie case had been made out and remanded Joyce back to Brixton prison for a week, from whence he returned for a formal committal hearing to send him to the Old Bailey to stand trial on the charge of high treason.[18] After the second court hearing, MI5 officer D. H. Sinclair approached Joyce's defence lawyer on what can only be interpreted as a 'fishing expedition'. In a memorandum he wrote after the discussion, Sinclair said he enquired of Head as to the barrister the defence proposed to brief. Sinclair claimed Head told him he would start off with Derek Curtiss Bennett KC, but added there might be somebody else later on. The conversation continued to discuss the merits of various barristers, with Head saying: 'He would like to go to Ireland and arrange for some leading King's Counsel from there with a great deal of fight in him to come across and assist the defence'. The conversation ended with Head telling Sinclair: 'he felt that Joyce really had got a defence, which would enable them to put up a very good fight indeed.'[19]

The court proceedings and the delay in getting a response from New York prompted a further prosecution conference on 5 July 1945. Those attending included prosecutor Byrne, together with representatives from MI5 and Special Branch. The status of the evidence was reviewed and the issues of US and Irish citizenship discussed. Byrne also told of the way his mind was working with regards to the issue of allegiance:

Mr Byrne stated that he had had the opportunity of discussing the whole legal question with Sir Oscar

[17] Ibid.
[18] Ibid.
[19] Memorandum, D. H. Sinclair, 28 June 1945. Joyce files KV 2/246/437b.

Dowson, legal advisor to the Home Office, and he had also reviewed the authorities. He had found with some assistance in Foster a passage which stated that in certain circumstances even an enemy alien owed allegiance to His Majesty: he did however point out that Foster, in writing this, was referring to judges' declaration made in 1707 at the time of the war against France and Spain.

Byrne also told the conference that he had now received the brief for this case and that the Attorney General was going to lead him and junior counsel Gerald Howard.[20]

The serious weaknesses in the prosecution case together with fears of an acquittal by an Old Bailey jury clearly worried MI5. G. E. Wakefield, on learning of a potential German witness for the prosecution, outlined his concerns in a file minute, saying:

> The potential importance of Wagner's allegation (that Joyce was not naturalised in Germany till 1943) is based on the pessimistic assumption that Joyce is finally acquitted in this country on the grounds that he has never been a British subject. Moreover, if he was naturalised in 1940, before America was at war with Germany, he would not, presumably, have committed Treason against the USA. He would therefore go scot-free. If, on the other hand, he was not in fact naturalised till 1943, he would, I imagine, have been committing Treason against the USA.

Summing up his nightmare scenario, he observed: 'An acquittal whether at the Old Bailey, or by the Court of Criminal Appeal or House of Lords, must inevitably create a public outcry, which no amount of legal argument will be able to silence'.[21] It was not simply criticism from within Britain; there were also concerns about the

---

[20] Memorandum, D. H. Sinclair, 5 July 1945. Joyce files KV 2/246/443b. Byrne was referring to Sir David Maxwell-Fyffe KC, PC, MP, Attorney General in the Churchill government. When this government fell later in July 1945 his successor, Sir Hartley Shawcross KC, PC, MP, inherited the case and went on to lead the Old Bailey prosecution team.

[21] G. E. Wakefield, 10 July 1945. Joyce files KV 2/246.

reaction of the Soviet Union to such an acquittal, as there had already been critical comment in the Soviet media concerning this and other treason cases.[22] (**documents 41 and 54**)

These fears were not allayed at the evidence review conference called by the Director of Public Prosecutions on 16 July 1945. In attendance were representatives from MI5 and for the first time the FBI, who were still pursuing enquiries in New York. The immediate problem was that the Joyce trial was scheduled to start two days hence. The conference learned that the defence counsel would ask for an adjournment till September, when it was hoped the issue of nationality would be resolved. The fears and frustrations of all present are evident in the notes Sinclair later prepared. As the prosecutors were still without the results of the New York enquiries, it was agreed not to oppose the defence application,[23] (**document 49**) so when Joyce appeared at the Old Bailey on 18 July 1945 the case was adjourned till the September sessions.[24]

Because the case was listed for hearing, the prosecution were obliged to serve a copy of the indictment on Joyce. There is a copy in the MI5 files and it contains three charges. In summary all three characterized Joyce 'as a person owing allegiance to our Lord the King'. He was accused of:

1. Between 18 September 1939 and 29 May 1945 giving 'aid and comfort to the said enemies in parts beyond the seas . . . by broadcasting to the subjects of our Lord the King propaganda on behalf of the said enemies'.
2. Becoming naturalized as a subject of the Realm of Germany.
3. This part of the indictment was identical to the first except the dates, which were between 18 September 1939 and 2 July 1940 (the period when Joyce held a valid British passport).[25]

---

[22] Radio Moscow kept up pressure on the British regarding cases relating to British renegades. See extracts from BBC daily digest of world broadcasts dated 5 June 1945 and 19 September 1945. Joyce files KV 2/246/399b and KV 2/247/502a.

[23] Memorandum, D. H. Sinclair, 16 July 1945. Joyce files KV 2/249/61a.

[24] Memorandum, 'Rex v. William Joyce', D. H. Sinclair, 18 July 1945. Joyce files KV 2/246/460a.

[25] 'Indictment against William Joyce, 17 July 1945'. Joyce files KV 2/99a.

The indictment provided clear evidence to Joyce and his defence team of the all-encompassing nature of the charges, suggesting the prosecution was keeping all options open, whilst gambling on the nationality issue being resolved in its favour. In fact it took a further nerve-racking month to obtain the relevant FBI reports and certified copies of court documents concerning his father's US naturalization and copies of the marriage certificate to his mother, and to receive a copy of Joyce's own birth certificate. This evidence is described in Chapter 1, and seemed to confirm William Joyce's assertion of US citizenship.[26]

Mounting a defence

In the meantime William Joyce, his family, friends and legal team had not been idle, though perhaps inevitably Joyce's first thoughts were for his wife Margaret. A minute sheet from the Joyce files indicates a request for a letter written from Brixton prison to be passed to his wife, then still being held in Brussels.[27] Once this link had been established, letters passed between the couple on a regular basis. Extracts from relevant parts of this correspondence survive on the Joyce files. For example, she wrote to him for the first time on 1 July 1945, worried at the lack of news about him and concerned that no one, not even the British intelligence officers who acted as postmen, knew anything about her case. The old fire was still in her belly as she enquired:

> What has happened to old Quisling? Have they caught that swine Ribbentrop? What is Russia doing about Japan?...Did they change your German money, or is that with mine here? If it is, I have the impression that a lot of yours was stolen. Something the handsome

---

[26] See Chapter 1, pp. 2–4. Thanks to the activities of a US agent, Ludlow and Co. obtained typescript copies of Michael Joyce's naturalization and marriage papers. On 15 July they asked the Foreign Office to assist in obtaining photostat copies of these documents so that they could be proved as relating to the same person. Joyce files KV 2/249/66a.

[27] 21 June 1945. Joyce files KV 2/246.

Intelli-gent [sic] Major Randall said at Luneburg gave me the idea that I had yours too.[28] (**document 46**)

On 4 July 1945 William's younger brother Quentin wrote his first letter to Margaret. It was accompanied by a covering letter addressed to Chief Inspector Bridges of Special Branch in which he asked Bridges to have the letter delivered; it was forwarded to MI5 for onward transmission. Although Quentin knew of her detention, at the time neither he nor William had any idea as to her whereabouts, and Bridges either did not know or refused to tell them. Quentin told her of the good spirits in which he found his brother, and of his health:

> He is improving every day. When I first saw him, he was far from well, having no colour at all. His limp was most pronounced and he was suffering a certain amount of pain from the wound he received. Now, after a couple of weeks in Brixton, he is pulling round in a miraculous manner. The wound has healed very well, and he is experiencing no pain from it at all. He is putting on weight, and he is gaining more colour every day.[29] (**document 47**)

The prison governor at Brixton kept MI5 informed of Joyce's visitors and correspondence, ensuring notes were made of the subjects discussed by visitors and correspondents with him. The earliest surviving example of this is contained in a 6 July 1945 letter from MI5 to Special Branch which listed Joyce's visitors as his brother Quentin Joyce, his friends and former business associates Mr and Mrs John Macnab, his mother-in-law, and three former political associates John Beckett, R. Barnett and McNeil Sloane. MI5 were evidently worried about the sensitive nature of the letter and emphasized the highly confidential nature of this information, clearly not wishing its clandestine activities to fall into the hands of

---

[28] Extract of a letter from Margaret to William Joyce, 1 July 1945. Joyce files KV 2/245/454b.

[29] Quentin Joyce to Chief Inspector Bridges and Margaret Joyce, 4 July 1945. Joyce files KV 2/246/454a.

the defence team.[30] One memorandum, dated 9 July 1945, chronicles visitors between 22 June and 2 July – Quentin Joyce and John Macnab being noted as the most regular visitors – mentioning: 'On June 22nd he told Quentin that he was drunk when he made the recording for his final broadcast'. Other conversations were monitored, of which one excited MI5:

> On July 2nd he said that 'upon one piece of information supplied this morning', his counsel were 'very hopeful'. He asked Quentin to see Mr Head and 'press the point about the High Commissioner as it was very important'.

In a margin note is the comment 'Does this mean the plan is Irish nationality? We must keep this in mind'.[31] (**document 45**)

Another visitor report dated 5 September 1945 contains details of a conversation between Joyce and his brother Quentin, when the conversation turned to the possibility of further charges made under the Treachery Act 1940. This was said not to worry an optimistic Joyce, as he claimed he was out of the country when the legislation came into force, adding:

> It may be claimed that his voice was in the country through the medium of the receiving set, his answer to that would be 'hang the voice not the throat from whence it came' claiming as an analogy a geometrical theorem 'a part you can never make a whole'. Loud laughter on both sides and the visit terminated Quentin saying he would call again tomorrow.[32]

It was not just the visitor reports, for contained in the Joyce files are extensive correspondence notes and a schedule. These are in a

---

[30] E. J. P. Cussen to A. Canning, 6 July 1945. Joyce files KV 2/246/443d.

[31] Memorandum, G. E. Wakefield, 9 July 1945. Joyce files KV 2/249/447b. There is also a reference to his correspondents, describing them as being: 'letters of sympathy from fascists etc, with occasional letters of abuse (or sheer insanity)'.

[32] Prison report of William Joyce's visitors, 5 September 1945. Joyce files KV 2/246/493a.

post-mortem report written by C. A. Hains, in which he remarked on Joyce's own style of letter-writing:

> William's letters were written in a precise and academic style with a biting classical wit. Added to this however was a thin, but none the less distinct line of almost 'guttersnipe' coarseness, which was all the more remarkable against the otherwise academic background.[33]

According to the correspondence schedule, the pre-trial letters Joyce received were written by people who wrote either in support and sympathy or who were described as merely 'abusive' or clearly 'mad' or 'lunatic' or, occasionally, 'religious mad'. Some were humorous – for example one man told Joyce his broadcasts were better than Tommy Handley whose hit comedy radio show ITMA ran throughout the war. Another told him: 'The only punishment for you is [a] quick death'. However, in the main the letters were from old fascists who had known or supported Joyce before the war. Remaining faithful to the cause, the letters were often virulently anti-Semitic, as one wrote: 'As a National Socialist and ex-soldier (1914–1918) I salute you . . . [your] broadcasts lit a candle that all the forces of Jewry will never put out'. Another, this time from a family, told him how much they 'admired his loyalty to his country's real good', and enclosed a parcel containing sardines and biscuits. In contrast one correspondent enclosed a bottle of rat poison, the schedule noting its retention by the prison governor.[34] (**document 59**)

Whilst it is understandable that MI5 and the prison service maintained a close watch on Joyce's visitors and correspondence, the Joyce files reveal other more disturbing MI5 activities. F3, the MI5 division that dealt with fascist subversion, managed to keep Quentin Joyce the subject of a Home Office warrant, enabling MI5 to tap his phone and intercept his mail. The latter point was of particular importance to Cusson, Wakefield, Sinclair and other MI5 officers who were closely connected with the Joyce case, and took the form of photostats of Quentin's relevant outgoing and incoming mail.

---

[33] C. A. Hains, 'Notes on the correspondence of William and Margaret Joyce', 14 January 1946. Joyce files KV 2/247/518a.

[34] Ibid.

These included letters to relatives in Ireland and America, people who could have information or documents that might assist the defence case. Perhaps more controversial was the interception and photostatting of letters written to Quentin by William Joyce's defence lawyers Ludlow and Co. and by his uncle, Gilbert Joyce. During the critical period leading up to the trial, the correspondence between Ludlow and Co. and Joyce's friend and former business partner John Macnab was also intercepted. Taken together it all provided MI5 and the prosecution with many valuable insights into the strategy and thinking of the defence team. (**documents 48, 50, 51 and 57**)

A curious omission from the Joyce MI5 files is the document that provided the prosecution with the key to open the door of success, for, when on 17 September 1945 the trial of William Joyce began at the Old Bailey, they had received what turned out to be a critical opinion on the law of treason. The distinguished international lawyer Arnold McNair, who was a member of the faculty of law at Cambridge University, wrote the brief. His opinion, in the event, provided the prosecution with a cast-iron case at the Old Bailey and in subsequent appeals; and it cost William Joyce his life.[35]

On trial for his life

William Joyce's treason trial got under way in court number one at London's Central Criminal Court, the Old Bailey, on Monday, 17 September 1945, and lasted a total of three days. The trial judge was Sir Frederick Tucker, with the Attorney General Sir Hartley Shawcross, PC, KC, MP leading for the prosecution and Gerald Slade KC for the defence. Two accounts of the proceedings survive on the Joyce files: one the official trial transcript, the other a lengthy article by the writer and journalist Rebecca West and published by the American magazine *New Yorker*; later this and another article formed the basis of a book she wrote on the subject. The official trial transcript is, by its very nature, a dry and colourless document, leaving Rebecca West's article to provide much of the depth and

---

[35] Information provided to the present author by Kurt Lipstein, Professor Emeritus in Law at Cambridge University.

colour generated by the occasion. Rebecca West's article drew a vivid word picture that described the devastation suffered by the old City of London, particularly the area around St Paul's Cathedral, which had been almost completely flattened during the course of the Blitz, which had also destroyed part of the Old Bailey complex; what remained she described as being boarded up and looking dingy and dark. When she first caught sight of him, Rebecca West described William Joyce as having nothing individual about him:

> except a deep scar running across his right cheek from his lower lip to his ear. But this did not create the savage and marred distinction that it might suggest, for it gave a mincing immobility to his mouth. His smile was pinched and governessy.

After placing the theatricality of the scene at the Old Bailey into a perspective her American audience might understand, she included descriptions of the frayed pomp of the setting, including the judge in his robes and the presence of the Lord Mayor of the City of London together with several aldermen, all of whom were dressed in the flamboyant costumes of office. However, what Rebecca West and all those members of the press and public present in court wanted to hear was the sound of Joyce's voice. They were both thrilled and disappointed, for the only words he uttered throughout the three-day trial were the words 'Not Guilty' when asked to plead; she described these words as 'the most impressive uttered during the trial'.[36] Then the proceedings got under way.

As the death sentence was mandatory for a conviction of high treason, Joyce's life was at stake. The issues were clear: was William Joyce a British subject and if he wasn't did he none the less have a duty of allegiance to the Crown? Battle commenced over William Joyce's nationality. In the light of the possible outcome, Judge Tucker told both sides to prove it one way or the other: that is, beyond reasonable doubt. This was to prove difficult, as both William and his father Michael Joyce had claimed to be either

---

[36] All quotes taken from Rebecca West, 'The Crown versus William Joyce', *New Yorker*, 29 September 1945, pp. 30–40. Joyce files KV 2/247/503b.

American or British nationals on different occasions and in different circumstances; indeed Michael Joyce went so far as to explain to his children that he was a naturalized American, but had lost it through some kind of failure to renew. To support Joyce's contention he was born a US citizen there was the evidence of official documentation revealed by the British consuls in Dublin and New York and by the investigation the FBI undertook. These purported to show Michael Joyce's birth in Ireland, his application to become an American citizen and the certification of US citizenship. There were also the copies of entries in the New York church and municipal records relating to Michael's marriage to Gertrude Brooke together with a copy of the birth certificate relating to their first-born, a son they named William. But as Michael and Gertrude Joyce had died some time before the court hearing, the issue was how could it be proved conclusively that these documents related to the self-same William Joyce in the dock? In themselves, the judge argued, the documents proved nothing, and although Joyce was present at his own birth he knew nothing about the event other than what he had subsequently been told. The prosecution argued, notwithstanding the documentary evidence, William Joyce had been born in Ireland, as he asserted on many occasions, including the fateful British passport application and renewals, and on many of the German documents.

The defence attempted to prove the handwriting and signatures of Michael Joyce found on the surviving official documents by entering other documentary evidence still in the hands of the family. To support this evidence, they brought along a handwriting expert who testified as to their common source. Surviving friends and relatives also gave evidence as to Michael and William Joyce's identity and nationality. Other evidence confirming American nationality was provided by a former Galway police officer, who had known the family when they lived in Ireland, and also identified First World War police evidence, sourced from entries in various English and Irish aliens registration files, which again confirmed their American nationality. (**documents 10** and **12**) In the end the weight of evidence was overwhelming. Sir Hartley Shawcross, leading the prosecution team, realizing he was beaten on the issue, ceased cross-examining defence witnesses. At the start of the trial's third day he asked permission to amend the first two counts of the indictment from 'a person owing allegiance' to read 'a British subject'. Allowing the amendment Judge Tucker said, 'I think it is a proper amendment to be made and so far as I can see I think it is one that is likely to be of assistance to the defence rather than the reverse.'[37]

The evidence proving American nationality and the amendments to the indictment effectively killed the first two charges. This left Joyce and his lawyers hopeful that they could also successfully defend the third and last charge. Equally, the prosecution now gambled everything on the McNair opinion. This meant the final outcome of the trial rested on the third charge, which read:

> On the 18th day of September, 1939, and on divers other days thereafter and between that day and the 2nd day of July, 1940, being then – to wit on the several days – a person owing allegiance to our Lord the King, and whilst on the said several days an open and public war was being prosecuted and carried on by the German realm and its subjects against our Lord the King and his subjects then and on the said several days traitorously conniving and intending to aid and assist the said enemies of our Lord the King against our Lord the King and his subjects did traitorously adhere to and aid and comfort the said enemies in parts beyond the seas without the realm of England, to wit, in the realm of Germany by broadcasting to the subjects of our Lord the King propaganda on behalf of the said enemies of our Lord the King.[38]

It was, the prosecution argued, a case resting on the proposition that so long as Joyce held a valid British passport he had, regardless of the felonious circumstance in which it was obtained, the protection of the Crown and therefore he owed a reciprocal duty of allegiance. After the expiration of the passport on 1 July 1940, they accepted he

---

[37] Trial transcript, pp. 105–6. Joyce files KV 2/250/2.
[38] Indictment against William Joyce, 17 July 1945. Joyce files, KV 2/249/99a.

was no longer under the Crown's protection and therefore his duty of allegiance ended. In these circumstances, the prosecution threw away all the work undertaken by MI5, Special Branch officers and the BBC monitoring service during the years between July 1940 and the end of May 1945. Equally they accepted the proposition that if Joyce had not feloniously obtained a British passport there would be no case to answer in a British court; that in September 1940, at a time before Germany and the United States went to war, Joyce renounced his US citizenship in favour of German was also lawful. As Rebecca West pithily pointed out: 'It was plainly no business of a British court if an American subject chose to become naturalized as a German citizen'.[39]

At the core of the third charge on the indictment was the nature of allegiance. It was argued as axiomatic that a British subject owes allegiance to the King, but, as the prosecution suggested, that was not the only form of allegiance, and it was to those other forms that the prosecution now turned. Sir Hartley Shawcross deployed the McNair opinion with tremendous effect. The origins of allegiance derived, he told the jury, in what he called the many 'old books on English law'; in fact he used Blackstone, Foster, Coke and other important texts. He put it to the jury that in treason cases judges often had the function of adapting old principles to new circumstances. He also argued that the courts had jurisdiction to deal with offences committed abroad, which struck at the security of the State; this he said had been recognized in international law and the concept was at one with the idea of any man, alien or subject, could be charged with treason. At the heart of the case, the prosecution alleged, was the concept of temporary local allegiance acquired when an alien entered Britain, at which point the alien received the protection of the Crown, and must in return obey all laws. If the alien commits an offence, such as treason, then that alien could be tried and be punished for the offence. In most circumstances, it was argued, local allegiance ended immediately the alien left Britain's shores. However, over the centuries, the law relating to local allegiance had developed, though very slowly – in support of his contention Shawcross relied on a 1707 declaratory

---

[39] Rebecca West, 'The Crown versus William Joyce', *New Yorker*, 29 September 1945, pp. 30–40. KV 2/247/503b.

judgement, which said local allegiance could be extended if an alien left his wife or goods in Britain and subsequently threw in his lot with the enemies of the Crown. The judgement stated that in these circumstances the alien was still obtaining the benefit of the King's protection and therefore the temporary allegiance still held. The prosecution contended that as Joyce left Britain in August 1939 using his British passport, it must be assumed he intended to return and also to use the passport to obtain the King's protection whilst he was abroad. Therefore his propaganda broadcasts between 18 September 1939 and 2 July 1940 were made whilst he still held temporary allegiance to the British Crown. The logic of this argument was that by adhering to the King's enemies in this way Joyce was guilty of treason.

Replying to the prosecution's argument, defence counsel Gerald Slade put up a valiant fight. He maintained that there were no precedents capable of sustaining the prosecution argument and, citing cases by reading from many of the same texts Sir Hartley Shawcross had used, argued the opposite opinion. He claimed that as an alien Joyce could not commit treason against Britain outside the country, also insisting that the advent of the passport in its modern form was a new phenomenon and the case law relating to the documents was insignificant. After returning from the lunch break on the third day of the trial, Judge Tucker announced his interpretation of the law, telling prosecuting and defence counsel:

> I shall direct the Jury on count 3 [of the indictment] that on the 24th August, 1939, when the passport was applied for the prisoner beyond a shadow of doubt owed allegiance to the Crown of this country, and that on the evidence given, if they accept it, nothing happened at the material time thereafter to put an end to the allegiance that he then owed. It will remain for the Jury, and for the Jury alone, as to whether or not at the relevant dates he adhered to the King's enemies with intent to assist the King's enemies.[40]

---

[40] Trial transcript, pp. 127–8. Joyce files KV 2/250/2.

As Rebecca West observed: 'This ruling meant that Joyce was going to die, and his death would be recorded in legal history as the most completely unnecessary death that any criminal has ever died on the gallows'.[41] After directing the jury to acquit Joyce on charges one and two of the indictment, the judge sent them out to consider their verdict on charge three – it took no more than twenty-five minutes for them to return with a guilty verdict. Joyce declined to say anything before the death sentence was passed – at the end of the proceedings he bowed to the judge, waved to his friends and family and was taken away.[42]

Joyce was not returned to Brixton prison, but rather to the condemned cell at London's Wormwood Scrubs prison: on 28 September he was moved again, this time to the condemned cell at Wandsworth prison, London. As the MI5 Joyce files show, the battle was by no means ended. A memorandum written by D. H. Sinclair on 22 September 1945 records the court proceedings, noting: 'It being understood that Joyce is lodging an appeal as soon as may be, it is intended to obtain a copy of the shorthand note from the Court of Criminal Appeal'.[43] (**document 53**)

The appeal: 'no case to answer'

On 27 September 1945, William Joyce lodged his appeal against conviction with the Court of Criminal Appeal. A typescript copy of the notice of appeal, headed 'capital case', is held on the Joyce files. It stated the fourfold grounds for the appeal and read:

1. The court wrongly assumed jurisdiction to try an alien for an offence against British Law committed in a foreign country.
2. The Learned Judge was wrong in Law in holding and misdirected the jury in directing them, that the Appellant owed allegiance to His Majesty the King during the period 18th September, 1939 to 2nd July, 1940.

---

[41] Rebecca West, 'The Crown versus William Joyce', *New Yorker*, 29 September 1945, pp. 30–40. Joyce files KV 2/247/503b.
[42] All references to the trial arguments are taken from the trial transcript. Joyce files KV 2/250/2.
[43] Note, D. H. Sinclair, 'Rex v. William Joyce'. Joyce files, KV 2/249/100a.

3. There was no evidence that the renewal of the Appellant's passport afforded him or was capable of affording him any protection or that the Appellant ever availed himself or had any intention of availing himself of any such protection.

4. If (contrary to the Appellant's contention) there were any such evidence, the issue was one for the jury and the Learned Judge failed to direct them thereon.[44] (**document 55**)

The appeal notice indicated Joyce was not applying for legal aid, and it is clear, though implicit, that he had obtained funds to pay for his defence team from unstated sources within the old fascist community. The appeal took place at the Royal Courts of Justice in the Strand on 30 and 31 October 1945, before the Lord Chief Justice, Lord Caldecote and two other senior judges, Humphreys and Lynsky. The prosecution and defence teams were unchanged from the original Old Bailey trial a month earlier, and ground covered in the appeal was exactly the same as at the original trial. William Joyce and his family and friends were present throughout the hearing and also when, on 7 November 1945, the Lord Chief Justice delivered a written judgment rejecting the defence arguments as to the point of allegiance and jurisdiction and dismissed the appeal.[45]

The case of William Joyce involved many important principles of law and aroused excitement and controversy in the country. In these circumstances the Attorney General, Sir Hartley Shawcross, allowed a further appeal, this time to the Supreme Court, the House of Lords, or at any rate a judicial committee made up of the most senior judges who were members of that chamber. The House of Lords appeal took place between 10 and 17 December 1945 and was heard by the Lord Chancellor, Lord Jowitt, sitting with Lords Macmillan, Wright, Porter and Simonds. A copy of the printed transcript together with the judgement survives on the Joyce files, as does the second article on the subject of William Joyce written by Rebecca West for the *New Yorker*. In her article, she described the change that had come over William Joyce's appearance during the course of his trials:

---

[44] Notice of Appeal, 27 September 1945. Joyce files KV 2/249/102a.

[45] Note, D. H. Sinclair, 'William Joyce – PF 44469', 7 November 1945. Joyce files KV 2/249/104a.

At the Old Bailey he had been jaunty and vulgar, with nothing to recommend him except his remarkable courage and his look of horseplay fun. Now the long contemplation of death had given him dignity and refinement.[46]

The House of Lords appeal heard the same arguments as had been aired at the Old Bailey and during the first appeal at the Royal Courts of Justice. The debate turned on a fine point of law as to 'whether an alien who has been resident within the realm can be held guilty of treason in respect of acts committed by him outside the realm'. This was, the court conceded, 'a question of law of far-reaching importance'.[47] In the end, after hearing all the evidence and following a lengthy period of deliberation, the House of Lords rejected the appeal. There was a single dissenting voice from Lord Justice Porter, who argued: 'the question whether that duty [of allegiance] was still in existence depends upon the circumstances of the individual case and is a matter for the jury to determine'.[48] It was a small point and it didn't really matter – William Joyce was going to hang. Rebecca West recalled her last sighting of the man who had played such an important part in British life during the war years. Witnessing his departure from Parliament, she noted:

The courage he showed in the dock had impressed nobody very much, since most of us had acquitted ourselves fairly well in danger, but he was doing very well for a prisoner who had lain four months under the threat of death, and for a little ill-made man surrounded by four drilled giants. He held his chin high and picked his feet up as the sergeants major bid, and though he held his chin so very high that his face was where the top of his head ought to have been and though his feet flapped on his weak ankles, his dignity was not destroyed but was made idiosyncratic, his very own.[49]

---

46 Rebecca West, 'William Joyce: conclusion', *New Yorker*, 26 January 1946, pp. 28–43. Joyce files KV 2/247/579b.
47 'Transcript of the House of Lords appeal and judgement in the case of William Joyce'. Joyce papers KV 2/247/525a.
48 Ibid.
49 West, 'William Joyce: conclusion'.

Joyce was not present when the Lords dismissed his appeal. The news was conveyed to him by the governor of Wandsworth prison. He had written about this possibility in his journal entry for 22 April 1945:

> I shall be glad when this damned war is over. No alcohol, no tobacco – not enough food – why life is no better than penal servitude in any case. How glad I shall be to get a real rest from this mean and menial work, even if only in the condemned cell.[50]

The final acts

In the meantime, Margaret Joyce remained in a Brussels prison awaiting her own fate. Like her husband, she had made a statement to Captain William James Skardon in which she set out her version of events, explaining why she came to Germany in September 1939 and her activities since that date. In the course of this statement, she claimed to have made her first broadcasts in September 1939.[51] Following on from her husband's conviction for treason, the problem arose as to what should happen to her. Was she, like her husband, guilty of treason and if so should she be put on trial? Other issues had to be considered, not least her nationality. When she went to Germany in August 1939, was she a British or an American citizen? Equally, did she acquire German nationality on the basis of her husband's application or in her own right? It was a tangled and messy situation and it got messier, despite attempts by Home Office lawyers and others to make some sense of it. There was clear and incontrovertible evidence, from her own admissions and the entries in her diaries, and a wide range of other sources both in Britain and Germany, that she began her broadcasting career in September 1939, soon after her husband's own microphone debut. Yet the same British authorities that prosecuted her American husband for this crime of high treason decided, in the end, not to prosecute her. Officially, the reason given for the decision was compassionate

---

[50] Journal, 25 April 1945 (KV 2/250/2).
[51] Statement, Margaret Cairns Joyce, 30 May 1945. Margaret Joyce files KV 2/253.

grounds – in fact, the web proved so complex that the Director of Public Prosecutions could not be sure of a conviction. Like her husband, the British authorities were in dread of a major state treason trial collapsing because of a jury's rejection of the same kind of evidence that had hanged others, including her husband.[52]

On 19 November 1945, MI5 brought Margaret Joyce to London so that she might visit her husband before his execution. In order not to excite anger among the population, the agency arranged that on arrival at Hendon airport she would be refused admission, and as an enemy alien, detained by Special Branch and lodged in Holloway women's prison in London. On 20 November, the couple met for the first time since their arrest the previous May. Although it had been agreed that Margaret could see her husband once or twice before her return to Brussels, in fact it became convenient to allow her to remain until after his execution. During this time, Margaret was given permission to write to her husband and communicate with her mother, but she was refused permission to see her brother-in-law, Quentin Joyce.[53]

During the final six weeks of his life, William and Margaret Joyce met regularly; this included the period leading up to and including the House of Lords appeal and thereafter till his execution. Until a short time before Joyce's execution the couple's correspondence was subject to prison censorship, though this did not prevent them maintaining a regular correspondence with each other. In the event it was personal, containing little to excite either the prison censors or MI5. Margaret Joyce's correspondence with other individuals survives in her MI5 file, including many letters of support she received from former members of the old British Union of Fascists and others. Like her husband the correspondence included a range of 'mad' and 'abusive' letters. After the rejection of Joyce's House of Lords appeal, Margaret told him if she were released she would go to live in Ireland. His reply contained vulgar abuse of the Lord Chief Justice. During his last days Joyce expressed his worries and concerns for Margaret's future, and despite all the previous violence

---

[52] See notes and reports, May 1945 to January 1946. Margaret Joyce files KV 2/253.
[53] Extract from Home Office file 897868/27, 23 November 1945. Margaret Cairns Joyce files KV 2/253/91a.

and bitterness, the couple appear to have reached a complete reconciliation. The prison reports suggest a devoted couple with William showing, at least to Margaret, a characteristic bravery in the face of death.

When a final plea for clemency was rejected, all hope of saving Joyce was lost. Several people who knew him from his pre-war fascist days and continued to believe his National Socialist propaganda wrote to Margaret telling her it was all for the best and he was too good and honest a man to live. The prison 'death watch' reports tell of his attitude as it was articulated in his final censored letters, in which he argued his judges were biased and, according to the report, he expressed himself in more and more arrogant fascist terms.

To the very last he maintained many of the attitudes defined in his early 1945 journal entries. Although he saw himself dying defending his ideals in the manner of a front-line soldier, he was also rueful at the thought of dying hated by the British and branded a traitor. In the end this was the dilemma he faced, best summed up in the master propagandist's own words. On 25 March 1945 he had written in his journal:

> Today I have sad and haunting memories. I yield nothing of my political opinions nor do I believe that I have acted wrongly, but I hate the idea of dying as England's enemy – or of being despised by those among whom I was once regarded as an ardent patriot. A damned nuisance.[54] (**journal**, see p. 277)

Joyce also maintained an unqualified belief in the after-life, something that was also a feature of his journal entries. A few days before his execution he bade farewell to his wife with the words: 'I prefer to believe that my work has not been in vain: and after I have died, I believe that I shall resume it'.[55]

---

[54] Journal, 25 March 1945. (KV 2/250/2)
[55] 'Notes on the correspondence of William and Margaret Joyce', C. A. Hains, 14 January 1946. Joyce files KV 2/247/518a.

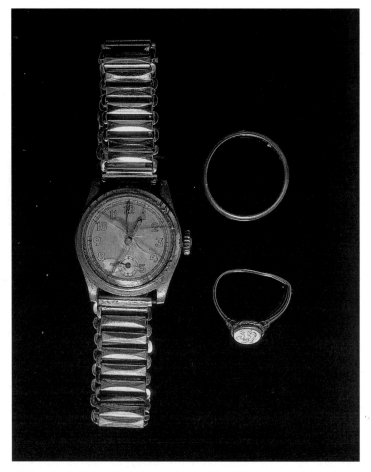

William Joyce's personal effects: his watch, signet ring and wedding ring. (KV 2/345/2)

Conclusion

At 9.00 a.m. on 3 January 1946 William Joyce was executed by hanging at Wandsworth Prison, London, three months short of his fortieth birthday. A small crowd maintained a vigil outside the prison to await the news of his execution, news that was posted as a notice of execution fixed on the prison gate. Newspapers reporting the event explained how the crowd was made up not just of people opposed to capital punishment, but included others, specifically old British Union of Fascists and National Socialist League comrades. The family did not appear, preferring instead to attend church service. Margaret remained in her cell at Holloway prison. After the execution there was a same-day post-mortem, then Joyce's body was, according to Home Office rules governing the disposal of executed criminals, buried in unconsecrated ground inside the prison walls. Shortly after the execution MI5 closed the files, by now swollen by bundles of prosecution papers, which then passed into the custody of the MI5 archives, until their review in the late 1990s and subsequent deposit at the Public Record Office, Kew (from April 2003 joining with the Historical Manuscripts Commission to form The National Archives).

William Joyce's journey through life ended with his execution as a traitor. His journal entries for those fraught early months of 1945 had often mused over his past and where it had delivered him – he evidently realized his likely fate. These entries, although occasionally regretful, were not self-pitying, a feature never found in the Joyce mentality. On 22 April 1945 he was in Hamburg still working, and shortly to make what became the final broadcast of his career. On that day he wrote:

> I realised this morning so clearly that, in the eyes of Englishmen, I have forfeited all claim to live in England or to consider myself English. I am very sorry: for I have now nothing left. Long before Germany's defeat became certain, I knew that I could never be at home here. Hamburg is better than Berlin – but still! Has it all been worthwhile? I think not. National Socialism is a

fine cause, but most of the Germans, not all, are bloody fools . . . England means so much to me, and I am old, well, in that spirit, I can take any punishment that is coming to me, but I am sorry for Margaret, whose outlook is quite different.[1] (**journal**, see p. 290)

Fears of a post-war resurgence of British fascism caused MI5 and others to hope that William Joyce would quickly be forgotten. These hopes had been articulated at his trial, when prosecutors told the jury that whilst Joyce's treason trial was important Joyce the man was of no consequence and would soon be forgotten, consigned to a footnote in the history of the Second World War. However, history proved them wrong. As William Joyce was the last man to be hanged in Britain for high treason, and given the nature of his extraordinary trial and conviction, he gained a second prominence every bit as important as his first. As a consequence his name and life remain of interest to the public, and since his death many books have been written about him and his extraordinary life and death. All highlight how during the early years of the Second World War Lord Haw Haw entered British folk memory. This folklore came complete with myths relating to a role many people believed he played as a spy-master controlling Nazi fifth-column agents in Britain, who were taking secret instruction from Haw Haw's broadcasts that enabled them to direct bombers to specific targets over Britain. In the end what is remembered is the Lord Haw Haw, the butt of much humour during the first months of the war; what is forgotten is the savage crowing beast of the terrible years 1940 and 1941, as are the hundreds of daily broadcasts in which he poured bile and acid on those figures and peoples who were the focus of his hatred.

Postscript

Within a few days of her husband's execution the British authorities deported Margaret Joyce, returning her to her Brussels prison. As the decision not to prosecute her had already been taken, British

---

[1] Journal, 22 April 1945 (KV 2/250/2).

officialdom, including MI5, found her something of an embarrassment. Essentially, there were no grounds for holding her in Brussels, especially after the Belgian press got hold of the story and put pressure on its government to get her removed. In a letter to the British authorities Margaret Joyce made it clear that she did not wish to return to Germany – if forcibly returned, she feared she might become a focus for Nazi sympathizers. Equally the German government of occupation told MI5 that if she did return she would be interned,[2] (**document 58**) at which point the MI5 files come to an abrupt end. It is known, however, that Margaret Joyce did eventually return to Britain, where she spent the rest of her life quietly in London, dying in 1972, aged 61.

The final twist in the drama of William Joyce occurred just over 30 years after his execution and goes unrecorded in his MI5 files – in August 1976, his remains were exhumed from Wandsworth prison and sent to Ireland for burial. On the day of the interment, one of Joyce's daughters from the first marriage arranged for a Roman Catholic requiem Mass to be said; this was followed by a religious service of committal, which took place in a Galway cemetery. Attending these services were his daughter, together with a number of surviving family members and former school friends. It is perhaps ironic and paradoxical that William Joyce, the complex man who was an Empire Loyalist and Black and Tan fighter, but who was executed as an infamous British traitor, should find his final rest among the nation whose existence he fought so hard to prevent. Though, in truth, perhaps everything that happened in William Joyce's strange and exotic journey through life proved in the end ironic.

---

[2] Papers concerning Margaret Joyce, January to February 1946. Margaret Joyce files KV 2/253/100b.

The MI5 documents on William Joyce

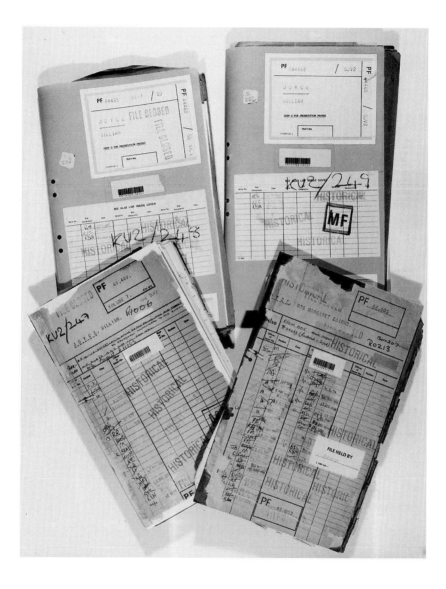

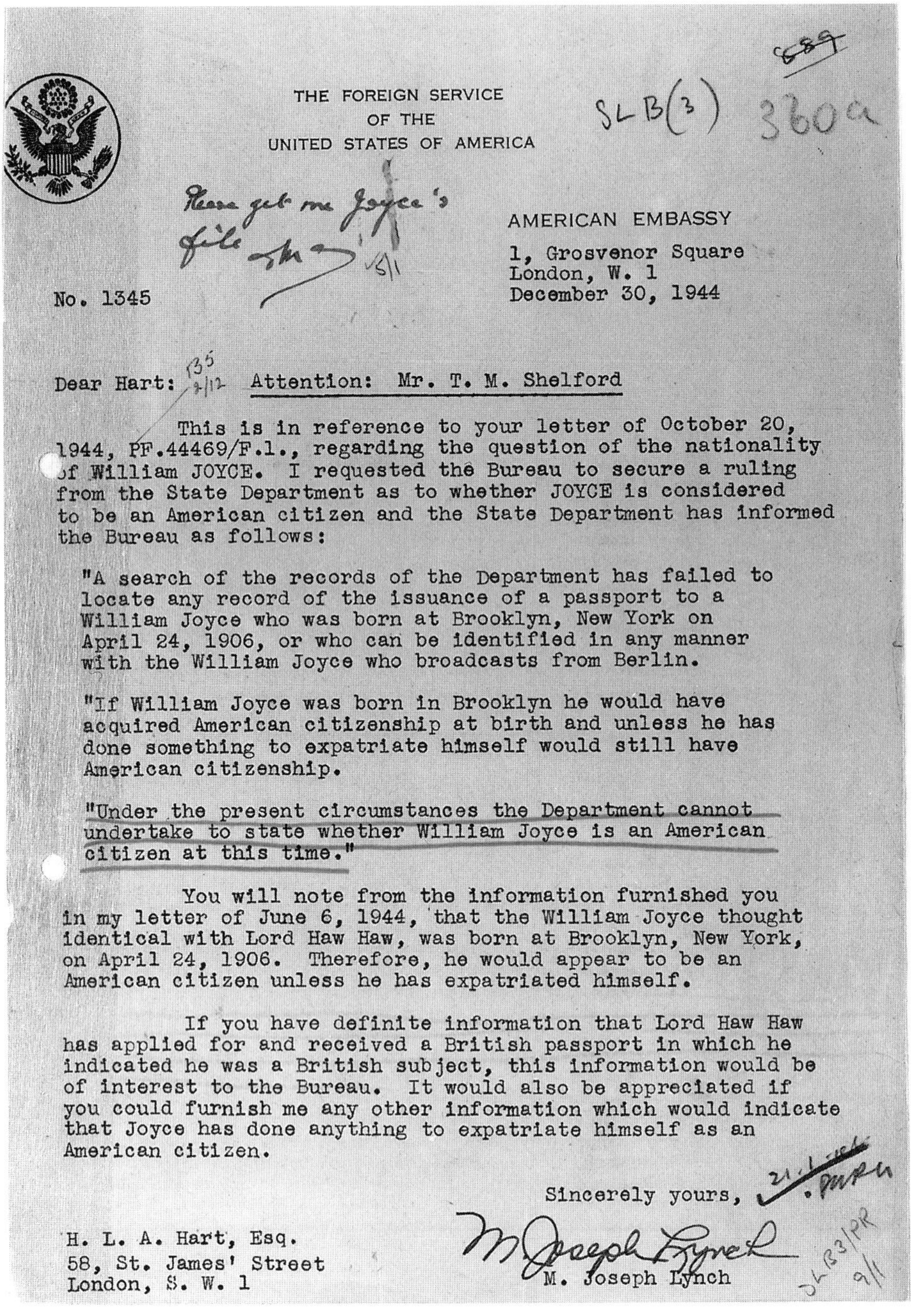

THE FOREIGN SERVICE
OF THE
UNITED STATES OF AMERICA

Please get me Joyce's file — [illegible signature]

AMERICAN EMBASSY

1, Grosvenor Square
London, W. 1
December 30, 1944

No. 1345

Dear Hart: Attention: Mr. T. M. Shelford

     This is in reference to your letter of October 20, 1944, PF.44469/F.1., regarding the question of the nationality of William JOYCE. I requested the Bureau to secure a ruling from the State Department as to whether JOYCE is considered to be an American citizen and the State Department has informed the Bureau as follows:

    "A search of the records of the Department has failed to locate any record of the issuance of a passport to a William Joyce who was born at Brooklyn, New York on April 24, 1906, or who can be identified in any manner with the William Joyce who broadcasts from Berlin.

    "If William Joyce was born in Brooklyn he would have acquired American citizenship at birth and unless he has done something to expatriate himself would still have American citizenship.

    "Under the present circumstances the Department cannot undertake to state whether William Joyce is an American citizen at this time."

    You will note from the information furnished you in my letter of June 6, 1944, that the William Joyce thought identical with Lord Haw Haw, was born at Brooklyn, New York, on April 24, 1906. Therefore, he would appear to be an American citizen unless he has expatriated himself.

    If you have definite information that Lord Haw Haw has applied for and received a British passport in which he indicated he was a British subject, this information would be of interest to the Bureau. It would also be appreciated if you could furnish me any other information which would indicate that Joyce has done anything to expatriate himself as an American citizen.

Sincerely yours,

M. Joseph Lynch

H. L. A. Hart, Esq.
58, St. James' Street
London, S. W. 1

1. Letter from the US Justice Department representative in London to MI5, 30 December 1944, concerning the great uncertainty existing at that time regarding William Joyce's true nationality. (KV 2/246/360a)

65-31206

SECRET – AIR COURIER
VIA U.S. ARMY AIR TRANSPORT COMMAND

Date: August 18, 1945

To: Mr. M. J. Lynch
Legal Attache
The American Embassy
London, England

From: John Edgar Hoover – Director, Federal Bureau of Investigation

Subject: WILLIAM JOYCE, with alias "Lord Haw-Haw"
TREASON

Reference is made to your letter dated July 19, 1945, setting out
a number of requests made by the British for additional investigation in the
captioned matter.

We have now been advised that on August 9, 1945, Special Agent Henry
O. Hawkins of the New York Office, in company with Special Agent Edward D.
O'Donnell of the Newark Office, contacted Mr. John J. Zigmund, Chief Clerk of
the United States Immigration and Naturalization Service Records, Common Pleas
Court, Jersey City, New Jersey, relative to the naturalization record of one
Michael Joyce. Mr. Zigmund displayed the original Declaration of Intention
and Petition for Naturalization and Naturalization of Michael Joyce. The
latter document, that is the Petition for Naturalization and Naturalization,
was filed in the County Clerk's Office, Hudson County, Jersey City, New Jersey,
on October 25, 1894. This document you will note contains number 423. When
Mr. Zigmund was informed that Special Agent Hawkins desired to secure photostatic copies of these naturalization records, he advised that he was prohibited by law from furnishing anyone with photostatic copies without a court
order; Mr. Zigmund explained that the Federal Law making it a felony to photostat these documents, is contained in Section 346 (A) (29), Naturalization Act
of 1940, Title 8, Section 746, United States Code. Continuing, Mr. Zigmund
stated that he would be in a position to furnish a certified copy of these
records without a court order.

Special Agent Hawkins, in company with Special Agent O'Donnell, interviewed Mr. Harold P. Woertendyke, Officer in Charge of the United States
Immigration and Naturalization Service, Room 803, 1160 Broad Street, Newark,
New Jersey. Mr. Woertendyke confirmed what Mr. Zigmund had previously stated
relative to the court order and advised that if the above records were
in the possession of the United States Immigration and Naturalization

2. Correspondence and documents from J. Edgar Hoover, head of the US Federal Bureau of Investigation, to M. Joseph Lynch, FBI representative in London, 18 August 1945. This collection supplied to MI5 was critical in proving William Joyce's US birth and American citizenship. It consists of a detailed account of the FBI investigation into the records of Joyce's parents' life in the United States, together with the 1945 applications made by Federal agents to access and copy records in the custody of the Hudson County District Court (not shown) and photostat copies of Michael Joyce's naturalization application, 22 July 1892, and grant of citizenship, 20 October 1894. (KV 2/246)

Service, the Commissioner of Immigration could give authority for securing photostatic copies, but, due to the fact that these records belong to and are in the custody of the Hudson County officials, it would be necessary to secure a court order.

Mr. Woertendyke advised Special Agents Hawkins and O'Donnell very confidentially and off the record that he had secured the naturalization certificate of Michael Joyce some few days previously and had given it to Commissioner Watkins in New York City. In addition, he stated that he had ascertained confidentially that two photostatic copies of Michael Joyce's naturalization record, which were secured by him for Mr. Watkins, were subsequently delivered to the British Consul General in New York City.

In connection with the inquiry in the last paragraph of referenced letter, Mr. Woertendyke stated that the final order as to the naturalization of Michael Joyce had been issued by Judge John Kenny when he signed his name to the order after the wording "He therefore prays he may be admitted to become a citizen of the United States." Mr. Woertendyke stated that in the old days the Petition for Naturalization and the actual Naturalization record in many courts were contained on one page as in this case.

Special Agents Hawkins and O'Donnell contacted Mr. Edgar H. Rossbach, Assistant United States Attorney, Newark, New Jersey, and had him prepare a petition and order to be presented to a judge of the Hudson County Court of Common Pleas in order that a court order might be secured to get photostatic copies of Michael Joyce's naturalization record. On August 9, 1945, the petition and order were presented to the Honorable August Ziegerner, Judge of the Hudson County Court of Common Pleas, Jersey City, New Jersey, who signed the order directing that the Clerk furnish to Special Agent Hawkins an exemplified photostatic copy of the Declaration of Intention and Petition for Naturalization and Naturalization of Michael Joyce. A copy of the petition and copy of the order signed by Judge Ziegerner are being enclosed herewith.

On August 10, 1945, this court order was presented to Mr. William H. Gilfert, Hudson County Clerk, Jersey City, New Jersey. Mr. Gilfert, in company with Special Agents Hawkins and O'Donnell, then proceeded to the Jersey Blue Print Company, 28 Tube Concourse, Jersey City, New Jersey, at which place the original Declaration of Intention and Petition for Naturalization and Naturalization were photostated in the presence of Special Agent Hawkins and Mr. Gilfert. After securing photostats of these documents, Mr. Gilfert and the Honorable Horace K. Roberson, Judge of the Hudson County Court of Common Pleas signed a certificate certifying that the photostats were true and correct copies of the original naturalization record of Michael Joyce. The exemplified photostatic copy of the Declaration of Intention and Petition for Naturalization and Naturalization, as well as the certified certificate mentioned above, are also being enclosed herewith. Each of these documents has been properly identified by Special Agent Hawkins.

- 2 -

2. (continued) Account of the FBI investigation into Joyce's parents' life in the United States.

On August 11, 1945, Special Agent Hawkins contacted Mrs. Elizabeth Ranger, secretary of the All Saints Catholic Church, 292 Henry Street, New York City, and examined the church register of marriages for May 2, 1905. He was unable to locate any record of the marriage of Michael Joyce to Gertrude Brooke. An examination was also made for several months prior and subsequent to May 2, 1905. This check likewise met with negative results. Mrs. Ranker advised that her church was the All Saints Catholic Church but that it is not a Roman Catholic Church.

Based upon the information received from Mrs. Ranger, Special Agent Hawkins contacted the Catholic Headquarters, New York City, and ascertained that the All Saints Roman Catholic Church is located at 47 East 129th Street, New York City.

On August 13, 1945, Special Agent Hawkins contacted Father Edward Bergin, Acting Head of the All Saints Roman Catholic Church. Before Father Bergin would furnish Special Agent Hawkins any information, it was necessary for Special Agent in Charge E. E. Conroy to contact Bishop McIntyre of New York City. Bishop McIntyre advised Special Agent in Charge Conroy that the British had previously made a request for photostatic copies of the marriage record of Michael Joyce and Gertrude Brooke but that he, Bishop McIntyre, refused to furnish the British the desired documents. He stated that he wished to cooperate with the Bureau and that he would instruct Father Bergin to make the records available to Special Agent Hawkins. Continuing, Bishop McIntyre stated that inasmuch as the marriage records were in a large bound book, it would be almost impossible to photostat the record in question without removing the book from the church. He said he did not wish to have the book removed from the church unless it was absolutely necessary. After the above arrangement was made by Special Agent in Charge Conroy with Bishop McIntyre, Father Bergin made the marriage records available to Special Agent Hawkins.

It was determined that under date of May 2, 1905, the church records reflect that Michael Joyce and Gertrude E. Brooke were married at the All Saints Church, the officiating priest being Reverend C. L. Crowley and the witnesses being John F. Ferris and Mary Naughton. It was further noted by Special Agent Hawkins that all the entries in the church records were made by Reverend C. L. Crowley and were not in the handwriting of Michael Joyce or Gertrude Brooke. Father Bergin stated that in the old days no further record was kept by the church and that all entries made in the church records were made by the Priest in attendance.

Father Bergin furnished Special Agent Hawkins with a certified copy of the above mentioned marriage certificate. This document is being enclosed herewith for the British. Inasmuch as the register at the All Saints Church did not contain the handwriting of Michael Joyce or Gertrude Brooke, no further efforts were made by Special Agent Hawkins to obtain photostatic copies of this record. Special Agent Hawkins has properly identified the enclosed certificate and can testify that it is a true and correct copy of the record appearing in the All Saints Church register.

- 3 -

While at the All Saints Catholic Church, Special Agent Hawkins requested Father Bergin to check the birth register on and about April 24, 1906, for a record of William Joyce's birth. This check was made with negative results.

While Special Agent Hawkins was checking in Jersey City, New Jersey, on August 10, 1945, in connection with this matter, inquiry was made of Mr. William H. Gilfert, Hudson County Clerk, relative to the voting lists maintained by the county from 1892 until 1910. Mr. Gilfert stated that all such voting lists had been destroyed and that no record was maintained by the county or state for that period of time.

A check of the Jersey City City Directory for 1915-1916 for the names Michael Joyce or John Duane, Michael Joyce's witness to his naturalization, met with negative results. Mr. Gilfert informed Special Agent Hawkins that no City Directory was in existence for Jersey City prior to 1915-1916.

A check of the records of the Identification and Record Bureau of the Jersey City Police Department relative to Michael Joyce and John Duane met with negative results.

A check of the current telephone directory for Jersey City, New Jersey, reflected two Mrs. M. Joyces, one residing at 135 Brome Street and a second residing at 40 Brome Street. Mrs. Mary Joyce, 135 Brome Street, was contacted for any information in her possession relative to one Michael Joyce who had previously resided in that city. She stated that she knew no one by the name of Michael Joyce and that all of her people had originated in Pennsylvania. She stated further that she had been residing in Jersey City for approximately sixteen years.

Mrs. Michael Joyce, 40 Brome Street, advised on interview that her husband and her husband's father were named Michael, but that she and her husband's family had originated in Gary, Indiana, and that she knew of no relatives of her husband that had resided in Jersey City or New York City during the 1890's and early 1900's. Mrs. Joyce was unable to furnish Special Agent Hawkins with any information that would be helpful in securing any data relative to the Michael Joyce who was naturalized in the Court of Common Pleas, Hudson County, New Jersey, in 1894.

Reference is made to paragraph three, page three, of your letter dated July 19, 1945, wherein the British requested that inquiry be made at the Central Register of Naturalizations, Philadelphia, Pennsylvania, to ascertain if the naturalization of one Michael Joyce, naturalized in Hudson County, New Jersey, in 1894, was recorded in the Central Register. It should be pointed out, as you were previously advised in Bureau letter of July 11, 1945, that the Central Office of the United States Immigration and Naturalization Service, Philadelphia, Pennsylvania, contains no copies of any naturalizations in the United States prior to September 27, 1906.

- 4 -

2. (continued) Account of the FBI investigation into Joyce's parents' life in the United States.

In the event the British make any further inquiries in connection with this matter, it is suggested that they be requested to furnish the Bureau more information relative to Michael Joyce and his family. It would be helpful to know whether Michael Joyce and his wife, Gertrude are living at the present time, and it would also be helpful to know whether or not Michael and Gertrude Joyce had any children other than William Joyce. It would also be helpful to know what occupation Michael Joyce followed while residing in the United States and further to know when Michael Joyce and his family departed from the United States.

You will note that only one photostatic copy of each of the documents comprising the naturalization record of Michael Joyce in the Hudson County, New Jersey, Clerk's Office was secured. It was not deemed advisable to request twelve copies of these documents from the Hudson County Clerk as requested by the British, nor could we reproduce them without violating the Statute mentioned above. In addition it was not deemed advisable to transmit such bulky enclosures across the ocean to you. You should tactfully point out to the British the reasons the Bureau has not furnished a dozen photostatic copies of Michael Joyce's naturalization record.

The information requested by the Bureau in the last paragraph of Bureau letter dated July 11, 1945, should be secured from the British and forwarded to us at your earliest convenience.

Enclosure

STATE OF NEW JERSEY.

Be it Remembered, That on the _22nd_ day of _July_ in the year of our Lord one thousand eight hundred and ninety _two_ before me DENNIS McLAUGHLIN, Clerk of the Court of Common Pleas, in and for the County of Hudson, (the said Court being a Court of Record, having common Law Jurisdiction and a Clerk and Seal), personally appeared _Michael Joyce_ an Alien, a native of _Ireland_ aged about _25_ years who, being duly sworn, according to law, on his oath, doth declare and say that he arrived in the United States on or about the _4th_ day of _May_ in the year of our Lord one thousand eight hundred and _eighty eight_ That it is bona fide his intention to become a Citizen of the **UNITED STATES OF AMERICA,** and to renounce forever all allegiance and fidelity to any and every foreign prince, potentate, state and sovereignty whatever, and particularly to the **QUEEN OF THE UNITED KINGDOM OF GREAT BRITAIN AND IRELAND,** whose subject he has heretofore been.

Subscribed and Sworn before me, this day and year above written.

DENNIS McLAUGHLIN, Clerk,

(SIGNED) _Michael Joyce_

STATE OF NEW JERSEY,

HUDSON COUNTY.

I, DENNIS McLAUGHLIN, Clerk of the Court of Common Pleas, in and for the County of Hudson aforesaid, do hereby certify that the foregoing is a true copy of the "Declaration of Intention to become a Citizen of the United States of America," of _Michael Joyce_ as the same is filed of record in my office.

IN TESTIMONY WHEREOF, I have hereunto subscribed my name and affixed the Seal of the said Court in the County aforesaid, this _22_ day of _July_ A. D. one thousand eight hundred and ninety _two_

CLERK.

2. (continued) Michael Joyce's naturalization application.

To the Judges of the COURT OF COMMON PLEAS in and for the County of Hudson, State of New Jersey:

The Petition of *Michael Joyce* a native of *Ireland*

Respectfully showeth:

That your petitioner arrived in the UNITED STATES OF AMERICA in the year *188__*

_____and that in pursuance of an act of Congress, entitled "An act to establish a uniform rule of *Naturalization*, and to repeal the acts heretofore passed on that subject," made a declaration of his intention to become a Citizen, conformably to the said act, before the

this Court

a CERTIFICATE whereof is hereunto annexed; that he has resided within the limits and under the jurisdiction of the United States for five years_____ and for ONE YEAR, at least, within the *STATE OF NEW JERSEY*: that he has never borne any hereditary title, or been of any orders of nobility in the kingdom whence he came, or elsewhere. He therefore prays he may be admitted to become a citizen of the United States

Michael Joyce

STATE OF NEW JERSEY, } ss:
HUDSON COUNTY.

I, *Michael Joyce*

the above-named petitioner, do, on my solemn oath, declare that the contents of my petition are true that I will support the Constitution of the United States; that I renounce and relinquish any title, or order of nobilty, to which I am, or hereafter may be entitled, and that I do absolutely and entirely renounce and abjure all allegiance and fidelity to any Foreign Prince, Potentate, State or Soverignty whatever, and particularly to the Queen of the United Kingdom of Great Britain and Ireland.

this __25th__ day of __Oct__ 189_ Sworn in Open Court, } *Michael Joyce*

John Kenny
Judge.

John Duane

STATE OF NEW JERSEY, } ss.
HUDSON COUNTY.

a citizen of the United States, being duly sworn according to law, says that he is well acquainted with the above-named petitioner, and that, to his knowledge and belief, he has resided within the limits and under the jurisdiction of the United States for *Five Years*, and for one year at least, within the State of New Jersey:_____

_____and that during the same period he has behaved himself as a man of good moral character, attached to the principles and Constitution of the United States, and well disposed to the good order and happiness of the same.

this __25th__ day of __Oct__ 189_ Sworn in Open Court, } *John Duane*

John Kenny
Judge.

2. (continued) Michael Joyce's grant of citizenship.

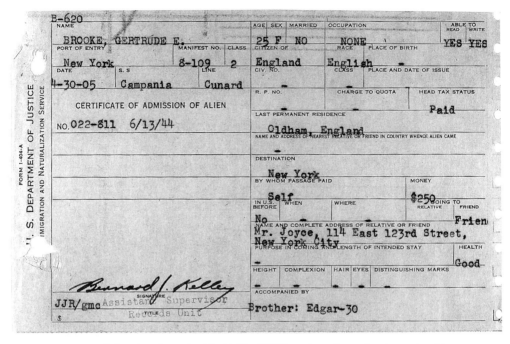

3. Immigration card showing the arrival in 1905 of William Joyce's mother to contract her marriage with Michael Joyce. This was included in MI5 and US documents relating to William Joyce's claim to US citizenship by birth. The set also includes a letter from the US Embassy in London enclosing a US Immigration and Naturalization Service report relating to the case, a typescript of the entry in the New York register of marriage and an MI5 note on the documents. (KV 2/245/337a)

*Type

EVIDENCE BEFORE ADVISORY COMMITTEE

OF

FRANK MARTIN JOYCE.

"My date of birth was 29.6.12. ..... I was born in the West of Ireland at Westport in 1912 and my family moved to Galway when I was very young and my father was manager of the Galway Bus Company. I was there till 1922, at which time the trouble was rife in Ireland, the Sinn Feiners and the I.R.A. were springing up, and my people, being Loyalists to this country, were given a week's notice to clear out of the country, or be shot. At this time my mother was nursing a child aged/about two days and it was a very serious shock to her. We had to leave the country and lose all our property and most of the money that my people had, in 1922.

..... My father was originally, I think, a building contractor in America some time ago, but in Galway he was the manager of the Galway Bus Company. "

Q. He was originally in America, was he?

A. That was before I was born actually; he was in the building line, a building contractor.

Q. Yes, and is he Irish?

A. He is Irish, yes.

Q. He is entirely Irish?

A. Yes.

Q. On both sides?

A. He was born in Ireland, and both his father and mother, so far as I can make out, were Irish too.

Q. And your mother?

A. My mother is English.

Q. When was your father in America?

A. It was previous to my birth. I am not sure over what period he was there, but he was there for some considerable time before 1912.

(This extract relates to Mr. Byrne's request for information as to the date when the JOYCE family moved from Ireland to England.)

S. L. B. 3.
5.7.45.

4. Evidence given before the Home Office Advisory Committee by William Joyce's brother Frank during his wartime detention for fascist activities. (KV 2/249/61b) It provides detailed evidence concerning the time the family spent in Ireland.

EXTRACT FROM NATIONAL REGISTRATION SCHEDULE.

ADDRESS AT WHICH REGISTERED:—
7, Allison Grove,
Dulwich, S.E. 21

ADDRESS TO WHICH REMOVED:—

E.D. LETTER CODE ABDM.   SCHEDULE NO. 31.

No. on Schedule	Surname and Other Names	Sex	Birthday (Day and Month)	Year of Birth	Condition as to Marriage	Occupation	Membership of Naval, Military or Air Force Reserves or Auxiliary Forces or Civil Defence Services or Reserves	No. of Ration Book Issued	Type of Ration Book Issued
1	JOYCE Michael Francis	M.	9.12.	1866.	M.	Vacuum Cleaner Salesman		R/31 096665	AE
2	JOYCE Gertrude Emely	F.	28.8.	1878.	M.	Unpaid domestic duties		R/31 096666	AE
3	JOYCE Gertrude Joan Brooke	F.	18.5.	1920.	S.	Dressmaker		R/31 096667	AE
4	JOYCE Robert Patrick	M.	12.2.	1922.	S.	Civil Engineer		R/31 096668	AE

I hereby certify that the above is a true extract of the schedule referred to.

Signature of F.E.O. Arnold ......   Date. 2/4/45.

4. (continued) A copy of the Joyce family National Registration entry made at the start of the Second World War, 18 October 1939. It shows Joyce's parents and younger brother and sister living at the family home in Dulwich. Both documents come from a file assembled during the summer of 1945 relating to the claim made by Joyce to have been born in the United States. Its purpose was to assess the validity of Joyce's claim to US citizenship, and it contains the workaday assessments made by various MI5 officers connected with the case. (KV 2/249/61b)

Copy filed in PF.44469 Ord. Vol.

K 12688/925/5.

With the Compliments
of the
Under Secretary of State
for Foreign Affairs

T. R. ⸻

Received 11.7.45.

54

TOP SECRET

2 0 JUL 1945

[Cypher]

DEPARTMENTAL NO. 1.

FROM NEW YORK TO FOREIGN OFFICE.

His Majesty's Consul General.
No. 385.   D. 6.36 p.m. 6th July, 1945.

6th July, 1945.   R. 2.20 a.m. 7th July, 1945.

- - - -

IMPORTANT.

    Your telegram No. 179.

    There is a record of nationalisation of one
Michael Joyce at King's County Court New York 4th
Judicial District Brooklyn.

    2. The Court seems unwilling to furnish a copy
or to inform me of date of nationalisation but I
am trying to secure this through the United States
Department of Justice.

O.T.P.

5. Telegram from HM Consul General, New York, to Foreign Office, London,
6 July 1945, showing the problems faced by diplomats and the FBI in their search for
Michael Joyce's naturalization papers. (KV 2/249/54a)

46138

New Yo. Nov. 2nd, 1917

25-2048-17-B, Form 5 H

A Transcript from the Records of the Births reported to the Department of Health of The City of New York.

The City of New York
Department of Health

STATE OF NEW YORK,

Registered Number

CERTIFICATE AND RECORD OF BIRTH 11596
OF

Name of Child ___ William Joyce

Sex	male	Color	white	Mother's Marriage Name — Gertrude Emily Joyce
Date of Birth	April 24/06			Mother's Name before Marriage — Gertrude Emily Brooke
Place of Birth (Street and No.) Borough	1377 Herkimer St.			Mother's Residence — 1377 Herkimer St.
Father's Name	Michael Joyce			Mother's Birthplace — England
Father's Residence	1377 Herkimer St.			Mother's Age — 26 yrs. Color — --
Father's Birthplace	Ireland			Mother's Occupation — --
Father's Age	36 yrs.	Color	--	Number of children born to this mother including present birth — 1
Father's Occupation	contractor			Number of children born to this mother now living — --

I, the undersigned, hereby certify that I attended professionally at the above birth and I am personally cognizant thereof; and that all the facts stated in said certificate and report of birth are true to the best of my knowledge, information and belief.

Signature,   Charles F. Yerdon
                                                         Physician
                                                         Midwife

Residence,   1276 Herkimer St.

Date of Report, May 7th, 1906

ALFRED E. SHIPLEY,   70   A True Copy, S. J. Byrne M.D.
Secretary,
Board of Health,
City of New York.   Assistant Registrar

6. William Joyce's birth certificate, from a transcript of birth records reported to the Department of Health of the City of New York. It provides conclusive evidence that Joyce was born in the United States. (KV 2/250/1)

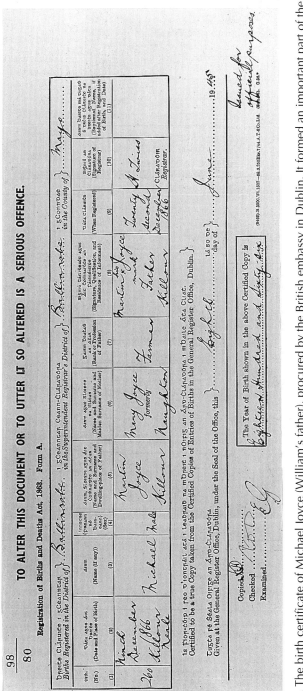

7. The birth certificate of Michael Joyce (William's father), procured by the British embassy in Dublin. It formed an important part of the prosecution and its hope of determining William Joyce's nationality. (KV 2/246/409)

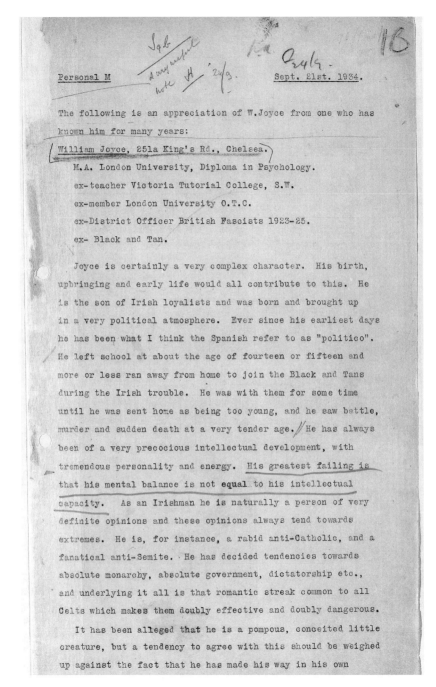

Sept. 21st. 1934.

The following is an appreciation of W.Joyce from one who has known him for many years:

William Joyce, 251a King's Rd., Chelsea.

    M.A. London University, Diploma in Psychology.

    ex-teacher Victoria Tutorial College, S.W.

    ex-member London University O.T.C.

    ex-District Officer British Fascists 1923-25.

    ex- Black and Tan.

    Joyce is certainly a very complex character. His birth, upbringing and early life would all contribute to this. He is the son of Irish loyalists and was born and brought up in a very political atmosphere. Ever since his earliest days he has been what I think the Spanish refer to as "politico". He left school at about the age of fourteen or fifteen and more or less ran away from home to join the Black and Tans during the Irish trouble. He was with them for some time until he was sent home as being too young, and he saw battle, murder and sudden death at a very tender age. He has always been of a very precocious intellectual development, with tremendous personality and energy. His greatest failing is that his mental balance is not equal to his intellectual capacity. As an Irishman he is naturally a person of very definite opinions and these opinions always tend towards extremes. He is, for instance, a rabid anti-Catholic, and a fanatical anti-Semite. He has decided tendencies towards absolute monarchy, absolute government, dictatorship etc., and underlying it all is that romantic streak common to all Celts which makes them doubly effective and doubly dangerous.

    It has been alleged that he is a pompous, conceited little creature, but a tendency to agree with this should be weighed up against the fact that he has made his way in his own

8. Report from agent 'M', 21 Sept 1934. 'M' was Charles Henry Maxwell Knight, a double agent who during the interwar period worked for various British fascist organizations and knew the Joyce family very well. This report, annotated 'a very useful note', provides remarkable insights into William Joyce's personality. Here Maxwell Knight describes Joyce as having: 'little stability due to over-developed intellect and Celtic temperament'. (KV 2/245/1b)

(2)

small world entirely by his own efforts and in the face of
very considerable difficulties.

In the first place, he is a very small insignificant
looking little man. He had practically no early education.
He was brought face to face with desperate situations and
happenings even younger than the average junior officer in
the war period, yet when he returned to England after the
Irish trouble he commenced to educate himself and achieved
comparatively brilliant successes. He was as fanatical in his
studies as he is in other directions, and several times during
his scholastic career he reduced himself to the verge of a
nervous breakdown. However he secured an excellent degree
with honours and other diplomas besides.

It was then (about 1927-28) his intention to take up
teaching as a profession with the object of breaking into
politics, and with that aim in view he threw himself wholeheartedly into the Junior Imperial League and soon became
one of their principal speakers in South London. However,
his natural aptitude for intrigue, his abhorrence of compromise, and his rabid opinions did not endear him to his
more peaceful colleagues, and after much strife he resigned.

He married, I think in 1927, a girl named Hazel Barr, whom
he met during his time with the old British Fascists 1923-25,
and has two little daughters aged six and four.

Regarding his associations with Fascism, little need be
said about his early efforts with the British Fascists. He
was in charge of a district in Battersea, was untiring in his
efforts and made himself so obnoxious to the Communist Party
that during the election of 1924 he was "razored" at one of
Mr. Hogben's meetings. (This he is not likely to have
forgotten.)

He was one of the earliest to join Sir Oswald Mosley's
BUF, and he has risen very rapidly until he now occupies a

(3)

13

seat at Mosley's right hand. He probably has many traits
in common with Mosley, though he would be a much more like-
able character in many ways. His political beliefs are
probably very mobile, but it is considered that his funda-
mentals are quite sound. I should not think that anything
could occur to shake his basic patriotism and he is violently
opposed to what can be broadly described as Bolshevism. In
his Fascist creed it is thought that he tends towards the
Hitler ideal rather than that of Mussolini. Under favourable
circumstances or where he thought his own cause would benefit
he would not certainly shrink from violence, but it would not
be unthinking, senseless, spectacular violence. He has at
times a very calm and cunning judgement. He obviously has
tremendous respect and admiration for Mosley himself, and
it is probably Mosley's independence of spirit and courage
that appeals to him.

If Fascism were to progress in this country and become
more powerful, then Joyce would be a man who would undoubtedly play a very prominent part in affairs. Should Fascism
wane or become discredited anything might happen to him;
for it is not thought that he has enough stability to make
him accept defeat very gracefully, unless his personal aims
could be definitely furthered on lines congenial to his
mode of thought.

His good and bad characteristics may be summed up as
follows:

Good: Boundless physical and moral courage considerable
brain power; tremendous energy and application; well read
politically and historically; very loyal to his friends;
a sense of humour; patriotic.

8. (continued) Report from Maxwell Knight on William Joyce.

(4)

Bad: Little stability due to over-developed intellect
and Celtic temperament; very violent temper at times,
at others extremely quiet and calculating; a tendency
towards theatricality; marked conspiratorial complex.
Celtic prejudices very deeply rooted; not to be swayed
by arguments where his inherent instincts are touched.

Moral temperament: As far as is known his moral temperament is no better and no worse than that of any other
young man who is over-developed intellectually. He does
not appear to have any very marked major vices; he is a
moderate smoker and as far as can be seen a fairly moderate
drinker with a tendency towards wine rather than beer and
spirits.   His code of personal honour is probably peculiar
but very rigid, and would be intimately bound up with his
personal likes and dislikes.

Tel. 3126

15, Shelburne Road,
Calne, Wilts.

June 26th 1945

Sergt. Chivers,
Wiltshire Constabulary,
Police Station, CALNE.

Dear Sgt. Chivers,

I see by this mornings Times that William Joyce (Lord
'Haw Haw') when charged yesterday stated that he had lived in
Galway, Ireland from 1909 to 1921. Also it is recorded that
when he applied, in 1933, for a British Passport he said then
that he had been born at Rutledge Terrace, Galway.

Now it so happens that I lived in Galway from 1911 to 1922
and one of my close acquaintances there from 1919 to 1921 was an
extraordinary youth whose name was William Joyce.

His father owned a short row of houses in Salthill, a suburb
of Galway, called as far as I can recollect Rutledge Terrace and
the family lived there. Later when the trams were scrapped in
Galway a new bus Company was formed, the Galway Omnibus Company
Ltd., and Willie Joyce's father became the manager.

Joyce senior was, so far as I remember, an American, or
rather what we called an Irish American, an Irishman who had gone
to the States, made some money and returned to his native country.

Willie Joyce, the son was about my own age, I am now 40 and
I see that William Joyce is given as 39.

I have stated above that he was one of my closest acquaintances and the reason for this was that I was an English lad and
Joyce was at that time very pro British (it was during the Trouble
period, as we called it, in Ireland) in addition we had certain
things in common, particularly a great interest in literature.
He taught me too to play chess and we spent hours together at
this pastime. Joyce was for a time very keen on hypnotism and
indeed every other -ism and on one occasion spent an hour trying
to hypnotise me but I didn't respond. He always spoke in an
exaggerated fashion and bubbled over with self importance. He
spent a considerable time in the barracks of the Black & Tans and
at Lenaboy Castle a large mansion on the outskirts of the town
which was then the Headquarters of the R.I.C. Auxiliary Cadets
(Royal Irish Constabulary). The townspeople, particularly the
anti British used to say that he was a Police spy and that he
swore away the lives of Irishman to the Auxiliaries. Certainly
he reviled in no uncertain fashion everyone who held anti British
views. There is no one more pro British than your extreme Irish
loyalist, he is almost a fanatic as Joyce certainly was and he
was heartily detected by, not only the ordinary local Irish
townspeople but even by the average loyalist too.

I am afraid that I rather liked his company and was a bit
proud of being the more or less only friend and companion of such
a firebrand pro Britisher but unfortunately I got myself tarred
with the same brush in the eyes of the younger element in Galway.
Even I went to Lenaboy Castle but in complete innocence.
Actually I doubt if Joyce was 'officially' a Police spy but I
have no doubt on the other hand that he interested the
Auxiliaries and they may have made use of him.

He used to carry around with him what he told me were small
'egg bombs' for personal protection in case he was attacked but
whether they were what he made them out to be I cannot say after
all these years.

One incident I have never forgotten, it was after a British
Officer together with a Police District Inspector and his

9. This set of documents dated 2 July 1945 is made up of MI5 notes and a
typescript copy of a letter written in June 1945 by one of William Joyce's former
school friends, Arthur Miles Webb, from his time in Galway, Ireland. It contains
fascinating insights into the childhood life and aspirations of the man and of MI5's
reaction: particularly the comment 'Value doubtful?' (KV 2/249/54b)

2.

were murdered one afternoon when playing tennis at a country house near Galway. The military funeral was coming from Renmore Military Barracks and the troops were marching with reversed arms, band playing and so forth. Joyce and I were there together in front of a crowd of people and as the coffins passed Joyce sprang to attention and, although dressed in ordinary clothes like myself gave a most elaborate and stiff salute, holding it with grim set face for two or three minutes with everyone gaping as much at him as at the cortege. I felt quite embarrassed at the time because he was not a soldier and had done this and I hadn't the courage to do it although I probably felt the same as he did. I have never forgotten this.

Now when the Irish gained their freedom and the Free State was formed the Crown Forces left Ireland. Joyce was thereupon likely to be left high and dry. I did not see him much about that time, I cannot remember just why. At any rate it was obvious that, as the former rebels who had been 'on the run' as well as those who were secretly members of the I.R.A. in the town all the time, were now coming out into the open and swaggering about with green uniform, many were out to settle old scores and Joyce was obviously one who would be dealt with. Many shootings took place at that time and patrols of these former I.R.A. men went about looking for old enemies and all trains were watched.

I did not see Joyce at that time but I was given to understand that he had joined the Army, a British Regt. then stationed in Galway and due to move back to England. I believe it was his mother who told me he had joined the Army, though she did not say the reason, actually I don't think his people ever took him very seriously or realised quite how he was involved in things in the town. At any rate I was given his address as Badajos Barracks, Aldershot and wrote to him there eventually but I think the letter came back as he gone on elsewhere. It is so long ago and, at that time it was not very important.

If this is the same William Joyce, and there seems little doubt this information may be of value to the authorities. If I am wrong and libelling an innocent man I am sorry and will apologise in advance for taking up your time in the matter.

Yours sincerely,

(Sgd.) A.W. Miles Webb.

The attached copy letter written by
Mr. Arthur William Miles-Webb of 15 Shelburne
Road, Calne, which has been referred to this
department by the Chief Constable of Wiltshire,
is forwarded for your information.

DEPUTY ASSISTANT COMMISSIONER.

9. (continued) MI5's reaction to Miles Webb's letter (sequence as preserved in the files).

STATEMENT OF Bernard O'REILLY of 73, Almonds Green, Liverpool 12,

who says :-

I am a retired Head Constable of the Royal Irish Constabulary. I retired on demobilisation on April 30th, 1922, and almost immediately afterwards I took up residence in Liverpool, where I have been ever since. For about 12 years of my service in the Royal Irish Constabulary I was a Sergeant and was stationed at the sub-station at Salthill, Co. Galway.

I have been shown a copy of a report, submitted by me to my Superiors relative to Mrs. Gertrude Emily JOYCE and her husband, Mr. Michael F. JOYCE, dated June 30th, 1917. Although it is twenty-eight years since this report was put in, I distinctly remember the circumstances attendant upon this enquiry.

The position in this matter was that a request had been received from the Chief Constable of Lancashire for an enquiry to be made as to why Mrs. Gertrude Emily JOYCE had not reported as an alien when leaving Shaw, Lancashire, some little time before.

At the time of the making of my report, Mrs. Gertrude Emily JOYCE was living with her husband, Mr. Michael F. JOYCE, at No.1 Ruttlidge Terrace, Salthill. Acting upon the request, I interviewed both Mr. and Mrs. JOYCE, whom I had known for some years as local residents and who, insofar as the Royal Irish Constabulary was concerned, were not considered as aliens and were not registered as such.

Mr. Michael F. JOYCE informed me that when in the United States of America, he had taken out naturalisation papers as a United States citizen, but that his claim to American citizenship had lapsed by his failing to register within two years after leaving the United States for Ireland.

Mrs. Gertrude Emily JOYCE informed me that when in Shaw, Lancashire, her husband, Mr. Michael JOYCE, had reported himself to the local police as an alien, but that he had told her that she need not do so, as it was for him to do so.

The report previously referred to by me was based on the information set out above given to me by Mr. and Mrs. JOYCE. Some time later I received instructions to caution Mrs. JOYCE for her failure to report to the Police as an alien and that should she go to Shaw again she should make a point of doing so. Apart from cautioning Mrs. JOYCE as requested, no further action was taken in the matter.

I would add that Mr. Michael F. JOYCE spoke with a very strong American accent, but I did not require him to produce naturalisation papers and he did not do so.

This statement has been read over to me and is true.

(signed) Bernard O'REILLY.

22.8.45.

[handwritten in left margin: Is this true →]

[handwritten at top right: 194..]

10. Statement of Bernard O'Reilly dated 22 August 1945. In 1945 O'Reilly was a retired member of the Royal Irish Constabulary. He had been based in Galway during the time the Joyce family were resident in that part of Ireland. The evidence in his statement helped the defence prove that the family were aliens; in fact US citizens. (KV 2/249/79a)

M.I.5   R E P O R T

Re W I L L I A M   J O Y C E

1.   William JOYCE was born on April 24th 1906, his father being
Michael Francis JOYCE and his mother Gertrude Emily JOYCE (nee BROOKE).

2.   There was at one time some doubt as to exactly where he was
born, mainly due to JOYCE's conflicting statements over a period of
years, but the almost certainly correct view is that he was born on
the date mentioned in paragraph 1 in Brooklyn, New York, and document
No.1 in Bundle 'A', which is explained hereafter, confirms this.

3.   A further question which arises, assuming JOYCE was born in
Brooklyn, New York, is whether he is a British or American citizen.
The view held by M.I.5 is that at all material times he was a British
subject for the reasons given later in this report.

4.   It is not thought necessary to go into JOYCE's history prior
to the outbreak of war in September 1939, but the following facts are
to be noted:-

    a) Between 1922 and 1925 JOYCE studied at the University of
        London, thereafter adopting the profession of private tutor.

    b) In 1923 he joined the British Fascists.

    c) In 1933 he became one of the earliest members of Sir Oswald
        MOSLEY's "British Union of Fascists" later becoming a key man.

    d) In March 1937 he was dismissed and in April 1937 founded the
        "National Socialist League", the purpose of which was to gain
        the support of all who believe in the principles of the B.U.F.
        but dislike its methods.

    e) On August 26th 1939 in company with his wife he left England,
        arriving in Berlin the following day.

5.   In mid-September 1939, reports were received that JOYCE was
broadcasting over the German Radio in English, but until April 1941 he
spoke anonymously and was popularly known in England as "Lord Haw-
Haw."

                                                        6..../

11. MI5 report on William Joyce, 13 June 1945. This was prepared shortly before Joyce's
return to Britain and sets out the case against him in preparation for the trial.
(KV 2/248/9a)

-2-

6.   On April 2nd 1941, JOYCE disclosed his identity over the German Radio in a broadcast monitored by the B.B.C., and if thought necessary, evidence can be adduced to prove this.

7.   In addition in a book written by him and published in Germany in 1940 under the title "Dammerung uber England" (Twilight over England) he admitted his broadcasting activities on behalf of Nazi Germany. It is hoped to make available a copy of this book in English; attention is drawn to the preface in which JOYCE writes of himself as "a daily perpetrator of High Treason".

8.   JOYCE continued his notorious anti-British and anti-Allied propaganda broadcasts almost until the capitulation of Germany. The last broadcast made by JOYCE was on April 30th 1945. As will be seen later in this report, a record of this broadcast is available and can be proved. It is to be noted that on the occasion of this last broadcast, JOYCE was under the influence of drink.

9.   After his broadcast of April 30th, 1945, JOYCE disappeared with his wife and nothing more was heard of them until May 28th 1945.

10.   On the last mentioned date, three officers, Captain A.A. Lickorish, Lieut. Perry and another (name not known) were gathering firewood on the Danish Border near Krussau, which is north of Flensburg.

11.   These officers were approached by a civilian who volunteered in French that a pile of good firewood could be found nearby. As he was moving off, the civilian made a remark in English, which aroused suspicion and one of the officers said point blank:-

    "You are JOYCE aren't you?" At this, the civilian, who was in fact JOYCE made a move towards his pocket, whereupon he was shot through the buttocks.

12.   After this shooting incident, JOYCE was removed to hospital. Search of his papers showed that he carried a German Passport in the name of HANSEN (Document No.8 Bundle 'A') but other papers found on

him.../

11. (continued) MI5 report on William Joyce.

-3-

him proved him to be JOYCE, a fact which he himself admitted.

13. On May 31st 1945, JOYCE was seen by Captain W.J. Skardon, Intelligence Corps (attached to M.I.5 Liaison Section, SHAEF), to whom he made a statement in writing under caution (Document No.9 Bundle 'A').

14. There can be no question but that JOYCE in broadcasting over the German Radio Nazi propaganda directed against Great Britain and her allies has committed a series of acts of treason. The evidence, which is available to prove his treasonable conduct and which is reviewed in the remaining paragraphs of this report, is thought to render the case against him conclusive.

Evidence

15. Nationality

As mentioned in paragraph 2 of this report, the better view as to JOYCE's nationality is that he is a British subject and in support of this, there are available:-

    a) His application of July 4th 1933 for a British Passport.

    b) His application for renewal of his British Passport dated September 24th 1938.

    c) His further application for renewal of his British Passport dated August 24th, 1939.

In all three documents, which will be produced by Mr. Godwin of the Passport Office, JOYCE describes himself as a British subject by birth though born in Galway, Ireland. The original passport issued to JOYCE is not available. (Document No.1 Bundle 'B'. Mr. Godwin's statement refers.

16. Acquisition of German Nationality

It is perhaps not inconvenient to deal with this aspect of the case at this stage rather than later in this report. In the statement under caution made by JOYCE, he states "In 1940, I acquired German nationality. I believe the date was September 26th, but the

certificate.../

−4−

certificate of naturalisation is not in my possession. The only
evidence I can offer in support of my statement is the entry in my
Wehrpass issued subsequent to my naturalisation when I am put down
as of German nationality."

Assuming that JOYCE is correct in saying he acquired German
nationality in 1940 – and there is no reason to doubt him on this
point as the Wehrpass (Document No.7 in Bundle 'A') confirms his
view – he would appear – having regard to the decision in R.v.Lynch
(1903) K.B.444 to have committed an act of treason by acquiring
German nationality at a time when England was at war with Germany.

Apart from JOYCE's admission in his statement and the Wehrpass,
no other evidence is available as to this act of treason.

17.   Recordings made of broadcasts of JOYCE's over the German
Radio during the course of the war.

As soon as JOYCE's identity was established as a broadcaster
over the German Radio in 1941, consideration was given to the
recording of a number of such broadcasts with a view to their being
available.

As a result of certain advice received, from the then Director
of Public Prosecutions, arrangements were made to take recordings of
broadcasts by JOYCE. These recordings were made by officers of the
British Broadcasting Corporation and whilst they were being made,
shorthand notes were taken by Special Branch Officers.

The dates of these recordings are as follows:-

January 30th 1943
April 8th 1943
July 12th 1943
August 30th 1944.

Broadly speaking the system adopted in the making of these recordings
was:-

(a)   Two B.B.C. engineers in a room at the B.B.C. Studios
        Maida Vale or elsewhere suitably adapted and equipped cut
        the records.

(b)...../

11. (continued) MI5 report on William Joyce.

-5-

(b) Two Special Branch officers who could recognise JOYCE's voice were present and took shorthand notes.

(c) The broadcast from Germany or German occupied territory was picked up by the B.B.C. at their Receiving Station at Tatsfield, Kent, and relayed to the room mentioned in (a) above by means of the B.B.C. land line system.

(d) In most cases, i.e. all with the exception of January 30th 1943, two sets of records were made, of which one set - the original set - was placed in cardboard or tin-plate containers and duly sealed. These original sealed containers are to-day in the possession of M.I.5 with the exception of that of January 30th.

On the occasion of the recordings of January 30th 1943, April 8th 1943 and July 12th 1943, the B.B.C. recording engineers engaged in the recording were:-

Mr.T.C.Burningham
Mr.F.H.Dart

Whilst the Reception Engineers on duty for those dates were:-

Mrs.G.M.Owttrim (January 30th)
Mr. H.V.Griffiths(remaining dates)

The Special Branch Officers concerned for these dates were:-

Inspector A.Hunt
Sergeant J.Buswell.

For the final recording on August 30th 1944 which took place at Crowsley Park near Reading the following were on duty:-

B.B.C. Recording Engineers	Mr.W.R. Arnell Mr. R.M.Lane
Reception Engineer	Mr.H.V.Griffiths
Special Branch Officers	Inspector A.Hunt Sergeant C.Rhodes.

Statements..../

-6-

Statements by all officers concerned (Documents Nos.2-14 inclusive in Bundle 'B') are submitted with this report. It is not thought necessary to comment in detail on these statements. Shortly put these officers prove the following:-

Recording Engineers	The cutting of the recordings, their sealing and identification. Reception of the land line relay.
Reception Engineers	The picking up of the German broadcast and relaying over the land line system. The fact that the broadcast emanated from Germany or German occupied territory.
Special Branch Officers	The transcript of their shorthanded notes and the identification of JOYCE's voice. The individual short-hand note of each officer is submitted, even though the difference between them is insignificant. It may be thought enough to rely on the note of Inspector Hunt only. (Documents 1, 1a, 2, 2a, 3, 3a, 4 and 4a in Bundle 'C'). The transcripts of all shorthand notes are in Bundle 'C'.

Two points arise in connection with the recordings made:-

a) Mr. Burningham, the Chief Recording Engineer for the first three broadcasts died recently and Mr. Dart alone will have to be relied upon.

b) The original sealed records of January 30th 1943 were surrendered to the B.B.C. for the purpose of testing the durability of the records made; this test was successful, but in the circumstances it may be thought unnecessary to put this recording and its attendant features in in evidence.

8.   Subject matter of the broadcasts in relation to the war.

January 30th 1943. This may shortly be described as a eulogy of Hitler with no particular significance.

April 8th 1943. For the most part, this deals with the situation on the Eastern Front after the appalling winter campaign experienced by the Germans in 1942/43. There are, however, references to Churchill and to Jews all of an abusive character.

July 12th 1943. At this time, as will be seen from the text, not merely was the battle for Orel raging, but the Sicilian landings were well established. JOYCE treats the latter in sneering fashion and contends that they do not discharge the obligation by the British to attack from the West.

August..../

11. (continued) MI5 report on William Joyce.

-7-

August 30th 1944. By this time, the invasion of the Continent was well established, the V.1. attacks on England gradually reaching their peak and Rumania had gone out of the war. All these matters are touched upon and there are also references to the abortive Warsaw rising and Soviet Imperialism.

19.   Arrest and taking of Statement under caution at Luneburg

The circumstances of JOYCE being found in the Flensburg area have been dealt with in paragraph 9, 10, 11 and 12 of this report. Unless thought essential, it is not desired to bring the officers concerned with JOYCE's apprehension over as witnesses.

As mentioned in paragraph 13 of this report JOYCE was seen in hospital at Luneburg by Captain Skardon to whom he made a statement under caution.   In this statement JOYCE makes the following admissions:-

a) He was born in Brooklyn, U.S.A. on April 24th 1906.

b) With his parents, he left the U.S.A. for Ireland and England in 1909.

c) At all times he and his people were counted as British subjects.

d) In 1940, he acquired German nationality.

e) In August 1939, he decided to leave this country.

f) He broadcast to Britain over the German Radio.

In addition the documents in Bundle 'A' apart from the statement under caution were found either in JOYCE's possession or at his lodgings and admitted by JOYCE to Captain Skardon to belong to him.   A statement by Captain Skardon (Document No.15 in Bundle 'B') is sent herewith.   Meantime the documents, where they are in German, have been translated by Mr. S.L.Salzedo, a copy of a statement by Mr. Salzedo as to his translations is included with this report.   (Document No.16 in Bundle 'B').   Copies of the translation follow the original German in each case.

The..../

-8-

The following points may be noted as to the documents (in numerical and date order):-

1. New York Birth Certificate

   This clearly shows that JOYCE was born as previously stated and as admitted by him.

2. Letter of June 26th, 1942

   This appoints JOYCE as "Chief Commentator for the group of countries 'England'".

3. Contract of July 3rd, 1942

   By this JOYCE is appointed Head Commentator in the English Editorial Department of German Broadcasting Station for Europe. His salary is 1200 marks a month and bonus. The contract is determinable on three months notice at the end of a quarter.

4. The Iron Cross, 1st September 1944

   This awards JOYCE the Iron Cross of War Merit 1st Class and is signed (facsimile) by Hitler himself.

5. Volksturm Certificate 21st December 1944

   This certifies JOYCE as being a member of the German Volksturm (or Home Guard) Berlin District.

6. Letter of March 29th, 1945

   This certifies the temporary transfer of JOYCE by the German Radio to Apen.

7. German military Passport dated April 12th, 1941

   Issued in the name of William JOYCE.

8. German Passport issued November 3rd 1944

   In the name of Wilhelm HANSEN.

9. Apen.

The makeshift German radio set-up at Apen was searched by Mr. Guy Della-Cioppa of P.W.D. A copy of his statement is sent with this report (Document No.17 Bundle 'B'). The material found by him has been examined. It is not thought to add anything to the

11. (continued) MI5 report on William Joyce.

-9-

evidence with the possible exception of the two records dated April
6th 1945 entitled "Views on the News". These are only part of the
whole broadcast. They have been heard by Inspector Hunt, Sergeant
Buswell and Sergeant Rhodes and a copy of their joint transcript
is sent with this report (Document No. 5 Bundle 'C'). The talk was
also monitored in its entirety by the B.B.C. and if thought
necessary their monitor can be made available.

21.   Hamburg.

Whilst JOYCE was still missing, Captain R.W.Spooner
Intelligence Corps (M.I.5 Liaison Section, SHAEF) had occasion to
go to Hamburg and examine a mass of material at the Radio Station
there (Document No.18 in Bundle 'B'). This material has been
further examined by M.I.5 and in principle nothing would appear to
add anything further to the case except two magnetophone records.
One of these has been discussed in paragraph 8 of this report.

These two recordings, both of which are by JOYCE, have
been heard by Inspector Hunt, Sergeant Buswell and Sergeant Rhodes.
Copies of their transcript shorthand notes are sent with this report.
(Documents Nos. 6, 6a, 6b, 7, 7a and 7b in Bundle 'C').

On the cardboard containers relating to these records they
are marked respectively Exhibit 1 and Exhibit 2. The dates of these
records can be fixed by reference insofar as Exhibit 1 is concerned
to the copy statement of SCHNEIDER (Document No.19 in Bundle 'B')
the Hamburg employee in whose presence it was made on April 30th 1945;
it is almost certainly JOYCE's last broadcast.

The date of Exhibit 2 is fixed by Fraulein BAUCKS as April
10th 1945 (Document No.20 in Bundle 'B'). An interesting thing to
note is that in Exhibit 2, JOYCE speaks in his usual sneering
boastful manner; in Exhibit 1, he is far from sober and rather
despondent. The German witnesses, SCHNEIDER and BAUCKS, can be
brought over to prove these records.

M.I.5.
13.6.45.

M.S./55.

LANCASHIRE CONSTABULARY,

PRESTON, 26th June, 1917.

From the Chief Constable of Lancashire.

To the Inspector General, Royal Irish Constabulary,
The Castle, Dublin.

ALIEN - G. E. JOYCE.

Sir,

I enclose herewith form A.R.-D, change report, in respect of the above named alien, who removed from Shaw to Rockbarton on the 8th instant without notifying the police of her intended change of address.

I should be glad to know whether this alien has reported her arrival in your area, to the Police at Rockbarton, and if so, will you kindly cause her to be interviewed and ascertain what explanation she has to give for failing to notify the Police at Shaw of her intended change of address, and inform me of the result.

I am,

Sir,

Your obedient Servant,

(Signed) W. Trubshaw.

Assistant Chief Constable,
of Lancashire.

C.I. Galway.
Transmitted.
Report as to A.
???
D.I.G. 27. 6. 17.

12. This evidence from police files in Lancashire during the First World War showed conclusively that the Joyces were regarded as aliens. (KV 2/249/76b)

M.S./55.

County of Galway W.R.
County Inspector's Office,
Galway, 28th June, 1917.

ALIEN - G.E. JOYCE.

For report please.

(Signed) G.B. Ruttledge.
County Inspector.

D.I. Galway.

District Inspector's Office,
Galway 29. 6.1917.

For enquiry and report please.

(Signed) ???????????

Sgt. Reilly. Salthill, 30. 6.17.

I beg to report that Mrs. Gertrude Emily Joyce is the
wife of Michael F. Joyce of No. 1, Ruttledge Terrace, Salthill
one of the most respectable, law-abiding, and loyal men in
this locality, and one who has been consistently an advocate
of the "pro-Allied" cause since the beginning of the war.

He returned from the United States to Ballinrobe, Co.
Mayo, in October, 1909, and Mrs. Joyce, his wife, also went
there on 2.11.1909, where they remained until May, 1913, when
they came to reside at Salthill where they have extensive
house property.

Mrs. Joyce was born an Englishwoman at 31, Manchester
Road, Shaw, Lancashire, and went to the States to marry her
husband. She states she was only three or four years there
altogether and she regrets very much not having reported her
departure to the police at Shaw, and says that as her husband
had reported himself and told her the matter was "all right"
she did not think a personal report was necessary.

Neither Michael F. Joyce, her husband, nor herself
consider themselves Aliens. The former asserts that he has
abandoned his claim as a Citizen of U.S.A. by failing to get
himself registered there within two years after leaving the
country for Ireland.

They were not considered as aliens here, and have not

been registered as such.

    (Signed)   Bernard Reilly S53,C10.

The D.I.

          District Inspector's Office,
          Galway, 1.7.1917.

Where was Mich Joyce born? If in Ireland, did he take out naturalization papers in the U.S.A.

    (Signed) ??????? D.I.

Sgt. Reilly.   Salthill, 2.7.17.

I beg to report that Joyce was born at Ballinrobe, Co. Mayo. He emigrated to United States of America and took out naturalization papers there. He left the United States in October, 1909, and has resided in the Counties of Mayo and Galway W.R. ever since.

    (Signed) Bernard Reilly S.53,C10.

The Dist. Inspector.

          District Inspector's Office,
          Galway, 3.7.1917.

Submitted - Please see "A". Under the cir.s there seems some doubt whether these people are aliens at all.

    (Signed) ???????? D.I.

The C.I.

          County Inspector's Office,
          Galway, 4.7.'17.

    Submitted.

        (Signed) G.B. Ruttledge.
             Co. Insp.

Inspr. General.

The Chief Constable of Lancashire, Preston.

    Transmitted.

        (Signed) W.W. Davies.

             D.I.G.

             5. 7. 17.

12. (continued) Evidence from police files in Lancashire during the First World War.

WILLIAM JOYCE

EARLY BROADCASTS

1.   The earliest report of the recognition of his voice was received on 18th September 1939, when he was reported to have broadcast as "William Joyce of the National Socialist League speaking to his English friends".

2.   Next day (19th September) a member of the public reported that the broadcaster at 12.15 a.m. that morning was JOYCE.

3.   On September 26th it was reported that JOYCE was broadcasting from Koln-Hamburg and also on D.J.A. short-wave at 12.15.a.m. nightly.

4.   October 4th is the earliest reference to the subject matter of his broadcasts. An informant, after saying he had recognised JOYCE's voice on the Hamburg-Koln and D.J.A. added that he had identified him also by "references to JOYCE's previous activities in this country and Eire".

5.   On October 6th a retired Inidan police officer who had been a B.U.F. officer described the subjects of JOYCE's broadcasts as practically identical with his old speeches, including one on October 1st about "power of International Finance behind the British Press" which informant described as "practically unaltered in form from the form which it took when he delivered the speech so often in England". He quotes a phrase used by JOYCE: "The General Manager of the Daily Express, Mr. R.D. Blumenfeld, whose Chinese name sufficiently denotes his racial origin". The broadcast was on the Hamburg-Zeesen and D.J.A.

6.   On November 26th a Naval Officer recognised JOYCE by (among other things) his pronunciation of "Hore-Belisha". Broadcasts generally about 8.10 to 9.15.p.m.

7.   On December 29th the "Sunday Pictorial" quoted JOYCE's first wife as saying that JOYCE "even tells the same stories that he used to tell me".

8.   On the afternoon of April 27th 1940 there was a broadcast from the N.B.B.S. (which started in February 1940) in answer to the Wolkoff letter (many of the N.B.B.S. broadcasts were by "the Professor", which had been JOYCE's nickname in early B.U.F. days.

9.   His first broadcast as "I, William Joyce" was on the 2nd April 1941.

13. This undated MI5 document sets out how Joyce came to be identified as Lord Haw Haw. (KV 2/247)

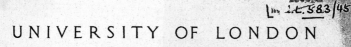

UNIVERSITY OF LONDON

SENATE HOUSE

TELEGRAMS: UNIVERSITY, LONDON

Temporary Address—
RICHMOND COLLEGE,
RICHMOND, SURREY.
Telephone: RICHMOND 2301.

TELEPHONE: MUSEUM 6000.

LONDON, W.C.1

19th July 1945.

CONFIDENTIAL

Dear Sir,

In accordance with your request, I have looked up our records concerning William Joyce, and his academic career at the University is as follows:-

He entered for the Matriculation Examination in September 1922. He gave as his date of birth 24 April 1906 and submitted a Birth Certificate in evidence of his age. This was, of course, subsequently returned to him. His permanent address at that time was 86, Brompton Street, Oldham, Lancs. He passed the examination in the 2nd division.

In October 1922 he registered as an Internal student of the University in the Faculty of Science at Battersea Polytechnic, giving as his address 10 Longbeach Road, Lavender Hill, Clapham, S.W.

He entered for the General Intermediate Examination in Science in July 1923 but failed in two of his subjects. // In October 1923 he registered as an Internal student of the University in the Faculty of Arts at Birkbeck College, giving as his address 3 Allison Grove, Dulwich Common, S.E.21. He took his Final examination for the B.A. Honours Degree in English (Subsidiary Modern History) in 1927, obtaining I Cl.Hons.

In May 1932 he registered as an Internal student at King's College for the Ph.D. Degree in Psychology. He left King's College during the session 1933-34. His address at that time was 41 Farquhar Road, Upper Norwood, S.E.19. He described himself as a Private Tutor of Languages and History at the Victoria Tutorial College, Eccleston Square, S.W.1.

Neither Birkbeck College nor King's College have any record as to his nationality or place of birth. King's College inform me, however, that he gave as the school at which he was educated St Ignatius College, Galway.

Yours faithfully,

K. N. Egan

Principal's Secretary

The Officer in Charge,
Room 055,
War Office,
Whitehall,
S.W.1.

Receipt ackd. in C.L. 584/45 of 21.7.45

KME/DA

14. Letter from London University, 19 July 1945, confirming Joyce's academic record, and an Internal MI5 letter revealing the agency's frustration at its inability to pin down the issue of Joyce's nationality. (KV 2/246/466a)

SECRET

Room 055,

WAR OFFICE,

WHITEHALL,

S.W.1.

G.L.583/45.   21st July 1945.

G.E.Wakefield, Esquire,
S.L.B.3/M.I.5.

Dear Wakefield,

As requested, I have tried to obtain from London University any records they may have concerning William JOYCE which would help to establish his nationality at date of birth, and I now send you original of a letter dated 19.7.45 which I have just received from the Principal's Secretary.

From this you will see that the only information approaching what is required is to the effect that when JOYCE entered for the matriculation examination in September 1922, he evidently produced a birth certificate which, if in the British form, would have given his date and place of birth but not his nationality, declared or otherwise.   This birth certificate would have been returned to JOYCE after perusal.

Unfortunately the University destroys all records of this kind after a lapse of ten years, so that the details given in this letter are all that now remain in the University archives regarding him.

In my view it would probably be a waste of time to pursue this line of enquiry through the University, and I do not know whether St.Ignatius College, Galway, would prove any more useful as a source of information.

Yours sincerely,

D.C.Orr.

DCO/AMR.

15. Letter from the teenaged William Joyce, 9 August 1922, setting out his military experience and skills, and asserting his British descent and loyalty to the Crown while acknowledging his US birth. This comes from a 1945 MI5 file relating to Joyce's London University Officer Training Corps application. (KV 2/245/301a)

I was informed, at the Brigade Headquarters of the district in which I was stationed in Ireland, that I possessed the same rights and privileges as I would if of natural British birth.

I can obtain testimonials as to my loyalty to the Crown.

I am in no way connected with the United States of America, against which, as against all other nations, I am prepared to draw the sword in British interests.

As a young man of pure British descent, some of whose forefathers have held high positions in the British Army, I have always been desirous of devoting what little capability and energy I may possess to the country which I love so dearly.

I ask that you may inform me if the accident of my birth, to which I refer above, will affect my position.

I shall be in London for the September Matriculation Examination, and I hope to commence studies at the London University at the beginning of the next academic

I trust that you will reply as soon as possible, and that your reply will be favourable to my aspirations.

Thanking you for your kind promise of interview,

I am, Sir,

Yours faithfully

William Joyce.

Extract from S.F.96/Brit/2 (307a).

331B

Notes by M. on Communist disorders at political meetings:

Case 2. Meeting in Battersea of Liberal opponent to Saklatvala 1924:
This meeting was stewarded by 11 British Fascists only. They were not
in uniform and had no distinguishing or provocative marks ... At the
conclusion of the meeting there was the usual attempt to rush the
platform, seeze the Union Jack etc. and it was in the course of the
ensuing melee that W. JOYCE (now an official of the B.U.F.) was
slashed across the face with a razor. The writer actually saw this
take place. There is little doubt but that the attack on JOYCE was
a serious assult little short of attempted murder. His life was
only saved by the action of a police officer who ran with JOYCE in his
arms the whole way to the nearest police station.

15.6.44.

16. Extract from a 1924 Special Branch report by agent 'M', Maxwell Knight, relating the slashing of William Joyce's face by communists at an election meeting. (KV 2/245/331b)

30/VI/34

Dear Mrs Bene,-

Please convey my sincere apologies to [Dr. Kutschke] for my failure to profit by his kind invitation to the Sommerfest.

As a matter of fact, I was about to leave Chelsea towards 10 p.m., when I became engaged in some street fighting which demanded my presence.

Believe me, I am sorry to have missed the occasion.

Heil Hitler!

William Joyce

WILLIAM JOYCE

W12YM

17. Letter of 30 June 1934 sent by William Joyce to a possible German agent, in which he boasts about his street fighting. It was intercepted by MI5. Note how Joyce uses the 'Heil Hitler!' salute to end the letter. (KV 2/245)

S.I. Form O.6.

2 4a.

EXTRACT.

Relating to JOYCE

Extracted from .... S.F. 96/British/2 vol.19. No............. 906a

Author of original .... M/F report .... Place and date of origin .... 24.1.37.

Extract made by .... EPR. .... on (date) .... 26.1.37.

JOYCE is apparently fed up about the loss of the uniform. From what I
was told, I feel certain that JOYCE had turned from the Napoleonic pose
to a copy of the Prussian officer. I hear that his manner had steadily
been becoming more parade ground like and that his head was cropped
closer that ever.before. From allusions to a certain irritability of manner
I would make a guess. that JOYCE feels in his inner man that he ought to be more
a leading light that he is. From what I saw on the night of the dinner,
and from what I have heard since I have come to conclusions which I will
advance for your considerations. I think that secretly JOYCE thinks O.M.
a conceited popinjay but has no intention of allowing anything of this to
see the light of day. Meantime he certainly throws himself into every activity
with unbounded energy and efficiency. The fact that JOYCE has been forced
to the background slighly is not to my mind that JOYCE's powers are waning
but that the heads realise the worth of the man and the danger to themselves
It will suit JOYCE to see O.M. in the limelight, preening himself and generally
providing publicity. JOYCE can afford to wait.
Meantime, JOYCE works hard. He does not model himself on the lines of the
ascetic Hitler. He drinks, plays about with women and plans. I is easy
to see that he is an expert at intrigue but temperiment does not allow him
to seek popularity. He is pleasant to those who do not oppose him but never
what I sould call friendly. I have been acutely conscious that he is irri-
tated sometimes to the point of insanity by the men above him, especially the
old men.
JOYCE, to my mind, is one of the most fascinating characters studies in
the movt. If this movt. does collapse, it will not mean the last of JOYCE.
If on the other hand the movt. succeeds in coming to power, I fancy that
one of the first things JOYCE will do is to try to bring about a purge
of the party. I am convinced that in reality JOYCE hates the second rate
politicians like BECKETT.
I cannot say that I can visualise JOYCE and O.M. working in harness for
long. JOYCE is skilful enough to hide what he thinks to a certain extent
but the pride and conceit of them both would be sure to clash. O.M. knows
that JOYCE is probably the most skilful and efficient officer that he
has at N.H.Q., and for that rea son he cannot afford to lose him. JOYCE
I am sure, realises that the British people would soon tire of the super-
ficial brilliance of O.M. I that event he would grab his chance.
JOYCE knows what he wants in life, and is out to get it. Ifeel somehow,
despite the fact that I dislike the man intensely, that in him there is
someone who might one day make history. With all his faults he remains in
my mind one of the most compelling personalities of the whole movt.

18. A series of MI5/Special Branch agent reports from 24 January 1937 chronicling the
collapse of the British Union of Fascists and the departure of William Joyce from its ranks.
(KV 2/245/24a, 28a, 29a, 29c, 30a, 31b, 33a, 36b, 40a)

28a

CROSS-REFERENCE.

Subject:— W. JOYCE

17.3.37   S.B. reports that W. JOYCE is intensely dis-
gruntled over the results of the B.U.F.
Election campaign. He believes his nomination
as candidate for Shoreditch was arranged by
Hawkins in order to discredit him, as Hawkins
fears his influence. He declares that headquarters did its best to sabotage his work in
the area.

29a

CROSS-REFERENCE.

Subject:— W. JOYCE

12.3.37.   S.B. reports that on Thursday, March 11th,
Sir Oswald Mosley held a meeting of senior
officials. At the end of the meeting many
were haded envelopes containing money and
a letter giving them a week's notice and
an intimation that there was no necessity
for them to come to the office in future.
Among those receiving notice was William
JOYCE.

S.I. Form O.6.

<u>EXTRACT.</u>

Relating to   William JOYCE

Extracted from   S.F.96/Brit/2   ....   No...................................   Vol 19 941a.

Author of original   S.B. report   ....   Place and date of origin 17.3.37

Extract made by   M.E.M.   ....   on (date) 19.4.37

"......Statements made by B.D.E. Donovan during the past few days supply confirmation of the theory that the financial crisis has been availed of by the organisation group to persuade Mosley to get rid of Beckett, JOYCE, and others of the Policy-Propaganda bloc. Several of the Organisation clique have been busily spreading rumours that JOYCE was guilty of conspiracy and treason against the movement, but they are totally unable to supply any confirmation of these allegations.

"JOYCE has been heard to emphasise that Mosley is losing his grip on affairs and is suffering from neurosis.....John A. Macnab is a friend of JOYCE and lives with him....."

18. (continued) MI5/Special Branch reports on the BUF and William Joyce.

<u>S.I. Form O.6.</u>

<u>EXTRACT.</u>

Relating to William JOYCE

Extracted from ...S.F.96/British/2.v.19... **No.**.........917x.....................

Author of original ...S.B..rport........ **Place** and date of origin .8.2.37.........

Extract made by ...M.E.M.................. on (date) ....23.3.37..................

    "There are indications that an internal crisis is developing
at Head Quarters, which may have far reaching effects on the
future of the movement.

    Neil Francis Hawkins, Director General of Organisation,
who has steadily been acquiring more power for his department
during the past two years, is now openly endeavouring to bring
under his control the Propaganda bloc, i.e. Policy, Publicity,
and Instruction of Speakers Sections, of which W. JOYCE, J. Beckett
and A. Raven Thomson have charge. These last named are resisting
the proposal and the relationship between the two groups - never
at the best of times good - has by no means been improved.....

    "Memoranda on the inefficiency of propaganda in both the
Southern and the Northern administrations have been handed by
Hawkins to Mosley "...The first intimation of these complaints
received by JOYCE, Becket and Thomson was the receipt of the
memoranda from Sir Oswald Mosley, together with the latter's
comments, couched in terms which made it clear that in general
he considered the accusations well founded....."

BK
14/37

R.3527.

S.I. Form O.6.

3/B

EXTRACT.

Relating to William JOYCE

Extracted from S.F.26/British/2.V.19..... No......943a............................

Author of original S.B. report........ Place and date of origin ...24..3.37......

Extract made by ...M.E.M................ on (date) ....21.4.37................

"......W. JOYCE has been formally expelled from the
British Union of Fascists...Bothe JOYCE and Beckett were
present at a "bottle party" given on the evening of 17th
March at the flat of Miss Walters, and Mrs JOYCE was also
there. There was much general talk to the effect that the
reductions in staff were nothing less than a scheme on the
part of the Organisation bloc to rid themselves of all who
stood in their way of obtaining full control. All agreed that
the true National Socialists had been driven out of the
movement and that they were being victimised becaus they had
tried to enlighten the Leader as to the true state of affairs
in the Organisation. No mention, however, was made of forming
any group of organisation in opposition to the B.U.F. and no one
broached the subject of future political activities,

"JOYCE was the most bitter in his comments. He said t
that Mosley was "not the man he thought he was", also that
after he had received notice to terminate his appointment
Mosley had...sent him an invitation to discuss affairs with
him. JOYCE refused this offer...Beckett and JOYCE are
maintaining close contact with each other....."

18. (continued) MI5/Special Branch reports on the BUF and William Joyce.

P.F. 44469.

CROSS-REFERENCE.

Subject: JOYCE.

5.4.37. **Source:** S.B. report.

Report deals with the first meetinfg of the NATIONAL
SOCIALIST LEAGUE an opposition movement to the B.U.F.
This has headquarters at 28, Fawcett St., S.W.10, private
address of JOYCE. JOYCE and BECKETT have inaugurated the
movement, and are joint directors of the venture. Report
gives text of a circular sent out to all districts of the
B.U.F. by them setting forth what they think to be the real
reason for their dismissal and their intention to found an
independent movement. Report gives names of those present
at the meeting, among them many B.U.F. members. JOYCE
gave an outline of events in the B.U.F. leading up to the
staff meeting of 11th March last at which he received notice.
He mentioned their dissatisfaction with the organisation
of the B.U.F., etc. BECKETT then spoke, giving an outline
of the aims they sought to achieve.

The opinion at B.U.F. headquarters is that the League is
not of great consequence, and Mosley will not believe that
disaafection exists, although there are indication that many
London branches are dissatisfied, and that it would not
take much to make them desert Mosley for BECKETT and JOYCE.

+O.F. 548/2 3a.   5.4.37.

Original in ....**dated**................

J.M.F. 10.4.37.

S. Form 81

S. Form 81/B.P./5000/5.43.

EXTRACT.

Extract for File No.: P.F.44469.   Name: JOYCE, William.

Original in File No.: S.F.96/Lancs/2.   Serial: 340a.   Dated: 10.4.37.
                                                               Rec'd 12.4.37.

Original from: C.C.Liverpool.   Under Ref.: 1743E.

Extracted on: 18.4.44.   by: V.A. Section: R.9.

Extract from C.C.Liverpool report of 10.4.37. re B.U.F. under ref.1743E.
enclosing copy of private B.U.F. document issued for the personal use and
information of District Leaders.
The Document shews that the services of 104 members of the National H.Q.
staff have been dispensed with as salaried officers, and indicates that
opposition propaganda may now be disseminated by William JOYCE and BECKETT,
two leaders of the movement who were previously both in receipt of salaries.
     The document states that most of those no longer on the salaried staff,
have offered voluntary service with the exception of JOYCE and BECKETT.

"Mr JOYCE on being informed that he could no longer be retained as a salaried
member of H.Q. staff, immediately refused either to speak or to write for the
Movement or to give any voluntary service. He even went so far as to write and
cancel his weekly order for Action. He also wrote to the Directors of B.U.F.
Trust demanding three months' salary despite the fact that being paid on a
monthly and not on a weekly basis he had already received a sum far in excess
of the two weeks' wages loyally accepted without complaint by most members of
the staff. He further proceeded without effect to endeavour to cause what
disaffection he could. He was accordingly informed by Mr. FINDLAY, on the
Leader's instructions, in a letter dated the 19th March that his membership
terminated by reason of his "conduct subsequent to being informed that he
could not be retained as a salaried member of H.Q. staff". He was further,

/informed

informed that he had the right of appeal to the Leader in the ordinary
way "if he was prepared to meet the case against him in person". He intimated that he would not do so and the termination of his membership is,
therefore, confirmed."

18. (continued) MI5/Special Branch reports on the BUF and William Joyce.

Pf 444 49A

No action without reference to A.D.S.B.

P.F.48221, P.F.47766
re Frank & Quentin JOYCE:) (brothers of William JOYCE)

Quentin JOYCE is employed at the Air Ministry;
P.F.48231
Frank JOYCE at the B.B.C. Quentin is about 20 years of age and Frank
about 24. When these lads were quite young boys I knew them personally
and always found them very sound. Quentin is described as liking his
work in the Air Ministry very much and hoping to get on well, while
Frank is a worshipper at the feet of Sir John Reith. There is no
evidence that either of these two young men is using his position in
any improper way, and as the information came to me as a friend I
should be reluctant to do anything which might prejudice their careers.
In any case, if it is deemed advisable to make enquiries, I suggest
that at least a month should be allowed to elapse before such are
instituted.

26.5.37.   M.

62 x

B.2c.

re William JOYCE:

I received a report yesterday from a very reliable but casual informant of mine who for the past six months on my instructions has been keeping in close touch with the National Socialist League.

of 539/3

My informant is a member of an organisation known as the "English Array" which is the major portion of the old "English Mistery".

of 539/3 — PF 513714.

The English Array is led by Lord LYMINGTON and although not very large numerically (I believe it numbers less than 3,000) it is composed of a very good type of man, different in every way from the Fascist type.

During the last few weeks while the present situation has been increasing in tension Wm. JOYCE has become more and more violently pro-German. In the course of his desire to further his own National Socialist League he made approach to Lord LYMINGTON with a view to co-operating with the English Array in their efforts to promote a peaceful solution to the Czech question, with the result that a rather loose body was formed called the British Council against European Commitments (see attached leaflet), the president being Viscount LYMINGTON and the hon. secretary John BECKETT.

Friction very soon developed between JOYCE and Lord LYMINGTON owing to JOYCE's very violent pro-German views, with the result that at a meeting held last weekend, JOYCE publicly refuted the programme of the Council and left the platform.

It is stated by my informant that JOYCE and John BECKETT have finally quarrelled and parted company. (I think this is reliable.) BECKETT maintains that while he does not wish for war and while he sympathises with the Fascist point of view, he would never take part in any activity which might be detrimental to the interests of this country in the event of war.

JOYCE, on the other hand, has in the presence of witnesses dissented from this view. JOYCE's personality, which is always highly emotional, has become more hysterical during recent weeks, and my informant gives it as his considered opinion that in the event of war with Germany he does not think JOYCE's loyalty can be relied upon. He thinks that JOYCE has been keeping in constant touch with the N.S.D.A.P. during the last week or so, and after the meeting of the British council, referred to above, my informant actually heard JOYCE say to a German who was present, speaking in the German language: "If there is war with Germany I will be shot rather than take any part in it on behalf of Britain". Then, with tears streaming down his cheeks he added: "But I am convinced that we shall one day see Germany the master of Europe".

27.9.38.   B.5b.

19. Report of 27 September 1938 made during the Munich crisis by Maxwell Knight and relating to William Joyce's activities and attitudes as they developed during the crisis. (KV 2/245/62x)

131a

In September last it became necessary to watch carefully the activities of William JOYCE owing to his strong pro-Nazi views, and a H.O.W. was imposed. As a result of this letters were seen addressed to him from Christian Harri BAUER in Berlin containing somewhat cryptic messages for his brother "Quentin".

Christian Harri BAUER was formerly in this Country as representative of the "Kyfhauser". He was suspected of engaging in espionage, and in November 1937 was made the subject of an exclusion circular.

Quentin JOYCE is employed in the Directorate of Signals at the Air Ministry and is understood to be in a position to obtain information of a highly confidential nature.

On 24.10.38. a H.O.W. was also imposed on Christian Harri BAUER and on 25.11.38. on Quentin JOYCE.

The following are some of the cryptic and significant remarks which have been noticed in the correspondence of these three persons:-

1. 10.38. Christian Harri BAUER, on board a Lufthansa aeroplane, to William JOYCE:-

> "Q. will have told you that I am going to switch the old footlights on and that I should be grateful for more information in that respect. You'll understand.
>
> You can tell him too, that Marseilles is O.K. He'll know."

6. 10.38. Christian Harri BAUER to William JOYCE:-

> "I am continuing this by hanging on a letter for Q. who will tell you about the 'scheme'. This only, of course, if the Person in question."

Enclosure to "Quentin":-

> "You will remember what I told you about marks. Will you try to look up the fellow and tell him, if he seems the sort of person, that he shall give you thirty p. You would then have to tell me quickly the rate of whatnot he would get if he bought reg. m. in London. If it's less, it does

20. A 28 March 1939 MI5 report relating to the mail intercepts obtained under a Home Office warrant. It shows the inconclusive results of these interceptions. The contacts with known German agents were not apparently sufficient to merit action. However they were used as evidence in MI5's application to the Home Office for detention warrants to be executed in the event of a declaration of war. (KV 2/245/131a)

- 2 -

not matter. I should be immensely grateful.
Funds & so on you know. I wish you look (?luck)
old man. Don't be cross, be quick about it.
Perhaps there is still time. Tell William
about it if you like."

19.10.38. Christian Harri BAUER to William JOYCE:-

"........very glad indeed to hear such
good news from you on the re-organisation
progress in connection with the League.

If you can spare an occasional half-hour
& if you think it advisable I should most
certainly be very glad to get the supp's
names (Q. will be able to tell you) as I
could probably make good use of them sometime."

....

"There may even be another enquiry just
to show you that I am still as inquisitive
as always."

16.11.38. William JOYCE to Christian Harri BAUER:-

"........I am hoping to get time at the
week-end to collect some material."

8. 12.38. Christian Harri BAUER to William JOYCE:-

"I just went through the latest information
which you were so kind as to pass on to me. I
am very grateful indeed because it is really
sound material with which one can really do
something. My great wish remains, I should
like to do more for your movement. There is
however, apart from the good chances I had
already, another one cropping up just now.

"I have stirred the pond at the Press
Dept. of the FO. Meaning, I made them very
anxious about you. Now they want to hear more
and by Jove they are going to get it. I am
really very pleased about this, for I know what
strings lead from this office to certain
places and as experience shows, it is far more
advisable to have not so many, but important
chaps, to 'know' then the whole apparatus....."
Meanwhile I want to thank you again for all
your kind and valuable help."

Note. We did not see JOYCE's letter to BAUER.

12.12.38. Quentin JOYCE to Christian Harri BAUER:-

"Congratulations on the result of the
Sudetan elections - it was a magnificent
performance. I suppose that the Memel result
will be equally excellent when it is published.
.... Please give my kindest
regards to your parents, Miss LAYNER,C.(E?)G.
................."

20. (continued) MI5 report relating to mail intercepts.

- 5 -

13.12.38.   Christian Harri BAUER to Quentin JOYCE:-

"Mr. REYMER brought the shirt along &
this very morning I received it by post
together with your letter card."

"It is unforgivable that I should not
have thanked you for the JBL magazine.
I got it all right. By the way, old man,
in all such cases where the material is not
too nauseating if you know what I mean send
it as printed matter by all means. It will
arrive here quite safely and you save a bit
of money after all, for those letters are
sometimes develish heavy and have to be paid
for accordingly."...................

".......there's a slight chance of my
coming to L. some time at the beginning of
next year.............First of all I should
have to find out whether your chaps at the
H.O. have got anything against me, as I was
rather active and in a way responsible for
certain developments regarding J laws over
there these last weeks........... It will be
a ticklish job to find out, because I cannot
do it through our Embassy for obvious
reasons."

"I have several irons in the whatnot but
the more the better so you don't mind my
asking you if you know of somebody perhaps
who knows somebody at the special departm.
at the H.O. - old man Cooper from the Aliens
department for instance. If so don't give
'em any titles or degrees. I would use my
plain pp. just Harri BAUER and nothing else
......"

14. 1.39.   William JOYCE to Christian Harri BAUER:-

"I hope that all goes well with you; to tell
you the truth, I have been wondering whether my
last "report" did not contain some blunder
that caused you to go up in smoke......"
"I am collecting some more material, though
perhaps not as quickly as you would wish.

Undated.   Christian Harri BAUER to Quentin JOYCE:-

"Thank you very much for your letter - not
to forget the fags.......What about the chap
from Cooks? I suppose he has other trips to
attend to just now."

"I wanted to let you know, above all other
things, how glad I was to get your message".

Note.   Not intercepted.

- 4 -

16. 2.39.   William JOYCE to Christian Harri BAUER.

"......Within a few days I hope to
be sending you some interesting matter.

11. 3.39.   Christian Harri BAUER to Quentin JOYCE:-

"Thanks a lot for your letter & fags
which arrived both safely here yesterday
evening."

Note. This was not intercepted.

16. 3.39.   William JOYCE to Christian Harri BAUER:-

"Congratulations on your spring
cleaning.......... Here I find no
excitement on the subject and indeed hardl
any interest; but in my opinion it would
be well to concentrate propaganda
resources on explaining Germany's
justification. Whatever politicians may
say, the English people have been growing
ever more friendly to Germany. What I can
do in my small way shall be done, as you
know...................................."

21. 3.39.   Christian Harri BAUER to Quentin JOYCE:-

"I am quite certain that one of these
days you will curse my shirt mania.........
An American Banker (for whom I am exacting
some private jobs here as a sort of honorary
secretary and the reasons for doing so you
will probably guess) is travelling to London
to-night and will stay there for a day. I
asked him to take a parcel containing two
shirts back with him.................Needless
to say I am very, very grateful indeed for all
you do for me, not because I simply take this
ting for granted but because I have a faint
feeling that you are - despite a few rude
remarks about me and my mania - going to
try to do your best"......................
"Thanks a lot for your 1/card which I received
as well for the letter (I shall answer) and
the Churchman's. They were a treat!"

Note. We did not intercept the 1/card or
letter.

B.2.c.
28.3.39.

20. (continued) MI5 report relating to mail intercepts.

B.

B.2c.

William Joyce

The following information regarding William Joyce has been given to me by a casual contact of mine, in whose honesty and reliability I have absolute faith.

1. Informant considers that Joyce is now a complete pro-Nazi fanatic, who will go to any lengths to further what he considers to be Nazi aims in this country.

2. John Beckett who was, of course, associated with Joyce in the B.U.F. and later still in the formation of the National Socialist League, recently told my informant that when the National Socialist League was started a substantial subsidy from Germany was forthcoming. Beckett considers that Joyce is still in receipt of funds from Germany for pro-Nazi propaganda.

3. It may be remembered that Lord Leamington is at present running a harmless organisation known as the English Array, this organisation is an off-shoot of the English Mistery. The publication of the English Array is the New Pioneer. Shortly after the September crisis Joyce was still in contact with Lord Leamington over the affairs of the Counsel Against European Commitments. On one occasion Lord Leamington was discussing the difficulties of producing a small paper. Joyce said to him that if Lord Leamington was prepared to devote some space in his paper to pro-Nazi propaganda he, Joyce, could guarantee considerable funds. Lord Leamington asked Joyce if he was really serious. Joyce replied that he certainly was. Whereupon Lord Leamington informed Joyce that they must therefore part company.

21. Report of 30 March 1939 from Maxwell Knight, highlighting the extent to which Joyce had become a 'pro-Nazi fanatic'. (KV 2/245/134a)

4. Joyce has recently been trying to persuade various organisations with whom he is in touch to assist him in getting up a declaration that under no circumstances whatsoever will the signatories take part in any war against Germany.

5. Regarding the National Socialist League. My informant considers that this organisation is making practically no progress and that numerically it is negligible.

B.5b. (M)

30.3.39.

21. (continued) Report from Maxwell Knight on Joyce.

22. Intercepted letter from William Joyce to German agent Dr Christian Bauer, 30 July 1939. The letter refers to the British politician Sir Philip Sassoon who had been private secretary to Home Secretary Sir Samuel Hoare before his death in 1938. Sassoon was Jewish and Joyce was trying to show Bauer what he believed to be evidence that Sassoon used his wealth to insinuate himself into British government circles. (KV 2/245/167a)

for such pro-Jewish creatures as P.
MALLON on the Board of Governors. I shall
make further inquiries: but of Reith I
have personal knowledge, and he can only
be accused of having obeyed orders. Indeed
the Govt. would not have moved him
from the B.B.C. if he had been easy to
handle.
    I send you a cutting re. Morley,
who, of course, wants to get back into
the Conservative Party. The G[...] press does not
seem to have noticed his recent
boast that Britain alone could beat
Germany. All that I hear convinces
me that he is under full sail
for a "safe" and profitable haven.
    Mrs. E. has been told by me
to send you a note. Of course she will
not expect you to waste any time on
her. Just a chat is all that
is needed.

22. (continued) Letter from Joyce to Dr Christian Bauer.

J. will quite probably be visiting Berlin
early in September. If so, he will
have an opportunity of explaining to
you the various factors which have
made me so useless of late. My
own affairs are in such an uncertain
state that I cannot say when I can
get across myself: but the sooner the
better.

Though I say it myself, I
think that the Editorial in the
August "Monthly News" deserves careful
study. Anyhow, it is the result of
much thought on my part.

I shall be out of Town till
Friday. Margaret & I are now living
on our own, and we find it much
better. Next week, I should get a
little rest, and thereafter my
nerves will be better. Thanks to the
Hebrews, my financial position is nil: but.

believe me when I say that each day, the feeling against them grows stronger. Even the Hampstead Chamber of Commerce has protested to Sammy Hoare about the trading methods that the "Refugees" employ. Hampstead was one of the least likely places in England to rise in revolt.

Well — may God strengthen your arm and may the great work go on! War is less likely than ever: but a bitter struggle is coming in this country.

With all the best wishes,

I am,

Yours ever,

William

Heil Hitler!

K817A2

22. (continued) Letter from Joyce to Dr Christian Bauer.

Name	JOYCE, William
Born	24.4.06. at Galway, Ireland.
Nationality	British.
Address	85 Onslow Gardens, S.W.7. and 177 Vauxhall Bridge Road, S.W.1. (National Socialist League).
Occupation	Private Tutor
Police District	Metropolitan.

After having left the B.U.F. as a result of a personal quarrel with other leaders of the movement, he formed the National Socialist League, a more violent-ly anti-Semitic and pro-German body than the B.U.F. He has identified himself unreservedly with the Nazi cause, maintains close contact with Nazi officials and has shown that he would be quite willing to take action inimical to this country in order to further the campaign against the supposed "world Jewish conspiracy". He is also on intimate terms with a German who is strongly suspected of having carried on espionage in this country.

He has on several occasions shown that he favours violent methods and through his whole career has shown him-self to be a man of unbridled fanaticism.

Recommend detention.

23. Undated memorandum prepared by MI5 and sent to the Home Office recommending Joyce's detention in the event of war with Germany. (KV 2/245/160a)

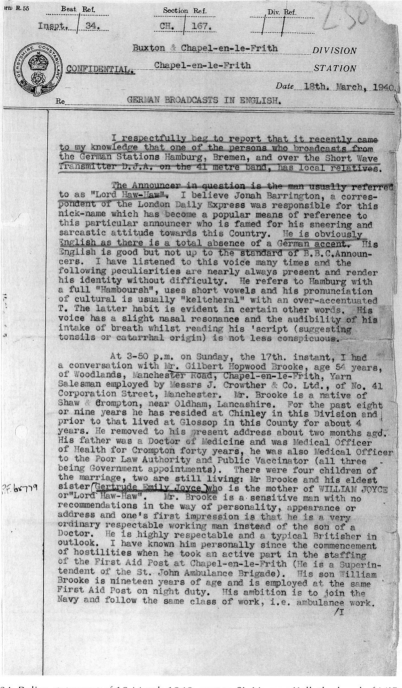

rn) R.55

Beat Ref. .... Section Ref. .... Div. Ref. ....

Inspt. / 34.   CH. / 167.

Buxton & Chapel-en-le-Frith   *DIVISION*

CONFIDENTIAL.   Chapel-en-le-Frith   *STATION*

Date 18th. March, 1940.

Re   GERMAN BROADCASTS IN ENGLISH.

    I respectfully beg to report that it recently came to my knowledge that one of the persons who broadcasts from the German Stations Hamburg, Bremen, and over the Short Wave Transmitter D.J.A. on the 41 metre band, has local relatives.

    The Announcer in question is the man usually referred to as "Lord Haw-Haw". I believe Jonah Barrington, a correspondent of the London Daily Express was responsible for this nick-name which has become a popular means of reference to this particular announcer who is famed for his sneering and sarcastic attitude towards this Country. He is obviously English as there is a total absence of a German accent. His English is good but not up to the standard of B.B.C.Announcers. I have listened to this voice many times and the following peculiarities are nearly always present and render his identity without difficulty. He refers to Hamburg with a full "Hamboursh", uses short vowels and his pronunciation of cultural is usually "keltcheral" with an over-accentuated T. The latter habit is evident in certain other words. His voice has a slight nasal resonance and the audibility of his intake of breath whilst reading his 'script (suggesting tonsils or catarrhal origin) is not less conspicuous.

    At 3-50 p.m. on Sunday, the 17th. instant, I had a conversation with Mr. Gilbert Hopwood Brooke, age 54 years, of Woodlands, Manchester Road, Chapel-en-le-Frith, Yarn Salesman employed by Messrs J. Crowther & Co. Ltd., of No. 41 Corporation Street, Manchester. Mr. Brooke is a native of Shaw & Crompton, near Oldham, Lancashire. For the past eight or nine years he has resided at Chinley in this Division and prior to that lived at Glossop in this County for about 4 years. He removed to his present address about two months agd. His father was a Doctor of Medicine and was Medical Officer of Health for Crompton forty years, he was also Medical Officer to the Poor Law Authority and Public Vaccinator (all three - being Government appointments). There were four children of the marriage, two are still living: Mr Brooke and his eldest sister Gertrude Emily Joyce who is the mother of WILLIAM JOYCE or"Lord Haw-Haw". Mr. Brooke is a sensitive man with no recommendations in the way of personality, appearance or address and one's first impression is that he is a very ordinary respectable working man instead of the son of a Doctor. He is highly respectable and a typical Britisher in outlook. I have known him personally since the commencement of hostilities when he took an active part in the staffing of the First Aid Post at Chapel-en-le-Frith (He is a Superintendent of the St. John Ambulance Brigade). His son William Brooke is nineteen years of age and is employed at the same First Aid Post on night duty. His ambition is to join the Navy and follow the same class of work, i.e. ambulance work.

/I

24. Police statement of 18 March 1940, sent to Sir Vernon Kell, the head of MI5. Early in 1940 the Derbyshire police discovered William Joyce's uncle Gilbert Hopwood Brooke living in its area. They interviewed him and sent his statement to MI5. The statement provides a great deal of important and detailed information about the Brooke and Joyce families together with insights into William Joyce and his upbringing. (KV 2/245/230b)

u R.55

Beat. Ref.	Section Ref.	Div. Ref.
Inspt. 34.	CH. 167.	

Buxton & Chapel-en-le-Frith *DIVISION*

Chapel-en-le-Frith *STATION*

-2- Date 18th. March, 1940.

Re GERMAN BROADCASTS IN ENGLISH (continued).

I understand his particulars have been taken by the
Naval Recruiting Authorities (believed Manchester) and he has
been informed that he will be sent for about August of this year.
William is a very respectable youth of good appearance and
has no interest in politics.

Mr. Brooke's sister, Mrs. Gertrude Emily Joyce met
her husband Michael Francis Joyce in County Galway, Eire, and
the marriage took place about 1903. Mr. Joyce is an Irishman
and a Catholic. Mrs. Joyce is a Protestant. Both retained
their original Faith and this has produced a most unhappy
married life. Mr. Joyce is now about eighty years of age and
his wife about sixty-two. They went to America shortly after
the wedding and Mr. Joyce obtained employment with an American
building firm. Leaving America about 1910 they returned to
Eire; either County Galway or Ayle near Westport, where Mr.
Joyce purchased property and spent his time keeping it in
repair.

Mrs. Joyce had five children as follows:-

(1). WILLIAM JOYCE, now about 35 years of age.				Married.
(2). Francis Joyce,	-do-	29 years of age.	-do-	-do-
(3). Quentin Joyce,	-do-	24	-do-	Single.
(4). Joan Joyce,	-do-	22	-do-	Single.
(5). Robert Joyce,	-do-	20	-do-	Single.

(handwritten left margin: PF 48221, PF 47766)

WILLIAM JOYCE who is the subject of this report was
born in Brooklyn, New York. He is understood to have no
Religion. He was educated at a Convent in County Galway and
at an early age developed a strong tendency to argue with the
Principals, expounding original theories on all manner of
things. This conduct, being alien to the atmosphere of a
Convent, was frowned upon, and he was eventually turned out.
Later, however, he proved that he was above the average in
intelligence and with the aid of scholarships, etc. he worked
his way to a University (either Oxford or Queen's College,
Galway) where he obtained his M.A. and Ph.D. Degrees. It was
at the time of the Irish Rebellion that he came to London with
his parents and lived with them at No. 7 Allison Grove,
Dulwich, S.E.21. This house is the property of his father.
William Joyce made a reasonable living by teaching languages
and coaching for the University in German. He was at one time
a very active member of Sir Oswald Moseley's Party but was
dropped by Sir Oswald because there was not room for two
Leaders of the Party. He later started some political
organisation on his own in London. Joyce is believed to have
been married twice (there is a doubt about his second association - Mr. Brooke never heard of their marriage). He divorced
his first wife about eight or ten years ago owing to her
misconduct and nothing of interest is known concerning her.
He met his second wife about four years ago whilst following
his political activities. She was a member of the British
Union of Fascists in the Eaton Mersey or Eaton Norris District
of Manchester. During his married life Joyce lived in
Kensington. He left this country for Germany just before the
outbreak of war, taking his wife with him.

/Francis

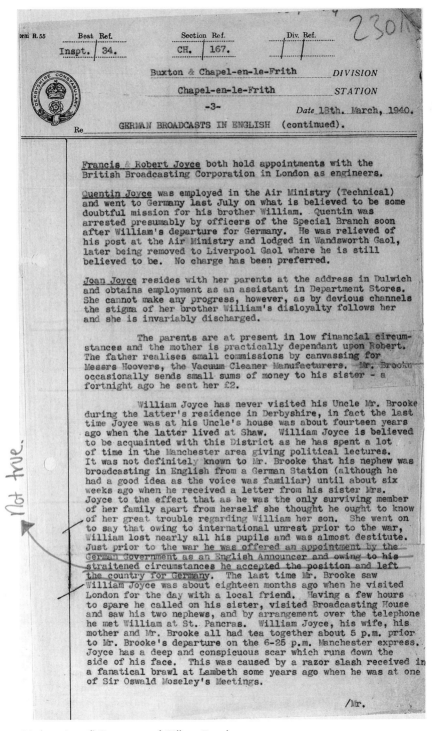

orm R.55

Beat Ref.	Section Ref.	Div. Ref.
Inspt. / 34.	CH. / 167.	

2301

Buxton & Chapel-en-le-Frith   *DIVISION*

Chapel-en-le-Frith   *STATION*

-3-   Date 12th. March, 1940.

Re GERMAN BROADCASTS IN ENGLISH (continued).

Francis & Robert Joyce both hold appointments with the
British Broadcasting Corporation in London as engineers.

Quentin Joyce was employed in the Air Ministry (Technical)
and went to Germany last July on what is believed to be some
doubtful mission for his brother William. Quentin was
arrested presumably by officers of the Special Branch soon
after William's departure for Germany. He was relieved of
his post at the Air Ministry and lodged in Wandsworth Gaol,
later being removed to Liverpool Gaol where he is still
believed to be. No charge has been preferred.

Joan Joyce resides with her parents at the address in Dulwich
and obtains employment as an assistant in Department Stores.
She cannot make any progress, however, as by devious channels
the stigma of her brother William's disloyalty follows her
and she is invariably discharged.

The parents are at present in low financial circumstances and the mother is practically dependant upon Robert.
The father realises small commissions by canvassing for
Messrs Hoovers, the Vacuum Cleaner Manufacturers. Mr. Brooke
occasionally sends small sums of money to his sister - a
fortnight ago he sent her £2.

William Joyce has never visited his Uncle Mr. Brooke
during the latter's residence in Derbyshire, in fact the last
time Joyce was at his Uncle's house was about fourteen years
ago when the latter lived at Shaw. William Joyce is believed
to be acquainted with this District as he has spent a lot
of time in the Manchester area giving political lectures.
It was not definitely known to Mr. Brooke that his nephew was
broadcasting in English from a German Station (although he
had a good idea as the voice was familiar) until about six
weeks ago when he received a letter from his sister Mrs.
Joyce to the effect that as he was the only surviving member
of her family apart from herself she thought he ought to know
of her great trouble regarding William her son. She went on
to say that owing to international unrest prior to the war,
William lost nearly all his pupils and was almost destitute.
Just prior to the war he was offered an appointment by the
German Government as an English Announcer and owing to his
straitened circumstances he accepted the position and left
the country for Germany. The last time Mr. Brooke saw
William Joyce was about eighteen months ago when he visited
London for the day with a local friend. Having a few hours
to spare he called on his sister, visited Broadcasting House
and saw his two nephews, and by arrangement over the telephone
he met William at St. Pancras. William Joyce, his wife, his
mother and Mr. Brooke all had tea together about 5 p.m. prior
to Mr. Brooke's departure on the 6-25 p.m. Manchester express.
Joyce has a deep and conspicuous scar which runs down the
side of his face. This was caused by a razor slash received in
a fanatical brawl at Lambeth some years ago when he was at one
of Sir Oswald Moseley's Meetings.

/Mr.

24. (continued) Statement of Gilbert Brooke.

n R.55 | Beat Ref. | Section Ref. | Div. Ref.

Inspt. 34.   CH. 167.

Buxton & Chapel-en-le-Frith *DIVISION*

Chapel-en-le-Frith *STATION*

-4-   Date 18th. March, 1940.

Re   GERMAN BROADCASTS IN ENGLISH (continued).

Mr. Brooke is greatly distressed by his nephew's treachery and would not under any circumstance have anything more to do with him. He has instructed his family at Chapel-en-le-Frith to say nothing to anyone of the relationship as he is ashamed and afraid of gaining unwelcome notoriety, especially if it comes to the knowledge of Press reporters.

Before leaving the Office Mr. Brooke reminded me that he may have supplied slight inaccuracies regarding ages, etc. but to be strictly correct was very difficult owing to the lack of close relations between the two families.

I understand several articles have appeared in the Press at different times regarding William Joyce and no doubt most of them were more informative than this report, but I have collected all the information possible in the slender hope that there may be some little point which is not already known to the Special Branch.

Inspector.

18 MAR. 1940

The Superintendent,
     Chapel-en-le-Frith.

Respectfully submitted. The knowledge that Mr. Gilbert H. Brooke was an Uncle of William Joyce - who, according to the Press, has been identified as "Lord Haw-Haw" - was obtained during a casual conversation Inspector Davies had at the First Aid Post at Chapel-en-le-Frith with William Brooke, a son of Gilbert Brooke, who is employed there.

An interview was consequently arranged at this Office with Mr. Brooke senior, on the afternoon of the 17th. instant when he supplied the information contained in this report.

Superintendent.

The Chief Constable,

COUNTY POLICE
HEADQUARTERS,
IRON GATE,
DERBY.
19 MAR 1940

REF. NO.

FOR THE ATTENTION OF M.I.5   BAG

A Personal Attack

As to the nature and quality of British propaganda, an amusing example has just come to my notice on which I am going to dwell because it is personal to me. For the first time since I have spoken on the German radio, I am going to speak very directly about the campaign of slander and libel directed against me. With indifference, complete indifference, I read in the "Daily Mail", and all sorts of other rags, some of them American, stories to the effect that I was an ex-actor, an ex-shipping clerk, an embezzler, a gangster, a sadist in family life, an unscrupulous mercenary, that I was born in several different countries, that I had dishonourably eloped with a girl from Manchester, who, incidentally, was and is my legal wife - that I was illiterate, that I could not speak English, and that I was insane.

All these imputations I disregarded as the mere filth of garbage hacks who knew that they had no law of libel to fear, and who were encouraged by the Government to make these ludicrous personal attacks. But now comes something different. It is worth taking up, not merely as a personal issue, but as a fine illustration of how British information is manufactured and from what source it comes.

The "Evening Standard" of 21st March last publishes an article beginning on the front page and headed: "Girl tells of Haw-Haw as spy in London; he had 300 agents". The article begins "Investigations into the former life of William Joyce, the traitor who has become notorious as Lord Haw-Haw, have disclosed a sensational story of his secret activities in this country". Sensational it is. I am supposed to have had 300 spies under my control - quite a large number; to have had secret codes; to have suborned waiters in the West End; to have been in close touch with the German Embassy; and to have met my co-conspirators in the house of an Italian lady of title. Hm-hm.

"Had I Been a Spy"

The credibility of these statements is revealed strikingly in this one sentence: the girl in the case says: "I was given a code for use if I had to send in reports. Each letter of the alphabet was represented by a symbol".

"Each letter of the alphabet represented by a symbol" - why, any intelligent agent who devised a code as transparent as that would deserve to be shot by his own masters! Had I wanted to spy upon England, I should have scarcely have proclaimed my admiration for Adolf Hitler as I did. I should scarcely have been arrested, as I was several times, for my National-Socialist activities. And if I could direct 300 agents under the noses of the police, who were watching me all the time, surely it would have been better for me to stay in England during this most important period, rather than abandon my personal position and my spies, and come to Germany?

And who is the lady whose legend is treated with so much respect by the "Evening Standard"? I recognise her photograph. Her name is given as Mary (Taverman) She was also known to some as the Baroness (Marovna?). Why, heaven knows. She interviewed me twice. And having been warned as to her idiosyncracies, I was careful to have witnesses present on each occasion. On the first meeting, she offered me a considerable sum of money if I would abandon my anti-Jewish propaganda. And on the second, she requested my help in blackmailing a public man, with whom she believed me to be on bad terms. She was shown out of my office. Subsequent enquiries revealed her to be a less distinguished member of the semi-social London underworld. This lady is the type of source from which British propaganda draws its data.

"I, William Joyce"

To conclude this personal note, I, William Joyce, will merely say that I left England because I would not fight for Jewry against the Fuehrer and National Socialism, and because I believe most ardently, as I do today, that victory a perpetuation of the old system would be an incomparably greater evil for

- 2 -

than defeat coupled with a possibility of building something new, something really national, something truly socialist.

But the story of the 300 spies is really worthy of British propaganda. It shows that any story, however fantastic, however unjustified, is given glaring publicity, provided that it serves the Government's ends and that refutation is difficult to offer. Sir Walter Moncton says that the work in his Ministry is not so romantic as that being done by the young. I beg to differ. It is more so, though far less honourable. The romancing continues in order that more young men may die in vain. Lies and illusions prepare the bloodshed of heroes.

25. (opposite and above) Transcript of William Joyce's broadcast for 2 April 1941. In the course of this broadcast Joyce attacked the *London Evening Standard* for an article accusing him of running a large spy ring in Britain. Stung by this accusation, he revealed his real name for the first time. Thereafter, until his final broadcast in 1945, he was introduced on-air as William Joyce. (KV 2/245/285)

BRESLAU (ENGLISH GROUP) 315.8 m. INENGLISH FOR U.K. 2230 9.9.43

"Views on the News" by William Joyce:

It will scarcely be a surprise to you if I devote this evening's Views on the News almost entirely to the developments which have taken place in Italy, and which have no doubt constituted a world sensation. Last night at this time a preliminary review of the situation was given by Roderick Dietze, who brought the day's events into focus and at the same time related the treachery of Badoglio to the broader and wider conspiracy to make a Bolshevik hell of Europe. I was especially impressed by his reminder that after the Duce had been betrayed red flags appeared in the streets of many Italian cities. This evening I am not pretending to review the Italian situation as a whole in a purely and chronologically objective manner. It is an occasion when I may be permitted to record some personal observations and impressions. Since as long ago as 1923 I belonged to the first Fascist movement in Britain, and then, as subsequently, regarded Benito Mussolini as one of the greatest men, not only of our century, but of our age. When Roderick Dietze mentioned the appearance of the red flag on the streets of Italian cities, I thought: "Yes, and it was in answer to this challenge of the bestial underworld that Mussolini first arose to save his country"....

I did not for one single moment believe that a great energising phenomenon like Fascism which has breathed new life into Europe, which bears the character of a creed for the ages, could be simply snuffed out by a couple of shifty old men, surrounded by jackals and parasites, who had consistently conspired against the front-line fighters. It did not seem compatible with the nature of historical development that a successful revolution should be abruptly undone by a handful of senile intriguers who had long shown the marks of subornation and moral decrepitude, and now I am more than gratified, more than satisfied to see that the Italian people have spontaneously formed a National and Fascist Government to vindicate their honour and pursue the fight for their rights.

Perhaps some of the malevolently minded commentators in the BBC, who to judge by their remarks listen to my broadcasts with close attention, might have expected me to show some sign today of embarrassment, or even depression. Well in that case they must be deeply disappointed. On 22nd June, 1941, when the Fuehrer drew the sword in Europe's defence against the Bolshevik colossus, I felt like all National Socialists that history was taking its rightful course and the hand of Providence was guiding the German nation. Today again I know that history is taking its rightful course, now that the Fascist banners have again been raised, now that patriotic Italians have taken up the torch that Badoglio and the recreant relic Savoy tried to extinguish. What matters most is that the dynamic urge of Europe to live in the light of her new faith should be strengthened and perpetuated. Like the phoenix from the ashes, Italy has arisen again, and whatever she may suffer, whatever trials may beset her on the road to victory, she has now once more recovered the spirit of ancient Rome and, come weal or woe, she has inscribed on her standards the Latin word: 'Resurgam' - 'I shall arise again'....

Eisenhower has done all the boasting necessary and far more. Now I expect it will be left to the British to bear the brunt of the fighting. And henceforth they will be facing serried ranks of resolute soldiers, without one traitor behind the lines, without a single venal creature to sell the passes.

- 2 -

To that extent our enemies are the poorer. Perhaps it seemed a brilliant
and cunning thing to contrive the downfall of a great patriot like
Mussolini and substitute for his Government, for his indomitable leadership,
a quivering mass of unwholesomeblubber interspersed with ancient bones.
But such a thing could not live. It could not survive. It has perished.
And now Germany and Italy can go into battle again, comrades in arms,
to defend the sacred cause of the European revolution. And once more the
soldiers of both nations know that they have the common purpose to wage the
struggle against vested powers, red front, and massed ranks of reaction, the
fight for freedom and for bread. It is well indeed that the canker has been
removed. Badoglio has surrendered, and the Axis lives again.

26. (opposite and above) Transcript of William Joyce's 'Views on the News', 9 September 1943.
The broadcast was made following the Italian king's dismissal of Mussolini as Italian leader. It
provided Joyce with the opportunity to indulge in reminiscences about his own youthful dalliance
with Italian-style fascism in 1920s London. (KV 2/246)

Copy *w st oo [UK] 25 (22)* report

METROPOLITAN POLICE

ENCL *extracts*
22 FEB 1943
TO......F.3.
REF.....

X William
JOYCE.X

Special Branch.
Metropolitan Police.
Scotland House.

19th   February   43.

hit.S

    I first knew William JOYCE as a speaker for the British
Union of Fascists and National Socialists, afterwards known
as British Union. On various occasions between 1934 and
1937 I was present in the course of duty at a number of
meetings of this organisation when JOYCE was a speaker.

    This man is also known to P.S. Buswell, who was also
present on various dates during 1936 and 1937 when JOYCE
addressed meetings of the British Union of Fascists and
National Socialists. We know his voice.

    On 30th January, 1943 P.S. Buswell and myself were
present at B.B.C. Studios, Delaware Road, W.2, when we
heard a transmission between 10-30 p.m. and 11-15 p.m.
The broadcast included a number of voices speaking in
rotation, one of which we recognised as belonging to William
JOYCE. Shorthand notes were made of parts of JOYCE's
remarks.

    In our presence a recording was made of the transmission
on four records, each of which we signed. A few minutes
later the fourth record was played over. It contained the
last part of JOYCE's speech as heard by us a few minutes
earlier.

    Attached are separate transcripts of the shorthand
notes taken by P.S. Buswell and myself.

a - Trunk

Inspector.

@ LONG. To—
@ Lord HAW-HAW
@ TREVOR

SUPERINTENDENT.

PF 44469 Vols 1 — 5. Supp. V

1/r 22/1/43.

R.
Please cross-refer to
S.F. 66 /U.K./ 25 (22)
and p.a.
F3.

24.12.43

27. This 19 February 1943 Special Branch report and transcript of one of
William Joyce's broadcasts was made in order to provide definitive evidence of
Joyce's treason at a future trial. Unfortunately, the proving of his US citizenship
at the trial ensured that none of this evidence could be used. (KV 2/245/287a)

Transcript of shorthand notes taken by Inspector Hunt, Special Branch, New Scotland Yard, S.W.1. on 30th January, 1943, at B.B.C. Studios, Delaware Road, London, W.2. on the occasion of a broadcast between 10-30 p.m. and 11-15 p.m. which included the voice of William JOYCE. Sections of JOYCE's remarks were recorded in shorthand. Parts of the broadcast were difficult to follow.

JOYCE said: "In this Proclamation which he addressed to the German people, the Fuehrer first called to account the fourteen years' struggle which preceeded the victory of January 30th, 1933. He described afresh how, after the world war which they had not wanted, the German people have suffered under the consequences of defeat of President Wilson's breach of faith contrary to dictate.

Again he called attention to the fact that all the injustices of the years 1919 to 1933 were perpetrated, not against National Socialist Germany, but against democratic Germany. Then the Fuehrer recalls the spoilation of the German nation by international Jewry. The misery of the economic crisis and unemployment which prevailed in 1932, the rupture of the German people...

At the turn of the year 1933, said the Fuehrer, Germany was threatened with complete bankruptcy and National Socialism was left with a terrible... to take over. The Fuehrer then gave a survey of the measures that National Socialism had taken to ensure immediate economic recovery. The consequence was that before the expiry of the year... the last of the unemployed were again at work...

These achievements were such that there was definitely nothing in the democratic countries to be compared to them. Only Fascist Italy had accomplished similar achievements...

There are roads to possibilities of solving the external problems in spite of all the Bolshevist catastrophies...

The German example to National Socialism succeeded year by year in making ever greater progress along the way to the restoration of Germany's right to live. New German fighting forces were built up only after the Fuehrer's peaceful proposals for loyal co-operation had been declined... Today on the 10th anniversary of the coming to power we can now recognise what would have happened if, on 30th January, 1933, Providence had not called National Socialism to power. For ten years before this time Bolshevism had been carrying out a systematic... program of vast dimensions with a view to the attack on Europe... on 22nd June, 1941....

The only reason is that in the year 1933 Germany feared a political, moral and material basis entitling her to the leadership in her struggle upon which the fate of the world depends. In former days there existed in Germany only two possibilities. Either the victory of the National Socialist revolution or the Bolshevist disaster. And now... there likewise exists... only these two alternatives. Either Germany, with the German forces of Europe as a whole, or else there will bear down upon this continent of ancient culture... Mongolian hordes destructive as they proved to be in Russia itself... Swamped over Europe the world would collapse and this result of human labour of a thousand years instead of being the most flourishing continent on the earth would be replaced by inconceivable barbarity. If National Socialism had accomplished nothing more than what already lies behind it, it would rank as one of the mightiest manifestations in the history of the world, but nevertheless, Europe would be lost to the marvellous progress of our movement...

Whatever blows of fate may fall upon us now they are nothing as compared with what all will suffer if barbaric hordes of the East swept over our part of the world. Every single life which is sacrificed in this battle will live in the generations of the future in recognition of the fact that in this way there cannot be... but only the survivers of the annihilated...

2.

National Socialism will carry on the fight fanatically. During last winter the Jewish leaders were exalting because in their eyes the collapse of the German forces appeared to be inevitable, but events transpired otherwise. In this winter they can entertain some hope, but they will find out that the strength of National Socialist ideals is greater than their aspirations or yearnings...

This strength will bind everyone to the fulfilment of his duty and will do away with anybody who opposes... National Socialism will wage this struggle until such time as there comes a new 30th January, that is to say, the day of... victory.

The Fuehrer's proclamation then expresses his gratitude to his soldiers for the... being enacted from the far North to the African desert, from the Atlantic to the wide steppes of the East, from the Aegean to Stalingrad, an epic which will survive more than one millenium. It is the Fuehrer's... to the home front to remain worthy of the heroic deeds done by the troops. The proclamation continues, the total endeavour of our nation must now be increased. The heroic fight of our soldiers on the Volga should be... to do his utmost in the struggle for the freedom of Germany and thereby in the wider sense for the preservation of the whole continent. It was the desire of our enemies to threaten peaceful towns and villages with weapons of gruesome destruction...

In the fracas which our foes forced upon us as they did before in 1914, the fracas which represents the be or not to be of our race, the Almighty will be the just Judge. Now our task is to fulfil our duties in such a way that before Him as the Creator of the Universe and in accordance with the... given by him for the battle of existence, we may stand without ever faltering...

From the ruins of our towns and villages there will emerge a new life which will develop further that stage in which we believe, for which we are working, a National Socialist Greater Germany.. In this day there will be for permanence a strength to protect the European family of nations in the future as well as against danger from the East. The Greater German Reich and its allies will, furthermore, have to secure in common these territorial areas which... are indispensable to the preservation of their material existence.

a. Hunt.

Inspector.

27. (continued) Transcript of one of Joyce's broadcasts.

COPY (Original in SF.91/1/24(3)

SECRET   Home Office,
                                  Whitehall,
                                    S.W.1.

                11th September, 1944.

Dear Mr. Shelford,

        This is to let you know that we
have asked the Foreign Office to
include in the list of persons to be
surrendered under the German Armistice
the names of:-

        William Joyce
        Margaret Cairns Joyce (wife of
                William Joyce)
        John Amery
        Major James Strachey Barnes
        William James Edward Percival
        John Alexander Fraser.

        . . . .

                Yours   sincerely,

                (signed) J. Nunn.

T.M. Shelford, Esq.,
M.I.5.

P.A. in Pf 44444 69 Joyce

        S.L A 14/10.

28. MI5 letter of 11 Sept 1944, showing that the names of
William and Margaret Joyce headed the wanted list of British
renegades. (KV 2/245/342b)

IM NAMEN
DES DEUTSCHEN VOLKES
VERLEIHE ICH

dem Hauptkommentator

William   J o y c e

in Berlin-Charlottenburg

DAS
KRIEGSVERDIENSTKREUZ
1. KLASSE

Führerhauptquartier, den 1. September 1944.

DER FÜHRER

29. Certificate in German signed by Adolf Hitler, 1 September 1944. The war merit cross, first class, and this accompanying certificate, were found among Joyce's possessions after his arrest in May 1945. The certificate states that the award is to 'the chief commentator William Joyce'. (KV 2/250/2)

- 5 -

incidentally I believe is related to Stewart HIBBERD of the
B.B.C. I had talked over many things with HIBBERD whilst
being in his company in the villa and we understood one
another very well, in fact it was he who first told me about
CHAPPLE's previous activities. I subsequently wrote a letter
to HIBBERD and told him that I intended to take drastic steps
to prove our suspicions. In fact I told him that whatever
reports he heard about me in the future he was to remember
this and also that I was British and a Commando. Shortly
after this I had become very friendly with CHAPPLE and although
he never took me completely into his confidence I was able to
form my own opinion about him, and in fact he consistently
attempted to fill my mind with the beauties of leading a normal
civilian life.

In the end he introduced me to a man by the name of ADAMI
who had come to the camp with members of the German Foreign
Office who passed themselves off as Y.M.C.A. representatives.
During our stay at the camp the Germans sent a number of influential Foreign Office people to give lectures on various
subjects ranging from world economy to racial theory. It was
after one of these lectures that CHAPPLE and myself were
approached by ADAMI and asked if we would broadcast on a
station which he was forming. CHAPPLE agreed and for reasons
of my own which I think are now clear I agreed also. In this
camp I had made friends with a New Zealand corporal by the name
of COURLANDER whom I had previously met but had never seen for
some months. CHAPPLE and myself were taken away to Stalag
IIID and given civilian clothes and from there we were taken
to a French P.O.W. camp where we were passed off to the French
as being civilian internees. We were called for daily by a
man in civilian clothes by the name of THEWS who took us to
the Reichsportsfeld where we found the German secret senders
were situated. The Germans made no bones about the matter and
it was either a case of making a broadcast on the first day
or getting out. I think it leaves little to the imagination
where we would at this stage have gone to if we had refused to
broadcast. It most certainly would not have been back to
Genshagen or for that matter any other P.O.W. Camp.

After about a fortnight, during which time I may say I
experienced being in an R.A.F. 2000 tonner, we were given German
passports with false names and allowed to live as civilians
in Berlin. Our work consisted of reading the British newspapers in the mornings and doing a ten minute broadcast at
2.30 p.m. This ten minutes was all that the Station, which
went under the name of Radio National, was allowed, therefore
I suppose each man was on the air for something in the region
of from two to three minutes. I had by this time discovered
that there were three other men broadcasting on this Station
whose names were PERRY, Sub.Lieut. PURDY and HUMPHREYS.
PERRY had previously worked on the editorial staff of 'The
Camp' which is the P.O.W. paper and also for the 'Signal' which
is a German publication similar to our 'Picture Post' and which
is published, I believe, in 17 different languages. PURDY I
have already mentioned as being in Kauenstrasse, and HUMPHREYS
whose first name is Reginald, as being a civilian internee.

The names that CHAPPLE and myself were given were Arthur LANG
and Pat MacCARTHY respectively, and PURDY went under the name
of Ronald WALLACE. The other two men retained their own
names, that is HUMPHREYS and PERRY. The Station had as its
main function to be a Fascist station run on the same lines

30. Extracts from the statement of Francis Paul Maton, Corporal, 50 Middle East
Commando. Corporal Maton was one of the prisoners of war recruited by Joyce
to make propaganda broadcasts for the Bureau Concordia. He made this detailed
statement in September 1944 and provides much detail about the life and career
of Joyce during the final phase of his career. (KV 2/245/342aa)

- 6 -

x sic

as the B.U.F. in England, and for this purpose John AMERY, BAILLIE STEWART, JOYCE and VERNON and FREEMAN, a pilot officer[x]. All of these were working at the Foreign Office and wrote talks. Both HUMPHREYS and CHAPPLE were rather literary-minded, in fact CHAPPLE had been a newspaper man before the war and so these two wrote all their own stuff, whilst PURDY and myself read the talks written by AMERY, JOYCE, STEWART and FREEMAN. PERRY had apparently been dissatisfied with the work at Radio National and so, as soon as CHAPPLE and myself went there, he returned to the Deutsche Verlag which firm prints 'The Camp', 'The O.K.' and 'The Signal'. It was during September 1943 that we went there and I believe the Station had only been going a couple of weeks at that time. During my stay at Radio National I found that the Germans had several other secret stations in Reichsportsfeld. The stations are called secret by reason of the fact that all of them are supposed to be in the country to which they broadcast, i.e. a station like Radio National was supposed to be in England and everything that was written for it had to be written from this viewpoint.

The other two stations broadcasting in English were known as Workers Challenge, which was a Communist Station founded by JOYCE, for which he himself wrote most of the stuff. There were only two men speaking on this station and I suppose for a period of practically three years only one man had actually spoken. His name is GRIFFITHS. He was a Welsh Guardsman captured in France in 1940. I think his first name was William. The second man to broadcast on 'Workers Challenge' was a man who went under the name of WINTER, but whose real name I believe to be COLLEGE. I say believe because I doubt very much if any person in Germany knows his name. He was a soldier, probably an officer, who came from Bath, and whom I believe to be from the North Somerset Yeomanry.

The other Station broadcasting in English was called N.B.B.S. which stood for New British Broadcasting Service. There were four men speaking on this Station and each of these four men also wrote talks and news items. Their names are James GILBERT, an ex-cadet officer of Woolwich and whose father is a high ranking Army Officer; he was wanted under 18B in May 1940 and he went across to Jersey and waited for the Germans to occupy it. He has been working for this Station since 1940 and is now married to a German girl by the name of Crystelle ARTUS, and is the father of two children. GILBERT, who is known as James to the Germans, served a 6 months' sentence in a concentration camp at WUHLHEIDE just outside Berlin for assaulting two S.S. men. The two S.S. men who had been guards over the premises were shot after being court-martialled for not shooting James at the time. James would not have continued working but he was not married at the time and his future wife was expecting a child. Subsequently GILBERT, after he was married and settled down, lived in the Tiergarten district and was bombed out on 22nd November 1943. The next man on the list of N.B.B.S. is a man under the name of John BROWN but whose real name is BANNING. This man previously worked in the Headquarters of the B.U.F. in London. The third man is a Lance Corporal of the K.R.R.'s by the name of Gerald SPILLMAN who was taken prisoner in Greece. The fourth is an ex-civilian internee who goes under the name of

30. (continued) Statement of Francis Maton.

- 7 -

✣ Put reference to cheat this again for details on other broadcasts

Donald PALMER and whose real name I do not know. There
are working at the Reichsportsfeld, the whole organisation
being known as Bureau Concordia, three other Englishmen, or
rather Britishers, by the name of John LINGSHAW, a Jerseyman,
HOSKINS, an ex K.R.R. man captured in France, and Peter
KOSAKA, a British subject born of a Japanese mother.
These men have all broadcast in the past but now only work
on listening **in** to **British** broadcasts and recording them.
Shortly after I went to Concordia, two other men came, one,
whose name is A/Wing Commander CARPENTER, and who was before
the war a personal friend of Goering. The other was a Polish
R.A.F. pilot whose real name I do not know but who calls
himself Julien KOWALSKI. His real first name is actually
Julian and he was shot down over Holland when flying a
fighter in June 1943. CARPENTER is an example of the Germans'
carelessness, because I believe that in a talk to a German
officer he had mentioned the fact that before the war he had
personally met Goering and so the Germans jumped to the conclusion that he was pro-German and sent him to Berlin in
civilian clothes. When he first came he made it quite clear
that he would not broadcast and only after much persuasion did
he write some anti-Jewish literature. This was never used
by the Station. Another example of German bureaucracy is the
fact that CARPENTER asked to be sent back to his Stalag but
owing to the fact that he had been transferred from the
Luftwaffe over to the Wehrmacht, his return was delayed for
four months, during which time he did absolutely nothing
except draw money from the German Foreign Office and live a
life of comparative luxury in an Hotel. He was eventually
sent away, but to where I do not know. I have heard two
stories. The first was that he was shot at SAGAN while
attempting to escape with the other forty odd R.A.F.
prisoners, and the second is that he did escape. The other
R.A.F. man KOWALSKI broadcast on a Polish Station which has
the same functions as the English one. Two other men who worked
at Concordia but who both left a week before I arrived there
were BARRINGTON, a civilian internee, and Llewellyn THOMAS,
also a civilian internee. BARRINGTON is now in a concentration camp for some sexual offence, and THOMAS is also in a
concentration camp for attempting to escape. He reached the
Swiss border but was handed over to the Germans by a Swiss S.S.
man.

In February 1944 I happened to bump into COURLANDER **who** was
now a member of the British **Free Corps** but who had previously
been **working** on the German **Empire** Sender. COURLANDER and
myself had talked matters over in Genshagen after I had spoken
to ADAMI and he told me that he would go to another Station
for the same reason. When **I** met him in Berlin he told me that
he was now working with the object of sabotaging the British
Free Corps and he implored me to join in with him as he said
he had no one there whom he could rely upon for help. I
immediately sent in an application to the Commanding Officer
S.S. Hauptsturmfuhrer ROEPKE asking to be allowed to join the
British Free Corps. He accepted my application but then the
trouble arose from ADAMI who said that he could not spare me
as we were now only four men. During February, PURDY was
arrested by the Gestapo for blackmarketing and was taken to
Stalag IIID from where the Germans were again stupid enough
to send him to Oflag IVC. He was immediately recognised in
the camp and the other British Officers threatened him with
his life. He was removed out of the Camp and placed in

- 8 -

solitary confinement in the German quarters. This cut
down ADAMI's staff to three men and so now it seemed impossible that I would get away so the whole matter became
a struggle between the Foreign Office and the S.S. Needless
to say the S.S. won and I went to the Free Corps at the end
of April 1944. The Free Corps people had sent down a man, an
Englishman Sergeant McLARDY of the R.A.M.C., an ex-
prominent member of the B.U.F. in Liverpool, to interview me.
He was a corporal in the British Free Corps and was using
the name WOOD. He told me that the British Free Corps had
over 500 men and he also told me many other lies which I
later realised the reason for. The British Free Corps had
its headquarters in Klosterstrasse Hildesheim and I arrived
there to find that instead of 500 men there were only 21.
I could find no apparent reason for this until I spoke with
COURLANDER who told me that he had been placed by the Germans
in charge of recruiting and had found it very difficult to
keep the numbers down to this level. As it was, most of the
men were either just adventurers or men who had been serving
sentences in German prisons and had been released to join the
B.F.C.

Another method which the Germans had used with a certain
amount of success was to bring men straight from the fighting
line in Italy, and therefore dazed by the war, to LUCKENWALDE
Interrogation Camp where they were treated much the same as I
had been, that is to say, ill fed, left without blankets
and sometimes beaten until they, out of desperation, offered
to join the Free Corps. Of course most of these men have long
since thrown in the project and been sent away to a special
camp where the Germans keep men who know too much. There was
one such man, a Canadian Corporal by the name of MARTIN who
had such ideas as I myself, but who unfortunately slipped up.
He was also sent to this Camp. During my stay at Hildesheim,
which was four months, I must say that the men did absolutely
nothing at all. In fact the only way that they served the
Germans was by the fact that they walked around in the British
Free Corps uniform. This uniform was the normal German grey
uniform with a ski cap and on the collar they wore three
leopards and on the right arm they wore a Union Jack flag and
on the left lower arm they wore an armband with 'British Free
Corps' in English but in Gothic characters.

I found out that the man in charge of the whole
organisation of the Free Corps was an ex-British Staff Officer
by the name of Dr. Vivian STRANDERS who had gone over to
Germany some time in the region of 1928 and had taken German
naturalisation and was in fact one of the earliest Party
members. During a talk with him he showed me his Party Book
and I was surprised to see that it had been signed by Hitler
himself. He had been working as a professor in the Berlin
University, but after it was bombed he was approached by the
S.S. to organise the Free Corps and was given a rank of S.S.
Sturmbannfuhrer, which is equivalent to the rank of Major.
STRANDERS has written many newspaper articles and books over
a period of ten years and struck me as being an idealist.
During my stay in Berlin, as I have already said, I was allowed,
by reason of holding a Rundfunk pass which was to enable me to
get into the Reichsportsfeld, to also get into the Funkhaus
which is the German equivalent of our own Broadcasting House.
I had already met JOYCE several times in the Reichsportsfeld
and he had invited me to go along to the Funkhaus and have
supper with him. This I did on many occasions and made use of
these opportunities to find out as much as possible about

30. (continued) Statement of Francis Maton.

- 9 -

something which I actually had no business to know. I am
referring now to the organisation of the German service
broadcasting in English of which JOYCE is the leading light.
There are actually very few English people working on this
Station. They are the following:-

> William JOYCE.
> Margaret JOYCE (his wife)
> JONES, an ex-civilian internee.
> Edward BOWLBY   "   "
> POWELL (a relation of BADEN POWELL)

The other English speakers are SCHNEIDER, a Young German
who speaks perfect English but who had never been to England,
DIETZE, the well known ex-B.B.C. commentator, also a German,
and Dr. SCHARDE, who is also more or less in charge of the
Editing of the Station. The whole organisation of both
Bureau Concordia and the English Redaction of the Reichrund-
funk is managed by a man by the name of Dr. Fritz HESSE who is
the right hand man of von RIBBENTROP. The Foreign Office man
for Genshagen and for Concordia is Professor HAVERKORN.
The immediate chief of the Bureau Concordia is S.S.
Sturmbannfuhrer Dr. HETZLER (Eric). The whole organisation
of the Foreign Office which deals with the propaganda to
England is known as the England Committee. Working hand in
glove with the England Committee is B.Q.M.S. BROWN, the Camp
Leader of Genshagen and Bombardier BLEWITT. These two men,
although still retaining their status as prisoners of war,
that is to say, living in the Camp, both hold German passes
and can wander about Berlin at leisure in civilian clothes.
On my arrival in Hildesheim I found that the man who was
more or less in charge of the British soldiers there was
Thomas COOPER who had by now reverted to his own name. He
had been promoted to the rank of Sergeant Major and was in
fact, when I left, about to be sent to an officers' school.

Courlander and myself, after the invasion started and
all recruiting had been suspended, began to think of a way
in which we could escape. However, as people do when labouring
under the threat of death, we constantly kept putting it off
until the break through of the allies which was during August.
We both considered that our easiest method of escape would be
to wait until the British advanced into Belgium by reason of
the fact that we found that the French people could not be
trusted as much as the Belgians. On August 28th, 1944, we
both asked permission to go to Berlin on the pretence of
going to Stalag IIID to see about mail, as both of us had not
received any mail from home for over 8 months. We arrived
in Berlin in British Free Corps Uniform on August 29th.
COURLANDER went to live with a girl friend by the name of
Karola BOEHM, Berlin Dachsische Strasse 8, and I went to live
with a very trustworthy girl friend of mine by the name of
Irene FRITZCHING, at 18 Reichstrasse Charlottenberg. This
girl I had made friends with at Concordia. She was an
American girl, that is to say, her parents were Germans and
members of the German Embassy in Washington, and she herself
had been born in America, educated there, and was in fact 100%
American in all respects. When America declared war on Germany
the family had been interned for six months in America and
finally repatriated back to Germany, much to their disgust.

- 10 -

There is another sister, who was in fact W/Commander
CARPENTER's girl friend, and these two girls did everything
to help both of us, CARPENTER and myself, at all times.
About three months ago the mother, father and eldest
daughter, whose name is Mercedes, left for Madrid and left
the young girl on her own in Berlin. We formed a platonic
friendship and I grew to trust her 100%. Before I left I
told her of my plans and left a great deal of information
and all my private letters and photographs with her. When I
first went to Concordia I took a room in Berlin, Maikowski
Strasse 7. This building was badly damaged in the October
1943 raid so I moved to Bismark Strasse II, where I lived
for two weeks before being bombed out in the November raid.
I then moved out to the Reichsportsfeld where I lived in a
small house along with GRIFFITHS and COLLEDGE until January
1944, during which month we were once again bombed out.

During this raid the complete tail of a Lancaster fell
some ten yards away and the body of the air gunner we pulled
out and saw that the Germans treated it with respect and
had it properly disposed of, because we knew that in some
cases the Germans had left the bodies of our air crews in
the wreckage for over 48 hours. The name on the parachute
was Sergt.McDAVITT, and Miss FRITZSCHING still has his name,
number and rank from the parachute at home. I then moved
to Reichstrasse and continued to live there up until the
time of going into the Free Corps. After that, whenever I
was in Berlin I always stayed there. We lived quite well
because her parents sent as much foodstuff as possible from
Madrid. While working at Concordia I received 300 marks a
month, but I know that I was the poorest paid Britisher
there, but still I did not grumble because I found that the
money was ample for my needs. I know also that the wage of
BANNING, SPILMAN, GILBERT, FREEMAN, VERNON, BAILLIE STEWART,
are over the 1000 marks a month rate, while other people
there and especially at the Rundfunk go over the 2000 mark.
JOYCE quite possibly, although he never openly discussed the
matter with, earns somewhere in the region of 4000 a month.
CHAPPLE, PURDY, HUMPHREYS, COLLEDGE, GRIFFITHS, HOSKINS,
LINGSHAW, BARRINGTON, were all earning between 400 and 600
marks a month. The Germans employed in these Stations were
badly paid, and the German office girls who worked ten hours
a day and who all spoke at least two languages fluently,
only received in the region of 198 a month.

All these people who I have mentioned as broadcasting
for Germany I have actually seen with my own eyes, and while
most of them have quite magnetic personalities, I think the
most outstanding person of them all is surely William JOYCE.
JOYCE is a man who many people have tried to describe, and
by reason of the fact that he is both universally known and
hated over here, they have been inclined I am afraid to let
their pens run away with them, and I don't think that anyone
has given an honest description of JOYCE. William JOYCE is
a man who, as we all know, has many faults, but JOYCE is an
idealist and it is quite possible that as an idealist he is
second only to Hitler himself. He is rather moody
and at times is nervous. He also beats his wife, who is
rather a fast woman, and has had affairs in Berlin with a

Wages - indicative of Status ?

30. (continued) Statement of Francis Maton.

- 11 -

large number of men. JOYCE surprised me by the amount of
courage he showed during some of the worst raids, and while
most of us were shivering down in air raid shelters JOYCE
stood alone on the top of the Reichsportsfeld making a recording of the raid. No doubt most people will have noticed
that during five years of war JOYCE'S sarcasm has somewhat
toned down, but I personally feel that this is not due to
any fear on his part but due to the fact that I am told
that in the early days of his career all his manuscripts
were written for him, and were just plain German propaganda,
cleverly interwoven with hate against our own country.
However, now JOYCE has risen into the position where he is king
pin of the whole show and I don't believe that he ever uses
manuscripts now. I have myself seen him sit down in front of
a radio, listen to the B.B.C. news, walk straight over to a
microphone and broadcast his well known 'Views on the News'.
Such a man is William JOYCE then.

From the 30th August till 1st September 1944, COURLANDER
and I just lazed around and in fact I did not see him till
the evening of 1st September, and I told him that the British
were advancing very rapidly and I knew that a troop train
was leaving Berlin for Brussels on 2nd. We decided that we
would jump this troop train at the Potsdamer, and in the
early hours of 2nd September we both arrived at the Potsdamer
in uniform which we had altered into a regular German S.S.
uniform. COURLANDER kept our British Free Corps arm bands,
Union Jacks, and collar patches for evidence. We journeyed
to the Potsdamer by the electric train and from there we
waited on the platform until the crowded troop train drew
in. We jumped on the train with no difficulty and stood in
the corridor for some five hours until we got a seat at
Brunswick. Most of the soldiers were tired and generally
fed up, and didn't bother to talk to us, but in any case the
normal German soldier is scared of an S.S. man and will not
under any circumstances ask him any questions. The only other
S.S. men on the train as far as we could see were Belgian
volunteers from the S.S. Division Langemarck, who for some
unknown reason were being returned to Brussels. I talked to
some of these men and when they asked me where I was going I
simply said "We have been ordered to report to the S.S.
Kommandanture in Brussels' and we did not know why, and the
general reply was 'It was just typical of the ungodly mess
that seemed to be developing'.

The train arrived in Brussels on the morning of 3rd
September, and when we arrived on the Station we found
much to our delight a state of chaos, owing to the fact that
the Germans were evacuating the city and men were just walking
in and out of the Station at leisure without any control being
exercised. I had been to Brussels before the war, knew my
way about, and with COURLANDER's knowledge of French he
walked brazenly through the town. It was now a matter of
touch and go whether the whole thing succeeded, so we went to
a house where an old woman was standing, in the Marie Louisa
Avenue, and asked her if she could make us some coffee.
She said she would and so we went inside and drank coffee and
then COURLANDER approached her straight cut and told her that
we were Englishmen and asked her if she would hide us until
the British came. The woman was overjoyed and offered us the

31. William Joyce's Deutscher Volkssturm (Home Guard) pass, 21 December 1944. (KV 2/250/1)

32. William Joyce's Deutsches Reich Reisepass. This false German internal passport issued to Joyce by the Gestapo in April 1945 is made out in the name of Wilhelm Hansen and backdated to 3 November 1944. It was found on Joyce's person when he was arrested in May 1945. (KV 2/250/2)

Die Deutschen Europasender
Hauptsendestelle Luxemburg
Zahlungsanweisung   Kassenbuch Nr. 00791

Die Kasse wird angewiesen,

Datum des Verpflichtungsschreibens

Herrn

William Joyce,
Luxemburg,
Hotel Alfa   lo.2.44 Ro.

Konto Nr.

DES 45.= 16o.--
DES 432= 4o.--

o.St.

Tonaufnahme

Ständiger Wohnsitz: Berlin-Charl.9,Kastanien Allee 29

nachstehendes Honorar auszuzahlen:
Wochentag, Datum, Zeit: 16.lo.,9.12.,15.12.,22.1.,22.3o

Titel der Sendung   **Views on the News**
bzw. Nr. der Aufnahme **Engl. Ausweichvorträge**
Art der Mitwirkung: **Man.u.Spr. à 5o.--**
                     2oo.--
Honorar RM
                     Zweihundert
(in Worten: Reichsmark

Die Mitwirkung in der Sendung bzw. Aufnahme Nr.
hat stattgefunden: (Datum und Name)

Obigen Betrag empfangen zu haben, bescheinigt

Luxemburg, den *11/II/44*
                                    (Unterschrift)
(Quittung ist erst an der Kasse bei Empfang des Betrages zu leisten).

Unter Vorbehalt der Genehmigung durch die Direktion
Buchungsvermerke :

Reichs-Rundfunk G. m. b. H.
Sender Luxemburg
Die Deutschen Europasender
Hauptsendestelle Luxembur

33. German radio payment slip by *Eurospasender* at Luxembourg, 11 Feb 1944. Evidence of high treason? This slip was made out to William Joyce for broadcasts he made in early 1944. (KV 2/250/1/10)

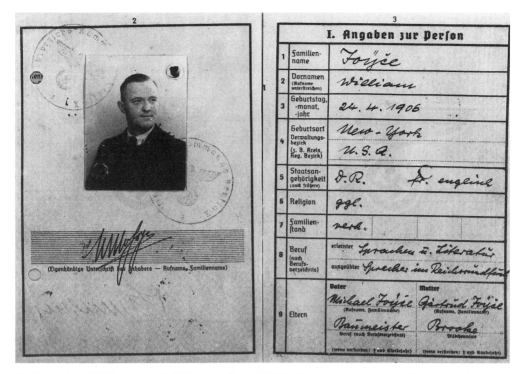

34. Pages from William Joyce's Wehrpass, issued 1941. Among Joyce's possessions when he was arrested in May 1945 was his German workbook. This document gives New York as his place of birth, describes his father as an architect and cites swimming, riding and boxing as his sporting qualifications. (KV 2/250/1)

3842

Hamburg Radio Station,

Germany.

21st May, 1945.

Statement of Edwin Hermann Frederick Lynn SCHNEIDER:-

1.   I reside with my parents at "KUCKUCKSBERG",
LUTJENSEE, Nr. Hamburg. I am 33 years of age. My father is
Hermann SCHNEIDER, and my mother Claire SCHNEIDER, nee SIMMONS-
LYNN who was British by birth. I was born in Germany and am
a German national.

2.   In January, 1942, I secured employment with the
Reichsrundfunk, at Rundfunkhaus, MASUREN ALLE, Berlin, and I
retained that employment until the occupation of Hamburg by
the British on 2nd or 3rd May, 1945.

3.   Throughout I was engaged in the English Redaktion,
of which the principal was always Herr Edward Roderick DIETZE.

4.   My sole duty was that of speaker in English of news
and commentaries, which were directed to England in the form
of propaganda. All my material was prepared for me and I
merely had to speak.

5.   I carried out this work from Berlin until 15th
March, 1945, when I was sent to Apen. At this place is
situated an amplifier station which was designed to amplify
the transmissions sent to Bremen from broadcasts originated
from the BREMERS Hotel in Apen.

6.   I remained at Apen until about the middle of April
when I was sent to Hamburg Radio Station, where I remained
until the occupation.

7.   Hamburg Station was linked with Apen through Bremen
by land line, but I understand there was an alternative line
through STADE.

8.   Throughout the whole of the time that I have been
employed by the ReichsRundfunk I have been intimately
associated in the broadcasts of William JOYCE, who I naturally
know very well.

9.   From January, 1942, until the middle of 1943 I
broadcast in English from Berlin at 1430, 1530, 1630, 1730 and
1830 daily, with the exception of two days off a fortnight,
when others deputised for me. My broadcasts all lasted for
15 minutes. That at 1430 was news, that at 1530 was the German
High Command Communique, which was repeated at 1630. At 1730
I introduced a feature programme of commentaries and music.
At 1830 I gave another news broadcast.

10.   During the same period, i.e. January 1942 until
the middle of 1943, JOYCE broadcast once daily only, viz.,
at 2230 or 2330 (I am not sure just now) and his item was
entitled "Views on the News". I believe that at the beginning
of this period he broadcast news items also. I was never

35. Statement of Edwin Hermann Frederick Lynn Schneider, 21 May 1945.
Edwin Schneider was one of Joyce's German colleagues at the *Rundfunk*. In this
important account Schneider tells of the final hours he spent with Margaret and
William Joyce before their disappearance from Hamburg. (KV 2/246/384z)

- 2 -

present when JOYCE made these broadcasts, but it was common
knowledge at the Rundfunkhaus and I also saw his name on the
daily programmes. JOYCE used to have either Wednesday or
Thursday off, and DIETZE used to deputize.

11.   All the above-mentioned broadcasts were on the
nominal transmission of "Bremen, Friesland and Calais".

12.   Owing to the bombing of Hamburg and the fear of
similar attacks in Berlin the routine was changed. The
Deutsche Europa Sender (DES) was evacuated to different
towns, and the English Redaktion was evacuated to Luxembourg.
I remained in Berlin, as did JOYCE.

13.   From the middle of 1943 until about 1st September
1944, when Luxembourg was taken, my duties merely comprised
feeding material to Luxembourg, by land line, where it was
recorded and broadcast as required. This material consisted
of news items, and commentories written by various people,
including BAILLIE-STEWART, HEWITT, Professor HAFERCORN and
JOYCE. In the latter days, before Luxembourg finished, much
of the news was broadcast from Berlin through Luxembourg,
to Bremen, Friesland and Calais as hitherto, and I did some
of this too.

14.   JOYCE still continued to broadcast his "Views
on the News" at 2230 hours each day, and I sometimes saw
him reading, through the studio window. He also wrote
scripts for broadcasting at 2330. This was broadcast by
various people, including myself, Barry JONES and Ralph
POWELL.

15.   From the end of August 1944 until the end of
September 1944 I was sent to Hilvershum, and then returned
to Berlin.

16.   At this time the daily news bulletins were being
broadcast from Apen, and the evening bulletins from Berlin.
The speakers were changed, and so at Apen JONES and POWELL
spoke in addition to HEYDEBRECK (a German), but alternately.

17.   For myself I took part in the evening programmes
from Berlin. These were at 1730 and 2030 (when feature
programmes were broadcast); 1900 to 2000 hours (headline
news headed "Jerry Calling", directed to the British
Forces) which was sent down the line to Apen; at 2130 (news
in English read by two people alternately); 2230 (JOYCE in
"Views on the News"); 2330 (news bulletin with commentories
by JOYCE, but read by speakers); and at 0015 till 0115
(headline news by "Jerry Calling" again).

18.   This programme continued to more or less the
end of February, 1945, and I took part in one or other
of these various broadcasts. During this same period I
announced JOYCE in his "Views on the News" two or three
times a week. I was present in the studio on these
occasions when JOYCE took over the microphone from me,
after my introduction, and then left the studio. Towards
the end of his broadcast he would ring a bell and I would
return to the studio as he was concluding his talk and make
a closing announcement that JOYCE had spoken.

- 3 -

situation, and this was followed by DIETZE, JOYCE, Mrs.
JOYCE, Fraulein - FRITZE (a secretary) and myself.

20.   At Apen I read the news in English alternately with
either JONES, POWELL or HEYDEBRECK, at 1730, 2030, 2130 and
2330 daily for a quarter of an hour each time. At 2230
JOYCE read his own "Views on the News". On several occasions
I announced him on the microphone and left him, then returned
when he finished, just as I had done in Berlin.

21.   We next went to Hamburg and during our stay here
I broadcast the news twice daily, viz., at 1730 and 2330.
JOYCE made his usual daily broadcasts of "Views on the News",
but at 2130. I introduced him on most occasions. These
transmissions were direct, but at intervening hours I fed
Apen with various short commentaries by JOYCE and Dr. EDWARDS
a German, known as the "Student of Politics", which Apen in
turn broadcast direct in their various bulletins. At Hamburg
I was the only broadcaster, apart from JOYCE, and a man
named HANSEN, who was only here for three or four days and
deputised for me on several occasions.

22.   The record (Ex. 2) played back to me today is by
JOYCE, and the introductory is by HANSEN.

23.   The record (Ex. 1) played back to me today was
made by JOYCE in my presence on 30th April 1945, at about
10 p.m. There were two broadcasts on the one "band". It
was extempore. I did not announce it.

24.   During the period I was at Hamburg JOYCE used to
prepare his own script, sometimes assisted by his wife. I
saw him on several occasions in his office (Room No.82) typing
his own script. I also saw his wife type some of it. They
had two or three typewriters which had been sent from Berlin,
and JOYCE had a small portable one of his own which he took
away with him. Mr. and Mrs. JOYCE also used one of the
studios in the "bunker" (air raid shelter) as an office and they
had a typewriter there too.

25.   I should mention that during my 2330 hours
broadcasts from Hamburg, I read commentaries by JOYCE, which
he gave me to read.

26.   I have been shewn by Captain Spooner a quantity of
typescript, marked Ex. Nos.1 to 193, covering a period from
9th April 1945 until 1st May 1945, which comprises news items
and commentories. Those bearing dates of 17th April 1945, and
thereafter were read by me from Radio Hamburg, either on
direct transmission or land line to Apen. All that material
was given to me personally by JOYCE for broadcast purposes.
Those bearing the originator's reference JY/MJ were undoubtedly prepared by JOYCE and typed by his wife. The news
items not bearing the originator's reference were translations of news items in German, made by Fraulein BENECKE,
a translator employed at Radio Hamburg.

27.   The typescript, bearing dates from 9th April 1945
to 16th April 1945 were originated in a similar way as the
foregoing, but as HANSEN was working as a speaker here
during that period I am unable to specify what was transmitted by him or me.

35. (continued) Statement of Edwin Schneider.

- 4 -

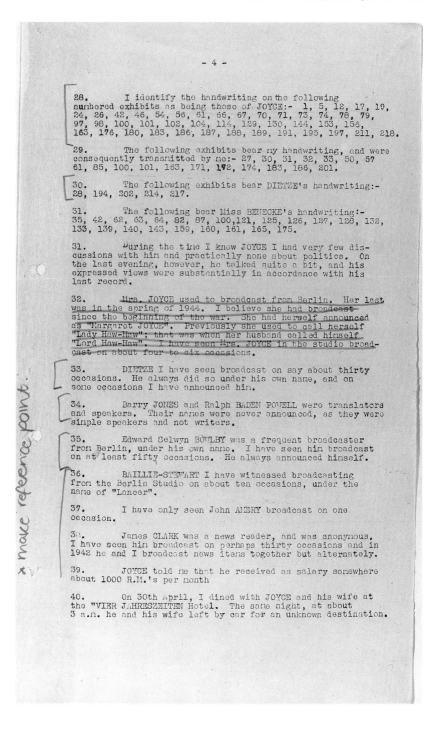

28.   I identify the handwriting on the following numbered exhibits as being those of JOYCE:- 1, 5, 12, 17, 19, 24, 26, 42, 46, 54, 56, 61, 66, 67, 70, 71, 73, 74, 78, 79, 97, 98, 100, 101, 102, 104, 114, 129, 130, 144, 153, 156, 163, 176, 180, 183, 186, 187, 188, 189, 191, 195, 197, 211, 218.

29.   The following exhibits bear my handwriting, and were consequently transmitted by me:- 27, 30, 31, 32, 33, 50, 57 61, 85, 100, 101, 163, 171, 172, 174, 183, 186, 201.

30.   The following exhibits bear DIETZE's handwriting:- 28, 194, 202, 214, 217.

31.   The following bear Miss BENECKE's handwriting:- 35, 42, 62, 63, 64, 82, 87, 100, 121, 125, 126, 127, 128, 132, 133, 139, 140, 143, 159, 160, 161, 165, 175.

31.   During the time I knew JOYCE I had very few discussions with him and practically none about politics. On the last evening, however, he talked quite a bit, and his expressed views were substantially in accordance with his last record.

32.   Mrs. JOYCE used to broadcast from Berlin. Her last was in the spring of 1944. I believe she had broadcast since the beginning of the war. She had herself announced as "Margaret JOYCE". Previously she used to call herself "Lady Haw-Haw"; that was when her husband called himself "Lord Haw-Haw". I have seen Mrs. JOYCE in the studio broadcast on about four to six occasions.

33.   DIETZE I have seen broadcast on say about thirty occasions. He always did so under his own name, and on some occasions I have announced him.

34.   Barry JONES and Ralph BADEN POWELL were translators and speakers. Their names were never announced, as they were simple speakers and not writers.

35.   Edward Selwyn BOWLBY was a frequent broadcaster from Berlin, under his own name. I have seen him broadcast on at least fifty occasions. He always announced himself.

36.   BAILLIE-STEWART I have witnessed broadcasting from the Berlin Studio on about ten occasions, under the name of "Lancer".

37.   I have only seen John AMERY broadcast on one occasion.

38.   James CLARK was a news reader, and was anonymous. I have seen him broadcast on perhaps thirty occasions and in 1942 he and I broadcast news items together but alternately.

39.   JOYCE told me that he received as salary somewhere about 1000 R.M.'s per month

40.   On 30th April, I dined with JOYCE and his wife at the "VIER JAHRESZEITEN" Hotel. The same night, at about 3 a.m. he and his wife left by car for an unknown destination.

make reference point.

- 5 -

Before doing so he gave me his bank book and his passport, saying that he might be back before the end of the year.

41.   I saw him leave in a car driven by a man wearing a Volksturm armband, but I do not know who e was. I do not know to whom the car belonged or who requisitioned it, but I think it may have been Herr GRUPE, the Intendante.

42.   All the typescript bearing the originator's initials 'ED' was prepared by Dr. EDWARDS and his wife (both Germans). HANSEN was a German.

43.   The pseudonym "Peter Calling" was Dr. Peter KRUGE, @ Peter ALDAG, a rumoured Gestapo member.

(Signed)   Edwin Schneider.

Statement taken, read over and signed by Schneider by me, R.W.Spooner, Captain, Intelligence Corps.

35. (continued) Statement of Edwin Schneider.

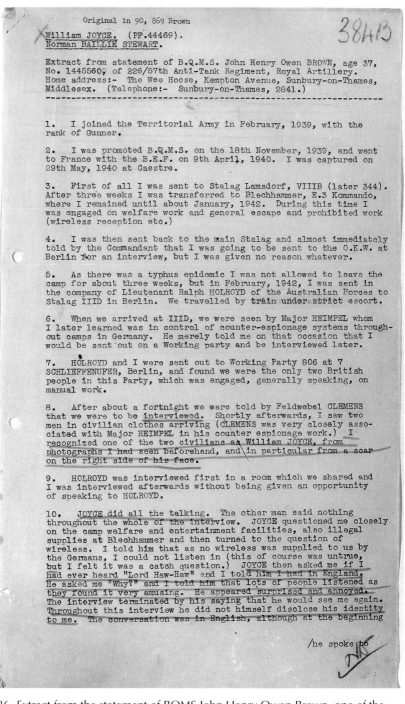

Original in 90, 869 Brown

William JOYCE. (PF.44469).
Norman BAILLIE STEWART.

Extract from statement of B.Q.M.S. John Henry Owen BROWN, age 37,
No. 1445560, of 226/57th Anti-Tank Regiment, Royal Artillery.
Home address:- The Wee Hoose, Kempton Avenue, Sunbury-on-Thames,
Middlesex. (Telephone:- Sunbury-on-Thames, 2841.)
----

1.   I joined the Territorial Army in February, 1939, with the
rank of Gunner.

2.   I was promoted B.Q.M.S. on the 18th November, 1939, and went
to France with the B.E.F. on 9th April, 1940. I was captured on
29th May, 1940 at Caestre.

3.   First of all I was sent to Stalag Lamsdorf, VIIIB (later 344).
After three weeks I was transferred to Blechhammer, E.3 Kommando,
where I remained until about January, 1942. During this time I
was engaged on welfare work and general escape and prohibited work
(wireless reception etc.)

4.   I was then sent back to the main Stalag and almost immediately
told by the Commandant that I was going to be sent to the O.K.W. at
Berlin for an interview, but I was given no reason whatever.

5.   As there was a typhus epidemic I was not allowed to leave the
camp for about three weeks, but in February, 1942, I was sent in
the company of Lieutenant Ralph HOLROYD of the Australian Forces to
Stalag IIID in Berlin. We travelled by train under strict escort.

6.   When we arrived at IIID, we were seen by Major HEIMPEL whom
I later learned was in control of counter-espionage systems throughout camps in Germany. He merely told me on that occasion that I
would be sent out on a Working party and be interviewed later.

7.   HOLROYD and I were sent out to Working Party 806 at 7
SCHLIEFFENUFER, Berlin, and found we were the only two British
people in this Party, which was engaged, generally speaking, on
manual work.

8.   After about a fortnight we were told by Feldwebel CLEMENS
that we were to be interviewed. Shortly afterwards, I saw two
men in civilian clothes arriving (CLEMENS was very closely associated with Major HEIMPEL in his counter espionage work.) I
recognized one of the two civilians as William JOYCE, from
photographs I had seen beforehand, and in particular from a scar
on the right side of his face.

9.   HOLROYD was interviewed first in a room which we shared and
I was interviewed afterwards without being given an opportunity
of speaking to HOLROYD.

10.   JOYCE did all the talking. The other man said nothing
throughout the whole of the interview. JOYCE questioned me closely
on the camp welfare and entertainment facilities, also illegal
supplies at Blechhammer and then turned to the question of
wireless. I told him that as no wireless was supplied to us by
the Germans, I could not listen in (this of course was untrue,
but I felt it was a catch question.) JOYCE then asked me if I
had ever heard "Lord Haw-Haw" and I told him I had in England.
He asked me "Why?" and I told him that lots of people listened as
they found it very amusing. He appeared surprised and annoyed.
The interview terminated by his saying that he would see me again.
Throughout this interview he did not himself disclose his identity
to me. The conversation was in English, although at the beginning

/he spoke to

- 2 -

The other interviewer

he spoke to his friend in German in the presence of both HOLROYD and myself. JOYCE's associate was about 30 years of age, medium height, medium build, dark hair; wearing English clothing and an Anthony Eden hat. The photograph of BAILLIE STEWART appears to be identical with this man, except that he was clean shaven.

11. HOLROYD later told me that he was asked for details of his escape in Italy. JOYCE had also made some very disparaging remarks about the British Empire, as at that time we had just lost Singapore.

12. Three weeks later, HOLROYD was taken away to a Strafe Oflag IVC, and I haven't seen him since.

....   14.5.45.

86. At my last meeting with War Office representatives, I was able only to give approximate dates of my changes of address etc. whilst a P.O.W., but I can now furnish the following information from my diary:-

15.7.40.	To Blechhammer E.3 working party.
31.1.42.	Leave for Lamsdorf Stalag 344 (formerly VIIIB).
9.3.42.	Leave Lamsdorf for Berlin with Lieut. HOLROYD.
16.3.42.	Have two visitors in afternoon. One definitely W. JOYCE.
22.4.42.	Two men arrive from Lamsdorf for trial.
30.4.42.	Lieut. HOLROYD leaves for Oflag IVC.
10.8.42.	Meet German Welfare Officer in Stalag.
15.8.42.	Back to Lamsdorf.
23.8.42.	Back to Blechhammer.
29.5.43.	From Blechhammer to Berlin. (Wahlheide working camp.)
12.6.43.	To Genshagen camp.
24.6.43.	First party arrives at Genshagen.
13.12.44.	Genshagen disbanded.
12.1.45.	Leave Lichterfelde camp Berlin for Lamsdorf.
5.3.45.	Leave Lamsdorf in cattle trucks.
10.3.45.	Arrive Memmingen, Stalag VIIA.
19.3.45.	Leave Memmingen in cattle trucks.
24.3.45.	Reach Hohenfels Stalag 383.
22.4.45.	Liberated by American 3rd Army.

23.5.45.

....

36. (continued) Statement of John Brown.

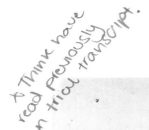

Think have read previously in trial transcript.

74 General Hospital,
Lueneberg, Germany.

31st May, 1945.

STATEMENT of William JOYCE, who saith:-

why didn't he say this?

I was born in Brooklyn, U.S.A. on 24th April 1906. My father was Michael JOYCE and my mother Gertrude Emily BROOKE. My father was born in Ireland in or near Ballinrobe and my mother was born in Lancashire at Shaw. I understand, though I have no documents to prove any statement that my father was American by naturalization at the time of my birth and I believe he lost his American citizenship later through failing to renew it because we left America in 1909 when I was three years old. We were generally counted as British subjects during our stay in Ireland and England. I was in Ireland from 1909 till 1921 when I came to England. We were always treated as British during the period of my stay in England whether we were or not. In 1940 I acquired German nationality. I believe the date was September 26th but the certificate of naturalization is not in my possession. The only evidence I can offer in support of my statement is the entry in my Wehrpass issued subsequent to my naturalization where I am put down as of German nationality.

I have been cautioned that I am not obliged to say anything. I understand that proceedings may be taken against me and that whatever I say may be written down and given in evidence.

(Sgd.) Wm. Joyce.

I take this opportunity of making a preliminary statement concerning the motives which led me to come to Germany and to broadcast to Britain over the German radio service. I was actuated not by the desire for personal gain material or otherwise but solely by political conviction. I was brought up as an extreme Conservative with strong Imperialist ideas but very early in my career, namely in 1923, became attracted to Fascism and subsequently to National Socialism. Between the years 1923 and 1939 I pursued vigorous political activities in England, at times as a Conservative but mainly as a Fascist or National Socialist. In the period immediately before this war began I was profoundly discontented with the policies pursued by British Governments, first because I felt that they would lead to the eventual disruption of the British Empire and secondly because I thought the existing economic system entirely inadequate to the needs of the times.

I was very greatly impressed by constructive work which Hitler had done for Germany and was of the opinion that throughout Europe as also in Britain there must come a reform on the lines of National Socialist doctrine although I did not suppose that every aspect of National Socialism as advocated in Germany would be accepted by the British people.

One of my dominant beliefs was that a war between Britain and Germany would be a tragedy, the effects of which Britain and the British Empire would not survive and I considered that a grossly disproportionate influence was exerted on British policy by the Jews who had their reasons for hating National Socialist Germany.

When/

la union 31.5.45

37. Typescript of the statement William Joyce dictated to British intelligence officer Captain Skardon from his hospital bed at Luneberg on 31 May 1945. In the event it was the last public statement he ever made. (KV 2/246/390b)

- 2 -

When in August 1939 the final crisis emerged I felt that the question of Danzig offered no just cause for a world war. As by reason of my opinions I was not conscientiously disposed to fight for Britain for Germany, I decided to leave the country since I did not wish to play the part of a conscientious objector and since I supposed that in Germany I should have the opportunity to express and propagate views the expression of which would be forbidden in Britain during time of war. Realising, however, that at this critical juncture I had declined to serve Britain, I drew the logical conclusion that I should have no moral right to return to that country of my own free will and that it would be best to apply for German citizenship and make my permanent home in Germany. Nevertheless, it remained my undeviating purpose to attempt as best I could to bring about a reconciliation or at least an understanding between the two countries.

After Russia and the United States had entered the war such an agreement appeared to me no less desirable than before for although it seemed probable that with these powerful allies Britain would succeed in defeating Germany, I considered that the price which would ultimately have to be paid for this help would be far higher than the price involved in a settlement with Germany. This belief was strengthened from month to month as the power of Russia grew and during the later stages of the war I became certain that Britain even though capable of gaining a military triumph over the Germans would in that event be confronted with a situation far more dangerous and complicated than that which existed in August 1939 and thus until the very last moment I clung to my hope of an Anglo-German understanding although I could see that the prospects thereof were small.

I know that I have been denounced as a traitor and I resent the accusation as I conceive myself to have been guilty of no underhand or deceitful act against Britain although I am also able to understand the resentment that my broadcasts have, in many quarters, aroused. Whatever opinion may be formed at the present time with regard to my conduct I submit that the final judgment cannot be properly passed until it is seen whether Britain can win the peace.

Finally I should like to stress the fact that in coming to Germany and in working for the German radio system my wife was powerfully influenced by me. She protest to the contrary but I am sure that if I had not taken this step should would not have taken it either.

This statement has been read over by me and it is true.

(Sgd.)   Wm. Joyce.

37. (continued) Statement of William Joyce to Captain Skardon.

War Office,
23rd June 1945

Statement of Alexander Adrian LICKORISH.
Captain, Reccanaissance Regiment.
R.A.C. Who Saith. -

On 28th May 1945 at about 7 p.m.
I was with another officer Lieutenant
Perry in a wood, a mile from
the Danish frontier near Flensburg
gathering fuel. A little earlier we
had seen an individual, a man
who was also in the wood and
as we were collecting logs at
7 p.m. he approa. turned towards
us and waving his stick
indicated some wood in a ditch.
Thereafter he remained near us
and presently spoke to us in
French but we ignored his
remarks except to thank him in
German. He seemed anxious to
help us find fuel and to talk
to us. After a while he said
in English "Here are a few
more pieces." I immediately
recognised his voice as that of
William Joyce. a broadcaster.

38. Statement of Captain Alexander Adrian Lickorish, 23 June 1945, describing
meeting the odd tramp-like figure who turned out to be William Joyce while
collecting wood on the German–Danish border. He also explains how he and his
colleague recognized Joyce's voice and how Joyce was shot during his detention.
(KV 2/248/39a)

on the German radio known as
William Joyce. I desired to
confirm my suspicions. and had a
discussion with Lieutenant Perry.
We evolved a plan as a result
of which when the man was
placing wood on our truck
Lieut. Perry taxed him saying
to him "You wouldn't happen to be
William Joyce would you?" He
put his hand quickly to his pocket
and Perry shot at his hand.
Joyce fell to the ground saying
"My name is Hansen." I rushed
towards him and searched him
with a view to disarming him.
Joyce said "I am not armed."
Looking through his pockets
I found in the inner jacket
pocket a Reisepasse in the name
of Wilhelm Hansen and a
Wehrpass in the name of William
Joyce.
We then treated his wound
by giving first aid. later
handing him over to the
appropriate military authorities
This statement has been read
over to me and it is true. a. a. Lickorish Capt

38. (continued) Statement of Captain Lickorish.

ARREST REPORT.

SURNAME JOYCE   FIRST NAME(s) William

ALIAS HANSEN, Wilhelm.

NATIONALITY CLAIMED GERMAN, formerly ENGLISH.

ADDRESS OF LAST RESIDENCE Not known.

OCCUPATION   Broadcaster on GERMAN Radio.

IDENTITY DOCUMENTS   Wehrpass No. BERLIN X/06/I29/47/I &
false Reisepass No. 281/44   (51844-P-42).

DETAILS OF ARREST: (a) PLACE   Kupfermühle, FLENSBURG.

(b) DATE   28 May 45.   (c) TIME   1930 hrs.

UNIT MAKING ARREST   65 F.S.Section

REASON FOR ARREST   Danger to security.

(further details to be written on back if necessary)

WITNESSES : NAMES AND ADDRESSES   Taken into custody by Capt.
LICKORISH and Lieut PERRY, G,
Press Control, FLENSBURG.

STATEMENT AFTER ARREST   NIL.
(attach on separate sheet if necessary)

PROPERTY: (Property taken from prisoner to be listed on back, together with description and
whereabouts of any other property relevant to the case.) Miscellaneous.

MILITARY OR CIVIL AUTHORITY TAKING CUSTODY OF THE PRISONER
II Armd Div HQ "I" Branch. 33 Casualty Clearing Stn.
Schleswig
Signature of person authorising arrest   Holcar   Rank Capt.
O.C. 65 F.S.Section.
Date 28 May 45

AG P BR--150M--26811ABCD--5-44   SHAEF AGO Form No. 7

39. Arrest reports relating to William Joyce, 28 May 1945. This file also includes lists of the property of William and Margaret Joyce on arrest. (KV 2/248/8a)

S E C R E T

SUBJECT:- William JOYCE

28 May 45

Col GS I

        At 1830 hrs today, Capt A A LICKORISCH,
Field Press Censor, attached Press Sub-Section No 4
Information Control Unit, FLENSBURG, and Lieut PERRY,
Editor of FLENSBURGER NACHRICHTENBLATT, and a member
of the same unit were gathering firewood on the Danish
Border at KRUSSAU M53/Y91, north of FLENSBURG.

        They were approached by a civilian who
volunteered, in French, the information that a pile
of good firewood could be found nearby.   The officers
thanked him, and as he was moving off the individual
made a remark in English.   This aroused suspicion
and one of the officers said point blank:-

        "You are Joyce, aren't you ?"

        At this Joyce made a movement towards his
pocket, whereupon he was shot through the buttocks.
He was then searched but found to have no gun.

        He was transferred to 33 CCS, FLENSBURG
where he was stripped, searched, medically examined
(including mouth), and given fresh clothes.   He now
has an all-night guard.   Medical authorities at the
hospital state his condition is serious, but not
critical.   Joyce carried a passport in the name of
HANSEN, but other documents found on him proved him
to be Joyce, a fact which he himself has admitted.

        These documents have not yet been fully
examined, but will be sent to this HQ tomorrow,
29 May 45.   It appears that Joyce, together with
his wife, who has also been arrested, and is now in
FLENSBURG jail, had been attempting to make his way

                        / northwards   .

39. (continued) Arrest reports on William Joyce.

- 2 -

northwards through DENMARK, but had turned back to
FLENSBURG as his funds were getting short, where he
and his wife stayed at the Bahnhof Hotel.   When
159 Inf Bde arrived at FLENSBURG Joyce and his
wife were turned out of the hotel, the formation
being unaware of their identity, and moved to
KUPFERMUHLE L55/X20.   It was here that Joyce's wife
was arrested.   She is described as an extremely
attractive woman.

      The two officers responsible for his
apprehension have been interviewed on the subject
by a Capt R HOWES, described as Public Observer,
HQ 11 Armd Div, and stated to have been with the Div
since D-day.   All three officers have been warned
not to discuss the matter, though it would appear
that Joyce's arrest is common knowledge in the area.

      On his way to hospital Joyce said to his
escorts:-

      "I suppose that in view of recent suicides,
you expect me to do the same.   I'm not that sort of
person".

      Joyces wife, together with her husband's
documents arrives this HQ tomorrow, ETA 1500 hrs.

28 May 45

(FORM No. 12C.A).
REF. No. ....
Sheet No. ....

WEST RIDING OF YORKSHIRE CONSTABULARY.

Statement of ....JOHN COWEN, Private No. 13010547,....
47 Tennyson Street, Nunroyd Estate,
GUISELEY.

xxxxxxxxd :

Occupation..Soldier, prev. Labourer.   Age..40 years.

STATES:– I am a Private soldier in the Pioneer Corps. I am at
present on leave with instructions to return, on the 23rd May,1945,
to No.45 Div. Troops Unit, Hardwick Hall, Sedgefield, Co., Durham.

.I joined the Army on the 21st Feb., 1940, as a volunteer,
and was posted to the Pioneer Corps, first to the 89th Company and
later to the 121st Company. I was in England until the 10th May,
1940, and·on that date we left Southampton and arrived at Le Havre
on the 11th May, 1940.   I was taken prisoner, by the Germans, at
Bolougne, France, on the 25th May, 1940, along with other 200 – 300
British troops.

We were marched from Bolougne to Seamir, Devrres, then
back through Seamir to Montreaus and to Cambria, arriving there on
the 31st May, 1940. We remained there until the 3rd June, 1940,
when we entrained to Trier, arriving there on the 6th June, 1940.
We left Trier, by train, the following day and arrived at Torun
(or Thorn) in Poland, on the 9th June, 1940, at Stalag XXA. From
this Stalag we were split up into various working parties, roadmaking
&c. On the 18th April, 1941, I was transferred to Stalag XXB at
Marianburg, West Prussia. I was put in a working party laying a
cable at.Guldenboden. On the 29th May, 1941 I was returned from this
working party to Stalag XXB.   On the 30th May, 1941, I was sent
with other thirteen British prisoners to work on a farm at Schablau,
Nr. Marianburg.   On the 13th June, 1941, whilst still at this farm,
just after dinner time, we were visited by the Official Welfare
Officer of Stalag XXB who was accompanied by a German wearing
civilian clothes; he was about 6' 2" in height, 38 – 40 years, he
stated he was a German newspaper reporter. This man spoke very
good English. We conversed together and I asked him why so much
German military stores and equipment were passing on a nearby railway
going towards Russia. He said Germany was going to strike Russia
first before Russia attacked them. I also asked him if there was
any truth about Hess having landed in England. He asked me how I
knew about this.and I told him I had learnt a little German whilst
being a prisoner and that I had overheard civilians who were working
with us discussing the matter – this was true and I had also heard
this rumour from other·prisoners. He seemed very surprised that we
knew about this.   He told me that Hess knew England could not
possibly win the war and that he (Hess) was contacting influential
friends in England with a view to England not continuing in the War.
He said this was his own personal opinion.   Later my camp number and
name were taken by the Welfare Officer.

On the 3rd September, 1941, I was recalled to Stalag XXB
Headquarters, I was there joined by Lance Corporal Cole (Home address
Leeds), Corporal Butterworth of the Black Watch, (Home address –
29 Church Street, Ridgemont, Bletchley), Private James Rice, of a
London Regt (Home address – 51 Dawes Street, Wellworth, London S.E.17),
and Corporal Thomas, also of a London Regt. (Home address – 22 Elbe
Street, London, S.W.6.)

The 5 of us left Stalag XXB at 1 a.m. on the 6th Sept.,
1941. We were not told where we were going.   We arrived in Berlin
about noon the same day, and were taken to Stalag 3D at Lichterfelde,
just outside Berlin.

Signature Witnessed by ....(OVER)..............

Date taken 20.5.45.....
By whom DC.243.Leng.
Time: From 4.pmto 5.40 pm.
Persons present None.

40. Police statement of Private John Cowen, 28 May 1945. This comes from a
file concerning police interviews and statements made by former prisoners of
war after the war relating to the attempts by Joyce to get them to participate in
wartime propaganda broadcasts and other activities. (KV 2/246/432c)

(FORM No. 12C.A).

REF. No. ....
Sheet No. ..2.....

WEST RIDING OF YORKSHIRE CONSTABULARY.

Statement of ....JOHN COWAN, Private No. 13010547......

continued :

At this camp we met a British Officer, Capt. Blacker - particulars of Regiment &c. not known. All the other prisoners at this camp were French. At this camp we were given a complete new outfit.

On the 24th Sept., 1941, two civilians came to interview the five of us who had come from Stalag XXB. Capt. Blacker also saw these two civilians and said one of them was William Joyce and pointed him out to us. The man stated to be Joyce was 5' 5" - 6" in height, medium build, pale and sallow complexion and had a cut scar on one side of his face (believed the right side) extending from his ear across his cheek to the corner of his mouth. He was wearing a navy blue pin striped suit.

Each of the five of us was interviewed seperately by the man stated to be Joyce. I was interviewed third, I don't know the order of the others. At the interview the man stated to be Joyce was accompanied by the other civilian referred to. I don't know who he was. He was about 5' 8", about 32-33 years, slim built and he took notes of the interview.

The man stated to be Joyce asked me how old I was, I replied "Thirty-seven".   Was I married?   I replied "Yes"
What family had I?   "Wife and five children."   Was I Labour, Liberal or Conservative?   I replied "I am a Trade Unionist and Labour".   He said "What did you do in civilian life?" I replied "Mining and labouring".   He then said "Did you volunteer for the Army?" I replied "Yes".   He asked why I volunteered when I had five children, I said "I am quite satisfied with things as they are in England and I thought it was my duty to fight for them".
He then asked "What do you think about the collapse of France" and implied that Great Britain had sacrificed the troops they had in France. I told him I didn't know what had actually happened there but we should know the truth at the end of the War. He then asked "What do you think of the conditions in Germany compared with those in England, I said "In my opinion conditions are better in England but Germany has two or three welfare schemes I have read about, which, if they were improved would be very good for England." I referred to German maternity and holiday schemes I had read about. I told I did not agree with Germany teaching Political doctrines in schools and teaching children to spy on their parents and neither did I agree with their Police and Gestapo systems. He said "The German people are used to it, you have your Police in England." I then told him the British Police protected our rights whereas the German Police forced the people into Political beliefs and made them do as they were told. He then asked me what I would say about the German system if I was allowed to speak over the wireless. I said, "As a British soldier it is not my duty to speak on the German wireless, and, if I do speak I shall probably get into trouble about it when I return to England." He said "You will not have any trouble about that, England can't possibly win the War." I then pointed out to him that although we had left the Continent of Europe we were still fighting in Africa. He then said "If you get back to England, what will you tell your wife and workmates about Germany". I replied "I will speak the truth and tell them that in my opinion conditions in Germany are not as good as those in England." He asked me about the German prison camps and I said "Considering we are prisoners of war we had nothing to complain about." The interview then closed.

Date taken ....

By whom ....

Time: From ......to......

Persons present ....

....

Signature Witnessed by ....

FORM No. 12C.A).

REF. No. . . . .
Sheet No. 3 . . . . .

WEST RIDING OF YORKSHIRE CONSTABULARY.

Statement of . . . . JOHN COWEN, Private No. 13010547. . . .

continued :

He said he would see me again in a few days but I did not hear further of him.

I asked the man who interviewed me if he was William Joyce but he evaded my question. I was later told by one of the four who accompanied me that the man had told him he was William Joyce – I don't know who this was.

The man stated to be Joyce spoke very good English with no trace of foreign accent.

I have not seen a photograph of Joyce and I do not remember having heard him on the radio.

I could identify him either from photographs or personally.

I do not know whether he interviewed Capt. Blacker.

We left Stalag 3B at 8 a.m. the 6th November, 1941 and returned to Stalag XXB at 3.30 a.m. the 7th November, 1941. I remained here until released by the Russians on the 27th January, 1945. We were then returned via Odessa to England, arriving at Liverpool on the 30th April, 1945.

(Signed)   JOHN COWEN.

Signature in official notebook of W. Leng D-o 243.

Date taken 20.5.45. . .
By whom D-o 243. Leng.
Time: From 4. . . .to5.40 p.m.
Persons present None.
. . . .

Signature Witnessed by W. Leng. D-o. 243. . . . .

40. (continued) Statement of Private Cowen.

3991B

Extract from Daily Digest of World Broadcasts. Part I.

Moscow in English 01.00 5.6.45.

Report by Analyser.

Visit to Joyce's Berlin Office.

Fourth instalment of a series of reports by our observer Analyser who is now in Berlin; William Joyce, English-speaking arch-Hitlerite, has been arrested. Before me lie the German secret documents shedding telling light on the treacherous activities of Joyce who, in one of his reports to his Chief, called himself "Goebbels' best propagandist". Many of the documents I am holding bear Joyce's signature. Others were penned by Goebbels and his immediate helpers in organising undermining propaganda for England and the U.S.A. I have also found several letters written to Joyce by certain British and German Fascists. There is a great deal of material here, all worthy of the closest study. In my report today I want to make some general observations about the traces of Lord Haw-Haw's activity that I found in Berlin's Radio House. Radio House is a large gloomy building whose architecture combines modernistic elements with an out-and-out prison style. From here Goebbels sent his Fascist propaganda through the air. Besides Germans, there were people of other nationalities, treacherously performing Hitler's underhand work, directed against the freedom-loving nations during the war. I tried to find out from some employees of Berlin's Radio House, who were working here before the Red Army arrived, whether any of the former employees of the English or American offices were still around. No, I was told. Somebody said that Goebbels's radio propagandists for England and America stopped working in Radio House a long time ago and that there were no traces of their general activity to be found. Narrow corridors lead to the editorial offices and studios. The building is intact, having escaped direct bomb hits, though the RAF and the Americans did effective bombing in this district. But quite a few Radio House window panes have been replaced by plywood. The plaster has come off in many places leaving uncovered brick. Somebody suggested I should look at the studios, from which there are no transmissions now. Here is a door without any sign except "No.123A". I enter a large room furnished with several desks. About a dozen automatic files lie on the top of one, but they are empty, their contents having been carefully removed. However, some papers have been left behind in one of them. A number of these deal with a certain woman who had joined the staff of the English Department - E.G. Dietze. I entered a studio. One can tell at a glance that this room was not used for broadcasting, but as an office. In a bookcase are the collected works of Goebbels with an inscription in English - a gift from one member of the English Department to another. The inscription contains this Latin quotation: "Morituri te salutant" - "the dying salute you". An interesting admission. Goebbels's mad radio dogs long ago sensed, it seems, that their dirty game was up. In one of the desk drawers I find a volume of articles by Herr William Joyce, which was published in German-occupied Holland in 1942.

There can be no doubt that the English material with which the Hitlerites cluttered the air was written in these very rooms. Opening another door I find myself in a small studio which was converted into a bedroom. Lying on the table are an American detective story and a German-English dictionary.

Further along is studio number eight. A piece of paper on the door reveals this as the office of William Joyce. The first thing that strikes my eye on entering this room is a pile of papers lying in disorder in a corner. The inhabitants of this room obviously left in a great hurry. Among the papers I find reports of the Listening Post and the German Digest of Enemy - that is, Soviet, British and U.S. - Information. Here are typewritten articles with German headings and English texts. The author, it turns out, is William Joyce and they are intended for broadcasts to England. I find dozens of these texts, giving a clue to

P.T.O.

41. Transcript of a Soviet broadcast made on 5 June 1945. The weakness of the prosecution case and the possibility of William Joyce's acquittal on the grounds that he was not a British subject owing allegiance to the Crown was the nightmare scenario for MI5. They were worried not just about British public opinion but also, as this suggests, about Russian reaction to such an acquittal. (KV 2/246/399b)

Lord Haw-Haw's activities. Among the papers, too, are copies of Joyce's
letters which he invariably closed with the words: "Heil Hitler",
followed by his signature. Here, too, are some letters addressed to
Joyce. Many of their authors bear English names. I also find many
cuttings from British newspapers with marginal notes and underlinings.
One of them is an editorial article called "Collaborator", from the
"Financial News" of 15th December 1944. Joyce underlined the statement that the fight against the collaborators must not be given too
wide a character. Joyce's interest in this editorial is understandable.
Sitting in the Berlin Radio House he knew what awaited him and he
indulged in wishful thinking about British kindness.

I want to point out that in all these documents Joyce expressed
his supreme loyalty to the cause of Hitler and Hitler Germany while the
Fascists, for their part, regarded him as their direct agent. In this
connection the following document I found in a forgotten file in Dietze's
desk is extremely interesting. It is Goebbels's decision on a report
sent in by Dietze. Among other things it says that the question of
decorating Lord Haw-Haw with the German Cross for his military services
has been laid aside lest it weaken his propaganda position. At the
same time Goebbels, as his Assistant, Dr. (? Wehrman), says in a letter
dated 2nd December 1942, intends to see to it that Lord Haw-Haw is
rewarded in some other way. I don't think any further proof is necessary to show that Joyce helped Hitler Germany in its fight against
Britain, the U.S.A., the Soviet Union and the other United Nations.
The very fact that Joyce was not given the German Cross, simply because
Goebbels feared to weaken his propaganda position, exposes the treachery
of this vile traitor and Hitlerite.

41. (continued) Transcript of a Soviet broadcast.

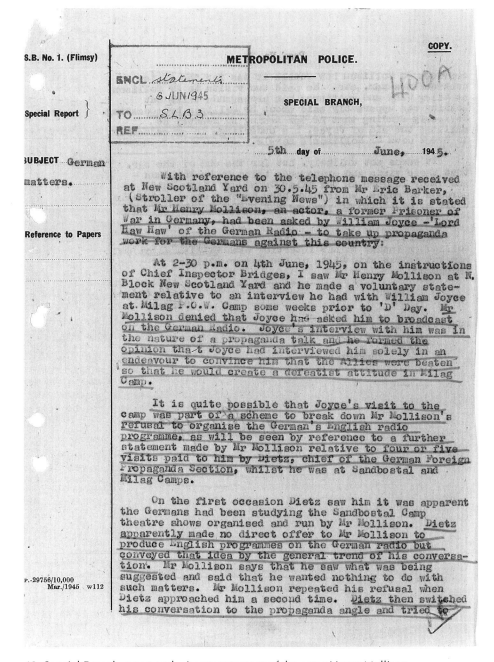

S.B. No. 1. (Flimsy)

METROPOLITAN POLICE.

COPY.

ENCL *statements*
6 JUN 1945

SPECIAL BRANCH,

TO S.L.B.3

REF ....

Special Report }

5th day of June, 1945.

SUBJECT ... German matters.

Reference to Papers

With reference to the telephone message received at New Scotland Yard on 30.5.45 from Mr Eric Barker, (Stroller of the "Evening News") in which it is stated that Mr Henry Mollison, an actor, a former Prisoner of War in Germany, had been asked by William Joyce - 'Lord Haw Haw' of the German Radio - to take up propaganda work for the Germans against this country:

At 2-30 p.m. on 4th June, 1945, on the instructions of Chief Inspector Bridges, I saw Mr Henry Mollison at N. Block New Scotland Yard and he made a voluntary statement relative to an interview he had with William Joyce at Milag P.O.W. Camp some weeks prior to 'D' Day. Mr Mollison denied that Joyce had asked him to broadcast on the German Radio. Joyce's interview with him was in the nature of a propaganda talk and he formed the opinion that Joyce had interviewed him solely in an endeavour to convince him that the Allies were beaten so that he would create a defeatist attitude in Milag Camp.

It is quite possible that Joyce's visit to the camp was part of a scheme to break down Mr Mollison's refusal to organise the German's English radio programme, as will be seen by reference to a further statement made by Mr Mollison relative to four or five visits paid to him by Dietz, chief of the German Foreign Propaganda Section, whilst he was at Sandbostal and Milag Camps.

On the first occasion Dietz saw him it was apparent the Germans had been studying the Sandbostal Camp theatre shows organised and run by Mr Mollison. Dietz apparently made no direct offer to Mr Mollison to produce English programmes on the German radio but conveyed that idea by the general trend of his conversation. Mr Mollison says that he saw what was being suggested and said that he wanted nothing to do with such matters. Mr Mollison repeated his refusal when Dietz approached him a second time. Dietz then switched his conversation to the propaganda angle and tried to

P.-29756/10,000
Mar./1945 w112

42. Special Branch report and witness statement of the actor Henry Mollison, 5 June 1945, in which he explains how as a civilian internee Joyce attempted to persuade him to take part in propaganda activities. (KV 2/246/400a)

Page No. 2.

convince Mr Mollison how futile it was for the Allies to continue the war, etc. He paid two visits to Mr Mollison at Milag Camp and continued his propaganda talks but nothing was apparently said about Mr Mollison broadcasting. Obviously finding that he was making no headway he enlisted the aid of Joyce, his underling, in an endeavour to break down Mr Mollison's morale.

It seems not unlikely, but for the end of the war, that these visits and propaganda talks to Mr Mollison - and other leaders in the Milag Camp - by Dietz, and perhaps by Joyce, would have been carried on at intervals until he consented to produce and assist in the German's English broadcasts.

Submitted herewith are statements made by Mr Henry Mollison relative to his interview with William Joyce and his interviews with Dietz of the German Ministry of Propaganda.

P. Fletcher
Sergeant.

Submitted.

Sydney James
Inspector.

J B Biggs
for SUPERINTENDENT.

42. (continued) Special Branch report.

PY.

METROPOLITAN POLICE.   STATEMENT OF WITNESS   No. 995

Special Branch   CO   4th   June   , 194 5.
Station.   Division.

Name : Henry Mollison   Age : 40

Address : "Oakleigh", Stanmore Hill, Middlesex.

Occupation : Professional actor.

Statement :   "I was in South America at the outbreak of war in September,
1939 and I left Rio de Janeiro on 30th June, 1940 by the s.s. "Delembre"
to return to this country for the purpose of joining H.M. Forces. On
Sunday 7.7.40 the ship was intercepted and shelled by a German sea
raider. I was the only passenger. The crew and myself were taken off
by the raider, "Vir", and with the others I was on the "Vir" for about
* and a half months. I was then transferred to a prison ship at sea
... I was on there for about six weeks. We arrived at Bordeaux on
ecember 13th, 1940 and were kept aboard the ship for about six days,
during which time we were bombed by the R.A.F., the Germans having
abandoned ship and left us to our fate. At the end of the six days we
were taken off the ship and put in a camp in Bordeaux. We were
transferred from Bordeaux to Paris and were there about three months
until being transferred to Sandbostal, near Bremen. We were finally
moved to Milag, the Merchant Navy Camp near Bremen. I organised the
camp theatre. The Germans became very interested in the camp shows -
t y did in fact record, unknown to us, one of our shows and later
broadcast it over the German radio. One day, date unknown, some few
weeks before D. Day I was taken from the camp to the Dulag, known to us
as the interrogation centre for Merchant and Royal Navy prisoners, and
I was shown into a small room where I met a man aged about 38; shortish,
of somewhat broad build; fair hair with very fresh complexion; blue
eyes; I noticed particularly that he had a scar across his right cheek
to the corner of his mouth. After some little conversation I commented
on the fact that he spoke perfect English and he said, "I was born in
York of English-Irish parents, and I have lived most of my life
in the North of England". I said, "You are an Englishman" and he replied
"No I am German. I am English by birth but I am one hundred per cent
German
by feeling and by adoption". He subsequently admitted that he was
'Lord Haw Haw'. He shook hands with me and started a conversation
which struck me as being in the nature of a propaganda talk to impress
on me the fact that England would lose the war and that she was
starving. London, he said, was a shambles and he gave me details which
tended to show that one thousand yards, presumably square yards, of
Piccadilly, one thousand yards of Oxford Circus, and one thousand yards
of Leicester Square, and the City of London had been laid waste by
bombing. He suggested that there were many Germany sympathisers in
England and that there was also a very strong anti-jewish feeling .
Unity behind Churchill, he said, was not all that British propaganda
made it out to be. He continually suggested that I should spread the
information he gave me amongst the other prisoners in the camp. He then

Signature ....

Signature
witnessed by ....

(Continue overleaf if necessary.)

M.P.-27665/30,000 Mar./1944 A4 (4)

42. (continued) Statement of Henry Mollison

(2)

said, "Well you take one platform and I will take the other". It is
suggested to me that he wanted to engage in a debate - he did all the
talking however. He stressed that the British had been talking about
the invasion of Europe for a long time but it had not taken place --
he wanted to know why. I suggested that Churchill had bluffed the
Germans by continual talking and propagating the possibility of an
invasion of Europe. He very bitterly resented my statement that the
Germans had been bluffed by the English and told me that the only time
they had been bluffed was by the Russians. The Russians had allowed
the Germans to see only poor equipment and ragged soldiers at the
frontier established by the Germans and Russians in Poland. Apparently
the Germans were led to believe that the Russians were easy and they
received a great shock when they came up against the true Russian
Forces. He went on to say that in the view of the German High Command
the invasion attempt would be made in the autumn, but stopped himself
and said, "Of course I cannot give away too many secrets as I am in th
know". He expressed the view continually during our conversation that
the invasion of Europe was impossible because of the strong German
coastal defences and then went on to say that if by any chance the
Allies should land, the Germans would allow the landing to mature and
then wipe out the forces by "throwing them back into the sea".
Continuing he said, "Then while you are preparing another invasion,
which will take at least a year, we would in the meantime turn to the
East with all our forces and smash Russia, then we would come back and
invade England". I gathered the impression that Joyce was telling me
all this to note my reactions and also in the hope that I would spread
defeatist propaganda in the camp. After I left Joyce Major Harvey,
senior medical officer of Milag was taken in to see him. I had,
however, mentioned to him as I came out that the man in the room was
'Lord Haw Haw'.

                              (signed) Henry Mollison.
          Signature witnessed by (signed) R.Fletcher, P.S.(S.B.)

42. (continued) Statement of Henry Mollison.

COPY. Original filed in PF.44469
Supp. Pros. vol. held by
S.L.B.1.

S.L.B.3. Mr Wakefield
    for information and retention.

411a

N O T E.

1. At a Conference held this morning at the Chambers in the Central Criminal Court of Mr L.A. Byrne, Treasury Counsel, there were present:-

The Director of Public Prosecutions	
Colonel Hinchley Cooke	M.I.5
Lieut. Colonel Cussen	"
Mr Morgan	Director's Office
Mr Jackson	" "
Captain Skardon	M.I.5
Mr Sinclair	"
Inspector Bridges	Special Branch.
Mr Wakefield	*M.I.5.*

2. Mr Byrne opened the Conference by saying that in his view the case was one which would be fought by the Defence, in all probability, on the technicality of whether JOYCE was a British subject owing allegiance to His Majesty. The position was that JOYCE was born in America on April 24th, 1906, and in his statement under caution suggested that his father had been naturalised American. In these circumstances he, Mr Byrne, felt that it was essential to prove that JOYCE was not an American, and he accordingly asked for further enquiries to be made as to the possible naturalisation of JOYCE's father, and that a witness who could speak as to the enquiries made should be available at the trial. The evidence was not evidence which need be put in at the Police Court, and indeed might not need to be put in at the Old Bailey, but he preferred to have it available in case the point was taken. Lieut. Colonel Cussen drew attention to the Passport Application and suggested that JOYCE, by his passport declarations, was to be regarded as a person owing allegiance to His Majesty. Mr Byrne stated that this was not necessarily conclusive, for which reason he was asking for this additional evidence. It was arranged that Mr Morgan and Mr Sinclair should confer as to exactly what was wanted.

3. A general discussion took place as to what witnesses should be called, and the following conclusions were arrived at:-

    a) Mr Godwin, to prove the Passport Application.

    b) Inspector Hunt to prove his familiarity with JOYCE's voice over a period of years, and the transcripts made by him from time to time, particularly that of the record of April 30th 1945.

    c) Captain Skardon, to prove the statement under caution and the documents found either in JOYCE's possession or at his lodgings, and admitted by JOYCE.

    d) Mr Salzedo, to prove the translations of the documents admitted by JOYCE to Captain Skardon.

    e) Mr Schneider, to prove the making of the record by JOYCE in his, Schneider's presence, of April 30th 1945, and to prove JOYCE's general broadcasting activities on behalf of the German Radio. In connection with this witness, Mr Byrne asked for an edited form of proof, confined to essentials.

4. It was also decided that some evidence of JOYCE's apprehension at Krussau should be given, and Captain Skardon undertook to take a statement from Captain Lickorish, who was responsible for this, and thereafter arrange for his and Mr Schneider's journey to England for the purpose both of the Police Court and Old Bailey proceedings. Mr Byrne also settled the charge.

Not used in trial

S.L.B.1.
14.6.45.

           D. H. Sinclair.

43. Notes of a meeting between the British prosecuting authorities, MI5 and Special Branch, 14 June 1945. This meeting was held just before Joyce's first court appearance. The notes show the deep concerns felt by all that Joyce might walk free on the grounds of his US nationality. (KV 2/246/411a)

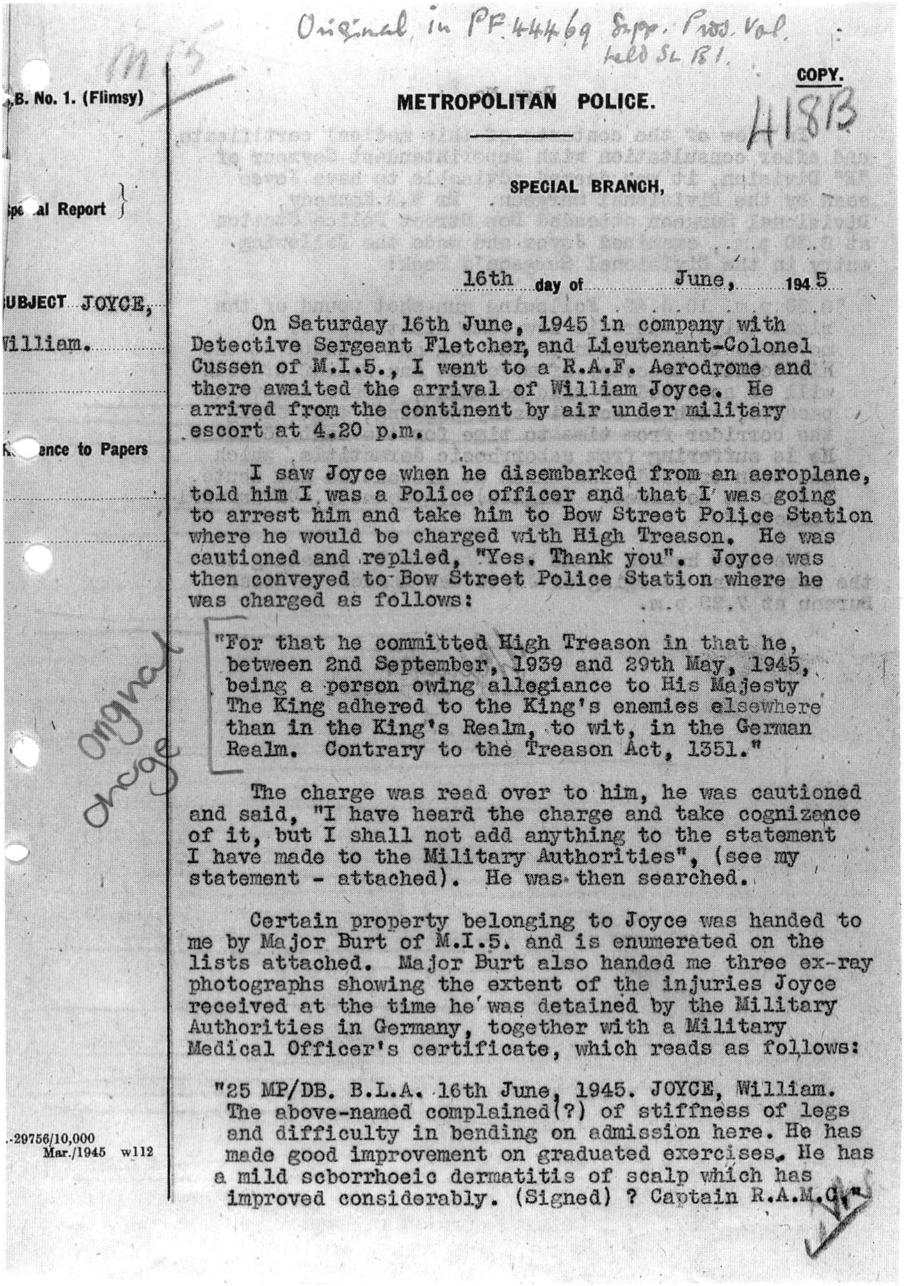

Original in PF 44469 Supp. Pros. Vol. held SL 181.

COPY.

,B. No. 1. (Flimsy)

METROPOLITAN POLICE.

418B

SPECIAL BRANCH,

Spe al Report

16th day of June, 1945

UBJECT JOYCE, William.

R ence to Papers

On Saturday 16th June, 1945 in company with Detective Sergeant Fletcher, and Lieutenant-Colonel Cussen of M.I.5., I went to a R.A.F. Aerodrome and there awaited the arrival of William Joyce. He arrived from the continent by air under military escort at 4.20 p.m.

I saw Joyce when he disembarked from an aeroplane, told him I was a Police officer and that I was going to arrest him and take him to Bow Street Police Station where he would be charged with High Treason. He was cautioned and replied, "Yes. Thank you". Joyce was then conveyed to Bow Street Police Station where he was charged as follows:

original charge

"For that he committed High Treason in that he, between 2nd September, 1939 and 29th May, 1945, being a person owing allegiance to His Majesty The King adhered to the King's enemies elsewhere than in the King's Realm, to wit, in the German Realm. Contrary to the Treason Act, 1351."

The charge was read over to him, he was cautioned and said, "I have heard the charge and take cognizance of it, but I shall not add anything to the statement I have made to the Military Authorities", (see my statement - attached). He was then searched.

Certain property belonging to Joyce was handed to me by Major Burt of M.I.5. and is enumerated on the lists attached. Major Burt also handed me three ex-ray photographs showing the extent of the injuries Joyce received at the time he was detained by the Military Authorities in Germany, together with a Military Medical Officer's certificate, which reads as follows:

"25 MP/DB. B.L.A. 16th June, 1945. JOYCE, William. The above-named complained(?) of stiffness of legs and difficulty in bending on admission here. He has made good improvement on graduated exercises. He has a mild seborrhoeic dermatitis of scalp which has improved considerably. (Signed) ? Captain R.A.M.C."

-29756/10,000 Mar./1945 w112

44. Reports and other documents concerning the arrangements made for the return of William Joyce to Britain. This collection includes a Special Branch report dated 16 June 1945 describing Joyce's return to Britain and his being charged with high treason, and a list of his property at that date (not shown). (KV 2/246/418b)

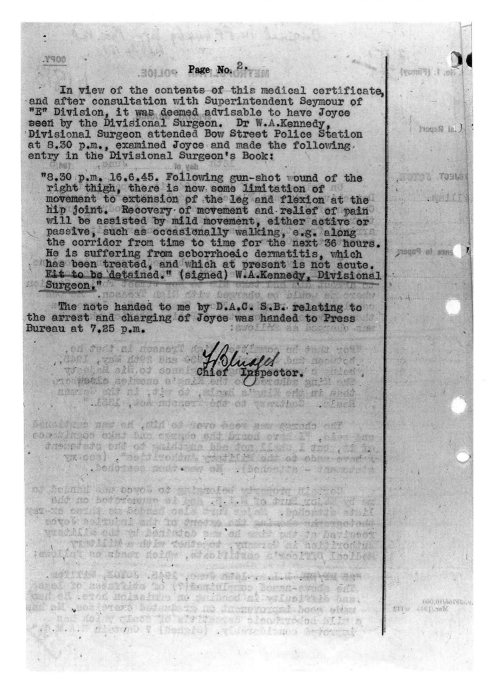

In view of the contents of this medical certificate, and after consultation with Superintendent Seymour of "E" Division, it was deemed advisable to have Joyce seen by the Divisional Surgeon. Dr W.A.Kennedy, Divisional Surgeon attended Bow Street Police Station at 8.30 p.m., examined Joyce and made the following entry in the Divisional Surgeon's Book:

"8.30 p.m. 16.6.45. Following gun-shot wound of the right thigh, there is now some limitation of movement to extension of the leg and flexion at the hip joint. Recovery of movement and relief of pain will be assisted by mild movement, either active or passive, such as occasionally walking, e.g. along the corridor from time to time for the next 36 hours. He is suffering from seborrhoeic dermatitis, which has been treated, and which at present is not acute. Fit to be detained." (signed) W.A.Kennedy, Divisional Surgeon."

The note handed to me by D.A.C. S.B. relating to the arrest and charging of Joyce was handed to Press Bureau at 7.25 p.m.

F.Bridges
Chief Inspector.

Original filed in PF44469 Supp. Prod. vol.

Special Branch,
16th June, 1945.

STATEMENT of Chief Inspector Frank BRIDGES, Special Branch
New Scotland Yard, S.W.1.

"At 4.20 p.m. on 16th June, 1945, I saw William Joyce on his
arrival in this country under military escort. I told him I was a
Police officer and that I was going to arrest him and take him to
Bow Street Police Station where he would be charged with High
Treason. He was cautioned and replied, "Yes. Thank you". Later
in the day he was charged with an offence contrary to the Treason
Act, 1351. The charge was read over to him, he was cautioned,
and he said, "I have heard the charge and take cognizance of it,
but I shall not add anything to the statement I have made to the
Military Authorities."

Frank Bridges

44. (continued) Documentation on the arrangements for Joyce's return to Britain.

Reference...

SPECIAL DETAIL FOR BRUSSELS, 16th June 1945.

Arrangements have been made for a special aircraft to leave Hendon Airport at 0900 hours carrying Major M. Johnstone, Intelligence Corps, and two other ranks, C.M.P.

The aircraft should reach B.56 at approximately 10.30 hours.

On arrival Major Johnstone will report to the officer in charge of Security Control in the main airport building, informing the latter that he is expecting the arrival from Brussels of Major Burt, Intelligence Corps, together with a passenger.

The party is scheduled to leave B.56 at approximately 1430 hours, and will put down at Odiham airport at approximately 1600 hours.

The journey to London will be completed by road.

Major Burt will proceed to Brussels by service aircraft on 15th June 1945.

14.6.45.

(117) Wt12861/1551
500,000 5/41 JC&SLtd
Gp736/210
(REGIMITE)

P.F.44469/SLB3

Arrangements regarding William JOYCE.

1.   Lt.-Col. Cussen, Chief Inspector Bridges and other
Police officers, will leave London by cars at 1000 hours
and will arrive at Headquarters, Hampshire County Police,
Winchester, at about 12 noon, where contact can be made with
them by telephone if necessary.

2.   As soon as the aircraft carrying Major Burt, Major
Johnstone, two C.M.P.s and JOYCE, is airborne at Brussels
(this should be about 1430 hours), Lt.-Col. Brooke-Booth,
SHAEF Mission to Belgium at Brussels, will telephone to Mr.
Sinclair conveying the information.

3.   Lt.-Col. Cussen will telephone from Hampshire to Mr.
Sinclair at about 1500 hours in order to see what the position
is.   At that time he will, if possible, give Mr. Sinclair a
telephone number where he can be contacted at the air station
(Odiham).

4.   In the event of the aircraft landing at a station other
than Odiham, Major Johnstone or Major Burt will telephone to
Mr. Sinclair in order that he may inform Lt.-Col. Cussen
where the aircraft is.   Lt.-Col. Cussen's party will then
proceed by car as soon as possible to the other air station.

NOTE: In order to speak to Lt.-Col. Brooke-Booth in case of
emergency, ask our switchboard to put through a priority call,
authorised by Lt.-Col. Cussen, to Lt.-Col. Brooke-Booth
personally at SHAEF Mission to Belgium, Brussels.

15.6.45.
EJPC/MKM

44. (continued) Documentation on the arrangements for Joyce's return to Britain.

Copy. Original 6 ... Sinclair
for Prosecution Volume.
6

447B

S. L. B. 1.
Mr. Sinclair.

William JOYCE.

You may like to have the following Note on the visitors and Correspondence reports.

A. VISITORS.

The regular visitors have been his brother Quentin and John McNAB.

1.   On June 22nd he told Quentin that he was drunk when he made the recording for his final broadcast.

2.   On June 28th Quentin said a cable had been received from the STANTONs in America.   William said "he remembered his mother telling him about a year or two before the war that his father was stateless, and he was wondering how she had obtained the information.   Maybe it was something to do with Insurance, as he remembered her saying about his father being younger than he had believed.   Quentin said he was trying to get some information about this and was going to write to Pennsylvania that day.   William said he believed his father became a naturalized American, but lost his American citizenship through failing to renew his papers.   If there was no record of it in New York, there might be in Jersey.   He said he supposed that the copy of "Twilight over England" which the Prosecution had got, was the copy Margaret had kept with her belongings.   A large number had been sold in P. of War camps.

3.   On June 29th he told Quentin that Mr. Head was getting advice from an American lawyer, and that, though the burden of proof was on the Prosecution, the Defence would have to have some evidence to put against theirs.

4.   On July 2nd he said that "upon one piece of information supplied this morning", his counsel were "very hopeful".   He asked Quentin to see Mr. Head and "press the point about the High Commissioner as it was very important".

B. CORRESPONDENCE.

This is nearly all of F.3. interest - letters of sympathy from Fascists etc., with occasional letters of abuse (or sheer insanity).

A letter from Leonard SINCLAIR suggests that the writer was one of the people who saw JOYCE off from Victoria in August 1939.

45. MI5 notes relating to Joyce's visitors and correspondence while on remand at Brixton prison in June and early July 1945. One note appears to confirm the view that Joyce was drunk when he made the recording of his final broadcast. (KV 2/246/447b)

S.L.B.3.   Colonel Cussen   86 13/7   8.A.

    I attach Margaret JOYCE's letter to William,
with extracts of the more interesting passages.   You
said you would send it on.

                              G.E. Wakefield.

S.L.B.3
11.7.45

                              For delivery on 16.7.45.

46. MI5 kept a close watch on the correspondence between Joyce and his wife, as these notes indicate. (KV 2/246/454b)

Extracts from letter from Margaret JOYCE to her husband
dated Brussels 1.7.45.

"I certainly got good and left behind this time! And now
they cant read the markings on my fleece and dont really know to
what flock I belong. Really, the young Intelli-gent who acted
as postman came along yesterday and wanted to know who brought
me here and why, because they have no papers about me at the
Intelli-gentsia and dont really believe in me. Fortunately, I
was able to tell him to whom I had been officially handed over
or whatever happened. It sounds a little as though the old
portcullis is beginning to creek. I dont know whether to be
glad or not. It would be nice to be in the same town or
country as you, but on the other hand an English prison, although
more civilised, no doubt, would certainly not be so homely as
this one. The nuns destroy the prison atmosphere, and the fact
that most of the other prisoners are also at least partly of
the right way of thinking, is very comforting.

However, nothing has happened yet, and in the meantime
the Intelli-gents are evidently making themselves responsible
for me, which is nice, because although in common with most of
their fellow-countrymen, they may be 'idiotes', they do know
their own job and are always extremely courteous and even kind.
Yesterday the "postman" brought along a nice A.T.S. officer to
see me in case there were any female oddments I needed ....
I am being well cared for and as we are "Obdachlos" and
"Arbeitslos", it is not too bad being here ....

I wish I knew what was happening. Neither the postman nor
the A.T.S. had the slightest idea as to whether you had been
committed for trial or not. That is the worst thing, not knowing
what is happening. Not only about us (which is frankly, Hell) but
in general.

What has happened to old Quisling? Have they caught that
swine Ribbentrop? What is Russia doing about Japan? ....
Did they change your German money, or is that with mine here?
If it is, I have the impression that a lot of yours was stolen.
Something the handsome Intelli-gent Major Randall said at Luneburg gave me the idea that I had yours too ..... Fortunately,I
managed to hang on to my cash until to got to Luneburg. The

Luneburgians were deathly honest, and the fact that some things
are missing is due to the fact that they are not expert packers
and not to ill will .....

If I should be taken to England and charged, I shall get
in touch with Head at once ...... I am the only one with a cell
to myself and British officers come to see me. My social
standing is something that would even get by in Boston.

3.7.45. Just got your letter.

(Sgd.) Your Wife.
Margaret.

454a

Your Ref. 300/FAS/254A
Our Ref: PF.66003/S.L.B.1.   11th July, 1945.

Deputy Assistant Commissioner,
Special Branch.

Rex v. William JOYCE.

Reference Chief Inspector Bridges' report dated 6 July 45 attaching copy of a letter received by him from Edwin Quentin JOYCE together with a communication addressed by the latter to Mrs. Margaret JOYCE.

The letter addressed to Mrs. JOYCE is being forwarded through official channels and Chief Inspector Bridges is at liberty to inform E.Q. JOYCE accordingly, if he wishes to do so.

NG

Colonel.

47. Correspondence of Quentin Joyce received by MI5, plus MI5 internal documentation (sequence as preserved in the files). The letter of 4 July 1945 reached Margaret in her Brussels prison giving her the first news of her husband's condition. (KV 2/246/454a)

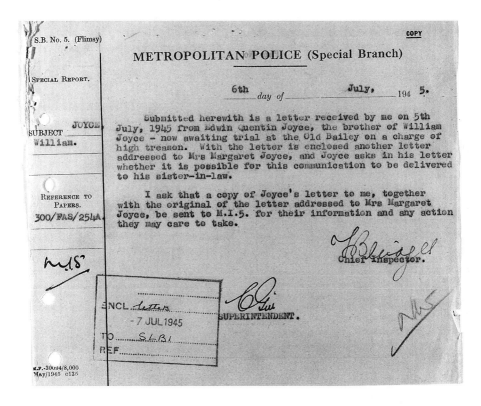

S.B. No. 5. (Flimsy)

COPY

METROPOLITAN POLICE (Special Branch)

SPECIAL REPORT.

6th _day of_ July, 194 5.

SUBJECT JOYCE William.

REFERENCE TO PAPERS.

300/FAS/254A.

Submitted herewith is a letter received by me on 5th July, 1945 from Edwin Quentin Joyce, the brother of William Joyce – now awaiting trial at the Old Bailey on a charge of high treason. With the letter is enclosed another letter addressed to Mrs Margaret Joyce, and Joyce asks in his letter whether it is possible for this communication to be delivered to his sister-in-law.

I ask that a copy of Joyce's letter to me, together with the original of the letter addressed to Mrs Margaret Joyce, be sent to M.I.5. for their information and any action they may care to take.

Chief Inspector.

ENCL. letters.

- 7 JUL 1945

SUPERINTENDENT.

TO S.L.B.I

REF

M.P.-30094/8,000
May/1945 c135

86, Underhill Road,

East Dulwich,

London. S.E.22.

4th July, 1945.

My dear Margaret,

In the hope that the Security Department will
have no objection to your receiving this short letter from me,
I am writing a few lines to enquire how you are getting on, and
to express the fervent hope that you are not finding your present
environment, wherever it may be, too oppressive.

I have been wanting to write to you for a long time - ever
since I read of your arrest and detention; but I hadn't the
slightest idea of your whereabouts. The many contradictory
Press references only succeeded in making the question even more
obscure.

First and foremost, I hope that you are in good health.
From the pictures I have seen of you in the Press and on the
news-reel, you certainly appear pretty fit.   Secondly, I hope
that you are not too uncomfortable where you are, and that your
custodians are treating you with due consideration.

Now, my dear Margaret, I know that your main source of
anxiety will be over William. Well, as you may have heard from
him by now, I see him very frequently - almost every day, in
fact, and his spirit is absolutely magnificent.   I have always
been considered a fairly cheerful sort of character myself; but
by comparison with him I must appear a real Dismal Desmond! My
first visit to him had a really tonic effect on me. I was amazed
by his cheerfulness and his complete indifference to his immediate
surroundings.   His only worry was that he had not been able to
get any news of you, and he was anxious for your sake. However,
he tells me that he has now received permission to correspond
with you, and that is a very great relief to him.

As regards his health, he is improving every day.   When
I first saw him, he was very far from well, having no colour at
all.   His limp was most pronounced and he was suffering a certain amount of pain from the wound he received.   Now, after a
couple of weeks in Brixton, he is pulling round in a miraculous
manner.   The wound has healed very well, and he is experiencing
no pain from it at all.   He is putting on weight, and he is
gaining more colour every day.   His only trouble at present is
from his ankle which has given him some pain at night. He is
receiving treatment for it, and I expect that in the course of
two or three weeks he will be all right again.   So, Margaret,
please don't worry about his health - he is doing better than

47. (continued) Quentin Joyce's letter to Margaret Joyce.

could be expected.

With regard to the forthcoming proceedings at the Old Bailey, please don't worry - I feel that everything will turn out all right. At this stage one cannot serve any useful purpose by discussing the case - we must contain ourselves in patience.

Your Mother called to see William last week, and she took the news very well. William will have told you about the visit in the letter he wrote on, I believe, the following day.

When I know that we are permitted to correspond, I shall write to you at greater length and let you have all the news. In the meantime, my dear Margaret, keep your chin up and keep smiling - the darkest hour always comes before the dawn.

With all best wishes and lots of love,

As ever,

Get help reading

Killour Neale
14th (7) 1945

Dear Quentin

I received
your letter in due time but
I was waiting to get some
information regarding your
father from some of his associates
the worst of it is those who
were very confidentel friends
of his are dead but I may run
accross some one later who woul.
be a help to us I have made a
dilligent search for a letter or
card of the date you mentioned
but did not run accross any
our friends in the united states
could have some valuable letters
if we only could get them.
If we could locate Tommy Stanton
he would be a help to us

47. (continued) Letter to Quentin Joyce from an Irish relative.

As regards me going to London I would certainly like to but presently I am not feeling very good I got a severe dose of the flue and I am not fully recovered from it as yet it stuck on to me for four or five weeks and almost paralyzed me I would like very much to help you out and I am very grateful to you for all your trouble regarding Willie. However if I feel fit later on I will let you know. We are sorry to hear of your mothers death as she was a friend whose company we much appreciated, may she rest in peace Hoping you will excuse this short letter I am dear Quentin faithfully yours. P. Joyce

C O P Y   86 Underhill Road,
                        East Dulwich,
                        London, S.E.22.

                        4th July, 1945

Chief Inspector T. Bridges,
Special Branch,
New Scotland Yard,
Westminster,
London, S.W.1.

Dear Sir,

re Mrs. Margaret Joyce

      I would very much like to communicate with my sister-in-law,
Mrs. Margaret Joyce, who is at present detained in, I believe,
military custody somewhere in Belgium.

      Very naturally, both my brother, William, and I would like
to get some news of her, and to satisfy ourselves that she is being
well cared for wherever she may be. My brother has been very
anxious because he has had no news of her since he was in Flensburg,
and although he has written to her, he has, as yet, received no
reply to his letters.

      I feel that she, also, must be very worried because she has
had no news of him, and I want to do my utmost to reassure her
that my brother's health is improving daily, and his spirits have
never been higher.

      I know that, strictly speaking, the Special Branch is not
directly concerned with my sister-in-law's position at present;
but I would be more than grateful for any assistance you could give
me in this matter. As I haven't the foggiest idea of the correct
procedure to adopt, perhaps you would be kind enough to advise me
on this point. I enclose a short letter which I have addressed
to Margaret, and if it is at all possible for you to have it sent
to the appropriate authorities for onward transmission and delivery,
I shall be most pleased.

      Assuring you of my sincere appreciation for any assistance
which you might be able to render me.

              I beg to remain,

                Yours faithfully,

                (Sgd.) E. Quentin Joyce

47. (continued) Letter from Quentin Joyce to Special Branch.

E. Quentin Joyce, Esq.,

86,Underhill Road,

East Dulwich,

LONDON, S.E.

LUDLOW & CO.
H.S.LUDLOW. C.B.V.HEAD.
SOLICITORS.

Amalgamating
HARRY WILSON & CO.
EDGAR SMITH & CO.

COMMISSIONERS FOR OATHS,
ENGLAND,TRANSVAAL
AND
AUSTRALIA.

TELEPHONE
TEMPLE BAR 7910.

BROAD COURT CHAMBERS,
BOW STREET,
COVENT GARDEN,
LONDON, W.C.2.

12th July, 19 45.

Our Ref.J.44.

E.Quentin Joyce,Esq.,
86, Underhill Road,
East Dulwich,
S.E.22.

Dear Mr. Joyce,

Re: YOUR BROTHER.

I am in receipt of your letter of yesterday.

Our Manchester Agent telephoned us this morning and stated that he had telephoned your uncle and was arranging to see him later in the day.

In case I am not in when you telephone tomorrow morning I am writing to inform you so that you can let your brother know when you see him that arrangements have been made for the three Counsel to visit him with me on Saturday morning.

I understand the case is to commence on Monday week the 23rd instant.

Yours truly,

[signature]

48. Correspondence between Quentin Joyce and Ludlow & Co (William Joyce's lawyers), 12 July 1945. During the period leading up to the Old Bailey trial MI5 received regular mail intercepts and photostats of correspondence between Quentin Joyce and his brother's lawyers discussing matters relating to the defence case. (KV 2/246)

Copy filed in PF.44469 Ord. Vol.

61 A

N O T E

1.   At a conference with the Director of Public Prosecutions, with whom was Mr R.L. Jackson, there were present:-

Lieut. Colonel Cussen	Security Service
Mr M.J. Lynch	F.B.I.
Mr Wakefield	Security Service
Mr Sinclair	" "

2.   The Director opened the conference by saying that he had called it because he understood that Mr G.O. Slade, K.C., who was leading for the Defence, was intending to apply for the case to stand over until the September sessions, and subject to anything that either M.I.5 or the F.B.I. had to say, he did not see how such an application could be resisted.

3.   The Director continued by saying that Mr Head, the solicitor for the Defence, had, through the Foreign Office, been making certain inquiries as to the naturalisation of JOYCE's father as an American citizen, and these inquiries were still under way, and it was now known that the British Consul in New York had found evidence of a Michael JOYCE being naturalised in Brooklyn; therefore as these inquiries were still far from complete it seemed to him that the application to stand over could not be resisted. An additional factor which made it impossible to resist it was that the inquiries instituted by the F.B.I. on behalf of M.I.5 were also still in progress.

4.   Mr Jackson suggested that the best course to adopt would be one which really placed upon the Defence the making of the application rather than that the Prosecution should make the application. The Director agreed with this, as did others present, and stated that he would consult with Counsel the following morning.

5.   A long discussion took place as to the inquiries which were being carried out in the United States by the F.B.I., and the Director intimated that subject to Counsel's view, he proposed to tell Mr Head that these inquiries were being made at the same time as the latter's inquiries were being made through the Foreign Office. His reason for telling Mr Head this was that H.M. Consul in New York was obviously having certain difficulty in making the inquiries and whilst he did not wish Mr Head to bind himself in any way by the result of the F.B.I. inquiries, he thought it only right that he should know that this was being done, and that, moreover, the inquiries were of an exhaustive character. At all times Mr Head would be left to pursue his own inquiries through the Foreign Office if he thought fit.

        The question of calling William JOYCE's uncle, Mr BROOKE, was also considered. Mr Wakefield said that he believed that this man was not at all favourably disposed to William JOYCE, but at the same time was not in the slightest degree anxious to give evidence in a case which would do him harm. Mr Jackson stated that considerations such as this were irrelevant, and that he would have to attend on the subpoena. On closer examination, however, of the evidence that could possibly be given by Mr BROOKE, it was felt that he would be of much assistance, as he was never in the United States at the time of the marriage.

6.   The question of what the Prosecution could adduce in evidence as a result of the inquiries was also discussed at length; the difficulties both from the Prosecution and Defence point of view were carefully considered. Both the Director and Mr Jackson stated that in their view the Marriage Certificate of Michael JOYCE and Gertrude Emily BROOKE would not be admissible, unless by some fortunate chance the parties at the time of the marriage were living at Herkomer Street, the address given as their residence in William JOYCE's birth certificate. The Director stated that in his view the Prosecution would have some difficulty in rebutting JOYCE's claim that any particular Michael JOYCE, who had been naturalised, was his father, unless it could be shown conclusively that the Michael JOYCE chosen from the point of view of age, address, and whether he was a bachelor or not, simply could not be William JOYCE's father.

7.../

- 7 -

7. The Director concluded the conference by saying that the inquiries were still of an urgent character, even though it was now almost certain that the case would be stood over until the September sessions, and he asked Mr Lynch if this could be impressed upon those making them in the United States. The Director invited Lieut. Colonel Cussen to attend with him upon Counsel on the following morning.

D. H. Sinclair.

S.L.B.1.
16.7.45.

49. (opposite and above) Notes of a meeting between the prosecution authorities and the security agencies, 16 July 1945. This again shows the worries felt about the apparent weakness of the prosecution case. (KV 2/249/61a)

160 Carteret Ave.

Jersey City,N.J.

July 31st,1945.

Dear Quentin :

In reply to your letter of July 21st,I find it very difficult to be of assistance to you because of the long period of time which has elapsed since your father was here. There were letters and papers of your father's which undoubtedly had his signature, but they wre destroyed long ago.

He worked for the Griffin Iron Works, now out of existence, for the Pennsylvania Railroad and the Naughton Construction Co. of Brooklyn. Naughton and a man named Freedman were partners with your father in this concern. I believe it is long out of business. John Ferris has been dead several years.

Would advise that your attorney try to trace the witnesses of the naturalization papers, as I do not know whether they are living or not. Lawyers have opportunities of securing information which others have not.

We are very sorry for the predicament your family is in and hope things may turn out for the best.

Sincerely,

Your Uncle,

E 84 H

50. Letter of 31 July 1945 received by Quentin Joyce from a relative in America regarding his brother's defence. This interception, and the accompanying MI5 memorandum, show how determined the agency was to obtain all the details it could about the defence case. (KV 2/246/479c)

LUDLOW & CO.
K.S.LUDLOW, C.S.V.HEAD.
SOLICITORS.
Amalgemating
«HARRY WILSON & CO.
EDGAR SMITH & CO.
COMMISSIONERS FOR OATHS.
ENGLAND,TRANSVAAL
AND
AUSTRALIA.
TELEPHONE
TEMPLE BAR 7910.

BROAD COURT CHAMBERS,
BOW STREET,
COVENT GARDEN,
LONDON, W.C.2.

25th September, 1945.

J. A. MacNab, Esq.,
6, Cleverton Street,
S.W.1.

J/44.

Dear Mr. MacNabb,

Rex v. Joyce.

I have very carefully considered the contents of your letter of yesterday and, not only because of your appreciation, I should like to say at once what very great assistance we and Counsel have had from you and Mr. Joyce in the matter.

The difficulty with regard to passport arguments is not only that the arguments must be good in themselves but to be any use they must be such as will commend themselves to the particular court before which Counsel is pleading.

If it is of any interest to you my own views to passports is that the primary object of them is not to confer protection on the holders but to be really a reference as to the bona fides of the holder given between one state and another state. If this is correct the question of whether something done by the holder of a passport matters to this country or not does not really arise until there is some complaint by the country into which the holder of the passport has arrived on the strength of the passport. In other words, in my view the strict position is that if Germany does not complain as to Mr. Joyce's conduct while the holder of a British passport this country should not have any complaint. These and all relevant matters are being considered by Counsel but, for the reasons which I have mentioned, only some of the arguments which you and Mr. Joyce may consider

valuable will be used in the Court of Criminal Appeal or as grounds of appeal.

If the case eventually goes to the House of Lords either one of the Counsel or myself will thoroughly investigate the position of passports from a historical point of view but there will be little hope of a lengthy argument based on such material finding any support in the Court of Criminal Appeal.

Yours truly,

51. Letter from Ludlow & Co to John Macnab, 25 September 1945. This mail intercept of a letter from William Joyce's lawyer to his friend shows that it was not only family members and lawyers who came under the scrutiny of MI5, but in fact anyone suspected of aiding the defence of his case. (KV 2/247/502b)

8ᵃ

S T A T E M E N T OF Mrs. Doreen Constance Abdel FATTAH of
126, Elgin Avenue, W.9.,   who says:-

        I have been in the employment of the British Broadcasting
Corporation since 1938.

        From September 1939 until December 1941, I was an English Monitor
in the Monitoring Service of the British Broadcasting Corporation. As
such my duties involved the monitoring of broadcasts over the German Radio
in English. All such broadcasts were until about late 1940 news items with
occasional comments by unannounced speakers.

        In the Monitoring Service of the Corporation, there was a great
deal of speculation as to the identity of the various speakers. One of the
speakers, who spoke with a cultured accent was to my knowledge dubbed by
the British Press as "Lord HAW-HAW". There was, however, another speaker
with an equally distinctive voice to whom the Press gave no appellation.
I myself christened him SINISTER SAM to distinguish him from the then
Lord HAW-HAW.

        I produce my original transcript of my shorthand notes of a broad-
cast made by SINISTER SAM on June 22nd, 1940, over Bremen.

        Later in the year 1940, the person whom I had christened SINISTER
SAM was announced over the German Radio as Lord HAW-HAW. I have no doubt
as to this, owing to the unmistakeable nature of the speaker's voice.

        Still later on and in about the middle of 1941, the speaker
christened by me as SINISTER SAM and announced as Lord HAW-HAW, was further
identified by being announced as William JOYCE.

        This statement has been read over by me and is true.

                            (signed) Doreen C. Abdel FATTAH.

8.9.45.

52. Statement of Mrs Doreen Constance Abdel Fattah, 8 September 1945. Mrs Fattah was
a member of the BBC monitoring service during the early years of the Second World War
and was responsible for making many of the transcripts of Joyce's broadcasts. In this pre-
trial witness statement she explains how in 1939 she came to name the then anonymous
broadcaster William Joyce 'Sinister Sam' to distinguish him from Baillie Stewart, the
original 'Lord Haw Haw'. (KV 2/249/87a)

Rex v. William JOYCE.

The trial of William JOYCE took place on Monday, Tuesday and Wednesday – 17th, 18th and 19th September, 1945 – before Tucker. J. at the Central Criminal Court. The Attorney General (Sir Hartley Shawcross, K.C.), Mr. L.A. Byrne and Mr. Gerald Howard (instructed by the Director of Public Prosecutions) appeared on behalf of the Crown, and JOYCE was defended by Mr. G.O. Slade, K.C., Mr. Derek Curtis Bennett, K.C. and Mr. G.C. Burge (instructed by Messrs. Ludlow & Co.).

2.   There were three Counts in the Indictment and of these, Counts 1 and 2 were amended during the course of the trial (see 99a). The third Count alleged that JOYCE owed an allegiance to the King between September 18th, 1939, and July 2nd, 1940, when his passport expired.

3.   A long legal argument ensued in connection with Count 3, it being contended by Mr. Slade that JOYCE, having proved himself to be an American citizen, could not possibly have owed any allegiance at any time to the King and indeed, the Court had no jurisdiction to try him in respect of an offence of treason not committed in this country. At the conclusion of this legal argument Tucker. J. ruled that during the currency of his British passport, JOYCE owed an allegiance to the King.

4.   Tucker. J. in the summing up directed the jury to acquit JOYCE on Counts 1 and 2 and then invited them on Count 3 to consider whether the prosecution had proved that JOYCE had broadcast propaganda over the German radio as between September 18th, 1939, and July 2nd, 1940; if the jury found that he had so done, then their verdict should be one of 'Guilty'. The jury, after a retirement of twenty-five minutes, returned a verdict of 'Not Guilty' on Counts 1 and 2 and a verdict of 'Guilty' on Count 3, and JOYCE was sentenced to death.

...

-2-

5.   It being understood that JOYCE is lodging an appeal as soon as may be, it is intended to obtain a copy of the shorthand note from the Court of Criminal Appeal.

S.L.B.1.
22.9.45.

53. Note on the MI5 file, 22 September 1945, showing the results of the Old Bailey trial and indicating the possibility of an appeal. (KV 2/249/100a)

for PA. 502a

Refs: P.F.44469/SLB3
         P.F.410,445/SLB3
Yr.Refs: 9/1660/44
          1/954/45   25th September, 1945.

                Rex   v.   William JOYCE.
                Rex   v.   John AMERY.

        I am sending to you herewith two copies of an excerpt
from the B.B.C. Digest which sets out certain broadcasts
made from Moscow on September 19th last.

        I hesitate to think what Moscow will say if it should
so happen that the House of Lords should take a view
favourable to JOYCE.   I am sure they will never understand
that the House of Lords in its judicial capacity is a
professional body, but that they will regard it as an inter-
vention by Reaction to save JOYCE at all costs.

        On the other hand, if the House of Lords accept the
Crown's view on the law, the reputation of that body in the
East will increase accordingly.

                                E.J.P. Cussen.

Theobald Mathew, Esq., M.C.,
Director of Public Prosecutions,
Devonshire House,
Mayfair Place,
Piccadilly, W.1.

54. Note on the MI5 file, 25 September 1945. Even after Joyce's Old Bailey trial MI5 lived
in fear of an acquittal in the House of Lords. This note and the accompanying transcripts
of Moscow broadcasts illustrate just how the pressure was being maintained.
(KV 2/247/502a)

Extract from B.B.C. DAILY DIGEST of WORLD BROADCASTS.
No. 2256. Date: Thursday, 20th September 1945.

MOSCOW IN ENGLISH   20.00   19.9.45   (MIIO)

"New Times" Article: "International Law"

British Reactionaries Seek to Protect John Amery

    John Amery, son of the Conservative Leopold Amery, ex-Secretary of
State for India and Burma, worked during the war in the service of the Nazis.
He unreservedly placed his talents, name and irreproachable English at the
service of Goebbels. John Amery toured the occupied countries, declaring that
only the German Army stood between civilisation and barbarism. He assured
Britain over the radio that it was in her interests to join the New Europe
and gloated over the effectiveness of the German bombing of London. But all
things come to an end and on 22nd April this year, Mr. Amery Jr., Englishman
and son of an English Cabinet Minister, was arrested by English troops.
Shakespeare would have loved such a situation - the tragedy of a highly
patriotic family, which suddenly discovered a traitor in its midst, who
betrayed his country and was brought before its Courts to receive merited
punishment; family and society unanimously turning their backs on their
contemptible offspring; a brother imploring to be allowed to carry out the
sentence on the criminal with his own hand and so on. However, modern
reality would have disenchanted the great English writer. It would be unfair,
of course, to say that John Amery's activities caused unalloyed gratification
to the British reactionaries. They would have preferred him to help Hitler
in more respectable ways, like F.A. Voigt, Eleanor Rathbone and others.
But putting aside sentimental talk about country and patriotism, John Amery,
after all, is one of their own and something had to be done to save him.
Time passed, but there was no signs of a trial. This extraordinary dilator-
iness aroused public comment. John Amery's father had an unpleasant quarter
of an hour when, on 29th June at an election meeting, he was asked by his
constituents why his son was still unpunished. "It has nothing to do with
me. It is a matter for justice," he replied. "That unhappy man's fate is
to be decided by the Courts of Law".

    Two and a half months after John Amery's arrest, he was brought to
London and finally even the date of the trial had to be appointed. The
Central Criminal Court in London proceeded with the case. Amery's protectors
were alarmed. But it appears that there are still sticklers for the law in
England, compared with whom some of Dickens's characters were mere infants.
At the last moment, when the trial had already begun, the Defence delivered
a knock-out blow. He declared that during the war in Spain, John Amery had
renounced the honour of British citizenship and had become a subject of France.
"Well if that's the case, of course, we can't try him," the judges declared
with a shrug of relief. The trial of John Amery has been delayed and his
brother, Capt. Julian Amery, has gone to Spain to ascertainhow they view the
matter over there: whether according to Fascist law an Englishman and son of
an Englishman can be tried for treasonable acts against England and whether this
double-dyed spy and Fascist really did put the betrayal of his country on a
legal footing by taking out Fascist citizenship. The judges are patiently
waiting for this obtuse psychological and legal problem to be cleared up.

MOSCOW IN ENGLISH   21.00   19.9.45   (MIIO)

Joyce Must Not Evade Punishment

Commentary by Mikhail Mikhailov

    Practically every hour, the BBC brings fresh reports from the Court
room where William Joyce, Lord Haw Haw, is facing trial.
I confess that every fresh BBC account leaves me more perplexed. The
impression one gathers is certainly peculiar, not because of the way the
trial is reported, but because of the way it is going. The reports are
vivid and I can visualise the proceedings in the London Criminal Court,
which, the newspapers say is so stuffy that the judges suffer some dis-
comfort in their wigs and gowns. Joyce, on the other hand, they say, is

feeling very pleased with himself. He smiles impudently and expects to get off scot free.

For six years Joyce helped the Germans. Listeners in the Anglo-Saxon countries know his voice. They remember his hundreds of frankly Nazi talks, his foul propaganda, directed first against Britain herself and also against her Allies. For six years Joyce slung mud at Britain and her statesmen, at the British people and all they hold dear. He talked of himself as an Englishman, but when he spoke English it was a traitor speaking, a creature who had sold himself to the Nazis, body and soul. Goebbels thought no end of Joyce, just because he was a 100 per cent Nazi, who spoke English as his native tongue. The only reason he did not get Joyce a German Military Cross was that it would have compromised Joyce as an Englishman. Times changed. Joyce's Berlin career ended. The British, who had warned Joyce repeatedly that he would be hanged as a traitor, could now keep their promise. Joyce found himself in custody and was brought to London. There the judges took an incredibly long time putting on their wigs. Finally they did get them on and the trial started.

As the Prosecution stated when the proceedings opened, Joyce is charged with the most heinous crime known to British Law. He is charged with High Treason on three counts. This statement seems to have made a big impression on everyone in Court except Joyce. He kept quite cool. The reason was not clear at first, but now it has been disclosed. Joyce is a sly as a fox. The Germans valued and paid him for being English, but Joyce could see what was coming and took precautions. He saw to it that he should have a daddy in New York, supposedly a naturalised US citizen and, therefore, a certificate to show that he himself was born in New York State. I say nothing about such a trifle as that William Joyce also produced a brother called Edwin Joyce, who told the Court a tearful tale of being bombed out by the Germans. The Court listened duly to Joyce himself, his brother and his council. Today we hear that two of the three charges have been quashed and the third hangs by a thread. No wonder Joyce is grinning. I can just see that grin. But joking aside, surely we are not to believe that an out-and-out traitor like Joyce is so easily to escape punishment. Naturally Courts cannot ignore the formalities or evade them, but there is a limit to everything. Joyce received a British passport more than once. He got a new one just before the war. He himself proclaimed he was a British subject. What more could be required? We remember the other recent traitor trial, that of John Amery. That trial was postponed as Amery claimed to be a subject of Franco. Now Joyce declares he's an American. He should be told that he has missed the bus. He was and remains a traitor and should be punished as such.

54. (continued) Transcripts from Moscow broadcast.

1.

<u>CAPITAL CASE</u>

528

FORM XXXIV.

To THE REGISTRAR of THE COURT OF CRIMINAL APPEAL.

NOTICE OF APPEAL OR APPLICATION FOR LEAVE TO APPEAL AGAINST
CONVICTION OR SENTENCE.

Name of Appellant............**William JOYCE**

Convicted at the (¹)............**Central ~~index~~ Criminal Court**
(1) Assizes, or County City or Borough Sessions.

Offence of which convicted (²)......**High Treason**
(2) e.g., Larceny, Forgery, Habitual Criminal.

Sentence................**Death**

Date when convicted (³)............**19th September 1945**
(3) Set out the actual date upon which the Appellant was convicted or sentenced.

Date when sentence passed (³)......**19th September 1945**

Name of Prison (⁴)............**Wormwood Scrubs**
(4) If not in custody here set out Appellant's address in full.

I the above-named Appellant hereby give you notice that
(5) If the Appellant wishes to appeal against conviction he must write the word "conviction." If he wishes to appeal against sentence he must write the word "sentence." If he wishes to appeal against both conviction and sentence he must write the words "conviction and sentence."

I desire to appeal to the Court of Criminal Appeal against

my (⁵) **conviction**

on the grounds hereinafter set forth on page 2 of this notice.
(6) This notice must be signed by the Appellant. If he cannot write he must affix his mark in the presence of a witness. The name and address of such attesting witness must be given.

(Signed) (⁶) **Wm. Joyce**

Appellant.

Dated this (⁷) **27th** day of **September** A.D. 19 **45** .
(7) If this notice is signed more than ten days after the conviction or sentence appealed against the Appellant must also fill in form IX., and send it with this notice.

<u>QUESTIONS.</u> (⁸)
ANSWERS.
(8) The Appellant must answer each of these questions.

1. Did the Judge before whom you were tried grant you a Certificate that it was a fit case for Appeal ?
   1. No

2. Do you desire the Court of Criminal Appeal to assign you legal aid ?
   2. No
   If your answer to this question is " Yes," then answer the following questions :—
   (a) What was your occupation and what wages, salary or income were you receiving before your conviction ?
   (b) Have you any means to enable you to obtain legal aid for yourself ?

3. Is any Solicitor now acting for you ? If so, give his name and address
   3. Yes.
   Ludlow & Co., Broad Court Chambers, Covent Garden, W.C.2.

4. Do you desire to be present when the Court considers your appeal ? (⁹)
   4. Yes
   (9) An Appellant is not entitled to be present on the hearing of an application for leave to appeal.

5. Do you desire to apply for leave to call any witnesses on your appeal ?
   If your answer to this question is " Yes," you must also fill in form XXVI., and send it with this notice.
   5. No

(26001) Wt.40140/4474 5,000. 11/43 A.& E.W.Ltd. Gp.685

[TURN OVER

55. Such was MI5's continued interest in this case they even obtained copies of Joyce's notice of appeal of 27 September 1945, which set out the grounds for such an action. (KV 2/249/102a)

2

Grounds of Appeal or Application.

These must be filled in before the notice is sent to the Registrar.

The Appellant must here set out the grounds or reasons he alleges why his conviction should be quashed or his sentence reduced.

If one of the grounds set out is "misdirection" by the Judge, particulars of such alleged misdirection must be set out in this notice.
The Appellant can also, if he wishes, set out his case and argument fully.

1. The Court wrongly assumed jurisdiction to try an alien for an offence against British Law committed in a foreign country.

2. The Learned Judge was wrong in law in holding and misdirected the jury in directing them, that the Appellant owed allegiance to His Majesty the King during the period from 18th September, 1939 to 2nd July, 1940.

3. There was no evidence that the renewal of the Appellant's passport afforded him or was capable of affording him any protection or that the Appellant ever availed himself or had any intention of availing himself of any such protection.

4. If (contrary to the Appellant's contention) there were any such evidence, the issue was one for the jury and the Learned Judge failed to direct them thereon.

Grounds of appeal.

55. (continued) Joyce's notice of appeal.

LUDLOW & CO.
H.S.LUDLOW. C.B.V.HEAD.
SOLICITORS.

Amalgamating
HARRY WILSON & CO.
EDGAR SMITH & CO.

COMMISSIONERS FOR OATHS,
ENGLAND;TRANSVAAL
AND
AUSTRALIA.

TELEPHONE
TEMPLE BAR 7910.

BROAD COURT CHAMBERS,
BOW STREET,
COVENT GARDEN,
LONDON, W.C.2.

28th September, 1945.

J. MacNab, Esq.,
6, Claverton Street,
S.W.1.

J/44.

Dear Mr. MacNab,

Rex v. Joyce.

I thank you for your letter of yesterday and I think the passport information which you give is important. Accordingly, I would like the original passport loaned to us until after the hearing in the Court of Criminal Appeal, if this is possible. In any event, I would like to have it deposited with us so that it can be photographed.

I saw Mr. William Joyce at Wormwood Scrubs Prison last night. He signed the Notice of Appeal and this was duly lodged this morning. Wormwood Scrubs Prison telephoned here and stated that Mr. William Joyce was being moved today to Wandsworth Prison but I expect that by the time this reaches you, you and Mr. Quentin Joyce will have ascertained that. As you and Mr. Quentin Joyce are so anxious to help, there is one matter on which I think you may be able to do so.

Long experience in the courts has shown me that the most convincing argument which can be used in a normal case is that of an analogy and what I would like you and Mr. Quentin Joyce to do is to try and think out within the next fourteen days the best analogy you can as to the attitude of the Crown in the present case.

For example, supposing J. falsely represented that he was the holder of the Victoria Cross. This, as you may know, carries with it the right to a small pension. Supposing that by fraud J. had got himself recorded with the authorities as the holder of a Victoria Cross so that the amount due for the Victoria Cross pension was being credited to him. Supposing before the first payment became due, J. had made an

G7954

Income Tax return setting forth all his income but in doing so had not included the amount which he would have received in respect of the Victoria Cross if his fraud had not been discovered. That being the position, the Crown prosecuted J. for making a false Income Tax return. If you think this out, you will see that the analogy is not quite perfect but something on the same lines is what I want.

Yours truly,

[signature]

56. Another mail intercept of a letter sent by William Joyce's lawyer to his friend John Macnab, 28 September 1945. (KV 2/249/101a)

CONFIDENTIAL.

COUNTER INTELLIGENCE BUREAU (BELGIUM),
c/o BRITISH MILITARY MISSION,
B.A.O.R.

From: Lt.Col.Brooke-Booth.   CONFIDENTIAL.

CIB/203/4.   29th October, 1945.

Dear

The following is an extract from a letter addressed to
Margaret JOYCE from J.A. MACNAB which has today been received
here:

24 Oct.

'I had been told that the case would not come up till Nov.
some time but today Q showed me a letter from lawyers to say
next Tuesday 30th has been fixed. So I had better send this
off to you without delay. Brief has already been delivered
to Counsel. I haven't W's permission but as the matter is
now so near I feel justified in mentioning the "find" about
which you have not asked him anything. It is a dual-nationa-
lity passport belonging to a friend of mine, or rather a brother
of one of my ex-camp-mates. It proves that under some circumstances a British subject, having a valid British passport
containing no false statements, can bear arms against the King
of England without being guilty of treason. Also that when
in the country of his other nationality he gets no protection
from the British Crown and is not relieved of his allegiance to
the other country. It follows that according to Tucker, L.,
the Crown demands from William while in Germany and a foreigner
a higher degree of allegiance than it demands from one of its
own subjects, whose passport is accurate while his is not.
Many other inferences can easily be drawn and I leave you to
do it.   ....'

The above is, no doubt, already known to you and in any case
it will reach you rather late I'm afraid but I thought you should
have it. The letter has been delivered to Mrs.JOYCE.

Yours

                                                    1577

Lt.Colonel E.J.P.Cussen,
Box No. 500,
Parliament Street B.O.,
LONDON, S.W.1.
MPS.

CONFIDENTIAL.

57. This letter of 29 October 1945, complete with manuscript additions, shows the real
fear that the court of criminal appeal might overturn the Old Bailey verdict. Curiously, the
Irish defence was never used. (KV 2/249/103a)

100 B

Ref: P.F.66003/SLB3
Yr.Ref: 897,868/52

19th February, 1946.

Dear Sir Frank.

Mrs. Margaret JOYCE.

Mrs. JOYCE was, as you know, brought to London in order that she might visit her husband before his execution, and thereafter she was taken back to military custody in Brussels. When she was landed here she was treated as a German, and the Immigration Officer formally refused her leave to land.

Our Liaison Section in Germany reported her return to Brussels to the Intelligence Bureau of the Control Commission, and suggested that she should now be moved from there to the British Zone in Germany. I am enclosing a copy of the memorandum addressed by our Liaison Section to the Intelligence Bureau on this subject, which I have marked 'A'.

We now have a reply from the Intelligence Bureau, which I have marked 'B'. This was mislaid in transmission, and the copy I am sending to you has been taken down over the telephone from the office copy of the Intelligence Bureau. You will see from it that they are opposed to her return to Germany.

Finally I am sending to you, marked 'C', a copy of a letter addressed by Mrs. JOYCE herself to Lt.-Col. Brooke-Booth, who represents the Intelligence Bureau in Brussels, in which Mrs. JOYCE asks that she should not be sent back to Germany and expresses a wish to go to Eire.

I am very anxious indeed to get this matter settled and, although, as Mrs. JOYCE is a German citizen not resident in the United Kingdom, you may take the view that the Home Office are not concerned, I shall be very grateful for your assistance. I say this particularly because I feel that the discussions which must take place should be conducted on a high level.

..... I have

Sir Frank Newsam, K.B.E., C.V.O., M.C.,
Home Office.

What was her Passport Situation?

58. How to deal with an embarrassment? Notes and correspondence from the Margaret Joyce file, including a letter from Margaret of 24 January 1946 asserting her desire to go to Eire. The file ends in 1946 with the British authorities wrestling with the problem as to what to do with her. In the end she returned to Britain and eventually settled in London. (KV 2/253/100b)

I have it in mind that, if you could yourself raise the matter with Sir Arthur Street, we might be able to secure the reception of Mrs. JOYCE in the British Zone in Germany without prejudice to any applications which she may make from there as to her future.

I mentioned this matter to Mitchell of this office yesterday (he, as you know, deals with Fascist activities), and we both felt that it would be most undesirable for Mrs. JOYCE to come back to the United Kingdom. The penultimate paragraph of Mrs. JOYCE's letter is a good illustration of her frame of mind, and it would be deplorable if she should become available to Fascist elements here as a stalking-horse of some nuisance value. The best way of preventing this is to secure that she is safely disposed of elsewhere.

You may feel that a discussion on this matter should take place and I should be grateful if you would consider suggesting to Sir Arthur Street that he should call a meeting for that purpose.

I am enclosing a second set of copies of the correspondence so that you may send them to him should you see fit.

Yours sincerely,

E.J.P. Cussen.

Enclosures
EJPC/MKM

58. (continued) Correspondence on Margaret Joyce.

COPY

CONFIDENTIAL

C/O HQ INTELLIGENCE CORPS (FIELD)
B A O R.

SLB3/NUR/35
Your Ref: CIB/B3/PF.225

'A'

22 January 1946.

FROM: M.I.5 Liaison Section

To: Brigadier Haylor, Intelligence Bureau, HQ BAOR.

Subject: Margaret Cairns JOYCE - widow of William JOYCE.

1.   It has been decided by the authorities in U.K. not to prosecute this woman, in effect on compassionate grounds. There is no lack of evidence implicating her in the treasonable activities of her late husband; but the authorities do not think that she need be punished further, and would like her to be returned to Germany as a German subject. She has been detained in military custody at the Reception Centre in Brussels since the beginning of June last, except for a short visit under escort to U.K. for the purpose of seeing her husband before his execution.

2.   Mrs. JOYCE is British by birth, having been born at Old Trafford, Manchester, on 14 July 1911. She did not acquire American nationality, or lose her British nationality, by her marriage to William JOYCE, an American subject, in February 1937. She was therefore a British subject when she went to Germany with her husband in August 1939.

3.   William JOYCE obtained German naturalisation in 1940. It is not known whether his wife was included in his naturalisation, and all efforts to trace the German records of his naturalisation have been unsuccessful. The opinion of the Legal Advice and Drafting Branch of the Legal Division, Control Commission for Germany (B.E.) has been obtained from which the following paragraphs are quoted:-

        "With regard to the effect of JOYCE's naturalisation on his wife's nationality, Section 16 of the Reichs-und Staatsangehörigkeits gesetz of 22 July 1913 (RGBl 583) provides that the naturalisation of the husband extends to the wife unless an express reservation is made in the naturalisation certificate. In the absence, however, of such a reservation, the wife is included in the naturalisation even if she is not mentioned in the certificate and has not signed the application. This may give rise to difficulties. The answers to the questions contained in paragraph 3 of the note appended to your memorandum are, therefore,

        (a) If Mrs. JOYCE was included in William JOYCE's naturalisation either expressly or by operation of law, she would acquire German nationality;

        (b) If she was expressly excluded from his naturalisation, she would retain British nationality.

        Divorce by itself would not make any difference to Mrs. JOYCE's nationality in German law. If she acquired German nationality before divorce, she would not lose it as a result of the divorce. Remarriage however, would cause her to lose her German nationality, if the man whom she married were not of German nationality. This is provided by Section 17(6) of the Reichs-und Staatsangehörigkeitsgesetz of 1913 which states that nationality is lost by a German woman when she marries a foreigner. If, not having acquired German nationality by naturalisation, she married a German, she would thereby acquire German nationality. That in itself would not amount to treason in English law (see Fasbender v. Attorney-General (1922) 2 ch. 850)"

4.   The opinion of the Legal Division on the effect of divorce and remarriage was sought because there have been reports that the JOYCEs were

divorced/

divorced and remarried during the war. The facts, however, on which these reports were based have never been precisely ascertained.

5.   It is probably safe to assume that Mrs. JOYCE was not expressly excluded from her husband's naturalisation, that she therefore acquired German nationality by being included in his naturalisation either expressly or by operation of law and that she has never lost the German nationality that she so acquired. It seems also safe to assume that the acquisition of German nationality by these means would not amount to treason in English law. She seems to have obtained German nationality by a combination of marriage and naturalisation, and would probably be held not to have committed an act of treason any more than any other British woman who claims German nationality by marriage to a German.

6.   In spite of the objections to the release of British renegades in the British Zone of Germany set out in your CIB/B3/5091/2 of 2. December 19 it would be appreciated if you would consider the application for the retu of this woman to the British Zone of Germany as sympathetically as possible, and as she has probably only German nationality, put her in the same category as such persons as HANSEN, STOETTNER, HUFFELD and DIETZE.

7.   It is suggested that it would be best for you to let the Minister of Occupied Germany and Austria have your views for communication to the Home Office, as Mrs. JOYCE's disposal is now a matter to be arranged between the Home Office and Control Commission for Germany. M.I.5 have attempted to get the Home Office to take up the disposal of Mrs. JOYCE with the Ministry for Occupied Germany and Austria; but the matter merely returned to M.I.5 from the table of an official in Civil Affairs Displaced Persons Branch, to whom it had apparently been referred by the Ministry. This explains the delay in referring the matter to you, and also suggests that the time has come for the Home Office to use the Ministry who are concerned, rather than M.I.5 who are not, as a channel of communication with you on the disposal of British renegades who are not to be prosecuted, but who are not wanted back in U.K. We should be grateful, however, if you would keep M.I.5 notified of your decision in this and other cases through this Section.

GHQ TPS
2451

Sgd: J.F.E. Stephenson, Major.
O.C. M.I.5 Liaison Section.

Copies to M.I.5 London
         Int. Staff, Brussels.

58. (continued) Correspondence on Margaret Joyce.

COPY

To: M.I.5 Liaison Section
From: Intelligence Bureau, HQ., BAOR.

5 Feb 46.

1.   Your letter dated 22nd January, reference conversation
Stephenson-Hinks. The reason advanced for returning Mrs. JOYCE
to Germany is, as we understand it, that it is not intended to
prosecute her in England as she is probably a German national.
We think, however, that she should not be returned to Germany
for the following reasons.

     If she is returned here we shall be bound to intern
her as a security subject. In the case of a German who was the wife,
prop and stay of a renegade Englishman whose task was to broadcast
propaganda trying to alienate Great Britain from the Soviet Union
and reconcile her to National Socialist Germany, we can hardly do
otherwise. This means that she will in fact be imprisoned without
trial in Germany for a considerable time. That happens to many Germans
but hardly fulfils the desire of the authorities in the U.K. that she
should "not be punished further", an intention which has now become known
to the Press (see "News Review" of 17th January). We also think it
undesirable that someone who, whatever her nationality, must popularly
pass for an English traitor should be thrown into civilian internment
as a German withother German security subjects.

2.   We feel therefore that the objections to returning her to
the British Zone of Germany are certainly no less strong than those
obtaining in the case of other renegades.

                       Sgd: D.G. Hinks
                         Lt. Colonel G-S.

               for Brigadier, Head of Int. Bureau

Intelligence Bureau,
CCG (B.E.)
c/o G.S.I.
H.Q. BAOR.

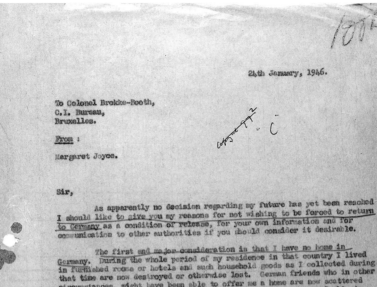

24th January, 1946.

To Colonel Brokke-Booth,
C.I. Bureau,
Bruxelles.

From :

Margaret Joyce.

Sir,

As apparently no decision regarding my future has yet been reached I should like to give you my reasons for not wishing to be forced to return to Germany as a condition of release, for your own information and for communication to other authorities if you should consider it desirable.

The first and major consideration is that I have no home in Germany. During the whole period of my residence in that country I lived in furnished rooms or hotels and such household goods as I collected during that time are now destroyed or otherwise lost. German friends who in other circumstances, might have been able to offer me a home are now scattered and have disappeared, or are themselves in custody. Even were I able to contact acquaintances, I must reckon with the possibility that owing to the strong measures taken against those in any way connected with the Government or public services of the Third Reich, there would probably be an understandable disinclination to assist me.

For this reason, too, I should find it impossible to obtain employment, even were I at the moment capable of earning my own living. I have only a small sum of money, rendered smaller by the devaluation of the mark and certainly not enough to live on for any length of time.

I should, owing to the continued difficulties of communication, be completely cut off from my relatives and friends in Britain, Eire and other countries. Were my husband alive this would be of little consequence but it is only natural that in the circumstances I should wish to turn to my next-of-kin. Hence my desire to go to Eire, which was my husband's childhood home, and from whence both our families originated. There I should be able to resume my studies of philology and have, I am told, a certain income.

One last but important point is that although I have no desire for any political activity, and no interest whatsoever in British politics of any kind, were I resident in Germany there would always be the likelihood of my being drawn into the inevitable reaction against occupation and the possible reaction against the continued Soviet encroachments, with both of which tendencies I feel a natural sympathy which would be greatly increased by direct contact with the conditions from which they will spring.

Should the authorities decide to continue to hold me in custody without trial, then I can only ask that it may be in some place where I am able to remain in communication with my friends.

I remain, Sir,

Yours obediently,

(Signed) Margaret Joyce.

58. (continued) Correspondence on Margaret Joyce.

pa in Joyce W 518a

Notes on the Correspondence of
William & Margaret JOYCE

During William Joyce's detention in Britain prior to his
execution on the 3rd January 1946 all correspondence between him and his wife
was submitted to this Office for censorship until after the failure of his last
appeal when we ceased to scrutinise the letters in order to reduce delay in
delivery. William's correspondence with third parties was censored for about
four months,while all Margaret's out-going letters have passed through our hands.
A schedule of extracts from William's correspondence is attached.

Fifty eight persons wrote to William expressing admiration,good wishes,
or friendship. In a few cases money was enclosed,either as a contribution towards
the cost of his defence,or for the purchase of cigarettes and such like comforts.
Nine of these persons wrote anonymously. Many of the JOYCE correspondents were
of course already well known fascists or 18b cases. There have however,been a
small proportion of illiterate or otherwise harmless fanatics,mostly of the
anti-Jewish variety. An unusual type of correspondent was an old clergyman,the
Rev.W.E. Farre of,11,Huntly Street,Grahamstown,C.P.,South Africa,who entered into
correspondence with Margaret,apparently out of pure kindness of heart. Throughout
all the JOYCE correspondence an undercurrent of moral support could be sensed
from the Catholic Irish type,and in many cases this was expressed in religious
terms. The main correspondents of the two JOYCEs were,William's brother Quentin,
Miss Scrimgeour,John Angus MacNab,and to a lesser degree Rosetta McNeil-Sloane.
These persons,although of political opinions similar to the JOYCEs,have figured
throughout in the capacity of personal friends. Special emphasis in this connection
should be laid on MACNAB. He is obviously a man of high culture and literary
ability. He is also a devout Catholic,to the point of fanaticism. But although one
may abhor his political views,considered from the point of view of pure friendship
his support of the JOYCEs throughout has been beyond praise. His letters have
been almost entirely in the religious strain,and this subject has now taken
possession of his mind to such an extent that he may well fade out of the political
scene altogether.

Perhaps every sensational trial produces its own crop of eccentrics. If
this is the case the JOYCE trial has been no exception. Twenty three letters were
received which were either abusive or meaningless. Thirteen of these were anonymous.
They ranged from one written by a P.T.R. RAYNER,who was apparently trying to 'pull
the leg' of the Security Service by suggesting that William had been given.
improper access to the telephone during his incarceration,to another from an
anonymous writer,who sent a bottle of rat poison to Willaim.

The JOYCE's main correspondence however,has been with one another,two
hundred and twenty three of these letters having been censored by this Office.
William's letters were written in a precise and academic style with a biting
classical wit. Added to this however there was a thin,but none the less distinct
line of almost 'guttersnipe' courseness,which was all the more remarkable against
the otherwise academic background. The main purpose behind their correspondence
was of course to maintain one another's morale,and considered from this point of
view the letters of both of them were quite admirable. The main contents were
typically fascist comments on the day to day news,and comments on the legal aspects
of William's trial. From time to time William complained that his Judges were
biassed against him,and this culminated in vulgar abuse of the Lord Chief Justice
in a letter written on the 19th December 1945,after the failure of his last Appeal.
The last letters of William to be censored by this Office found him expressing
more and more arrogant fascist views and adopting the attitude that he would die
as a front line soldier defending his ideals. On one occasion he even went so far
as to say "........I prefer to believe that my work has not been in vain : and
after I have died,I believe that I shall resume it.".

Apart from her parents Mr. & Mrs. E.R. WHITE of 18,Princess Road,
Crumpsall,Manchester,and the Rev.W.E. FARRE,mentioned above,Margaret's correspon-
-dents have been the same as William's. Immediately before and after her husband's
execution she seemed to be in a pretty pitiful state,although the indications
that she was able to maintain her morale in front of her husband. William himself

Correspondence

59. Notes on the correspondence of William and Margaret Joyce, 14 January
1946. Between Joyce's first remand into prison custody and his execution detailed
notes were taken of his conversations with visitors and correspondence. After his
execution on 3 January 1946, MI5 had the prison service compile this report
relating to Margaret and William Joyce. It contains important details concerning
Joyce's changing state of mind in the months leading up to his execution together
with a complete schedule of their correspondence. (KV 2/247/518a)

seems to have behaved magnificently as far as his wife was concerned, and judging by the correspondence, Mrs. JOYCE had been left fairly comfortable off as far as money is concerned. The last letters showed her taking consolation in the Catholic Religion, in which she was much encouraged by MACNAB. She has never shown any great concern as to her own fate, but she has expressed the hope that she may ultimately be allowed to settle in Eire.

S.L.B. 3
14th January 1946

C. A. Haines

59. (continued) Notes on the correspondence of William and Margaret Joyce.

William Joyce's 1945 Journal

This final selection of documents is made up of extracts from the journal William Joyce kept during the eight weeks or so between 27 February and 2 May 1945. The journal was written in a cheap notebook and covered a total of 112 pages. The contents provide valuable and detailed insights into his daily life and thoughts during this critical period. The entries are quite varied in length, ranging from the short and terse – with some hurriedly written; often, as he occasionally noted, whilst travelling or in air raid shelters – to lengthy discourses with detail spilling over several pages. Joyce used this journal not only to chronicle daily happenings but also to record the world-shattering events unfolding around him: events that led to the final collapse of his beloved Third Reich and the end of the Second World War in Europe.

The language used by Joyce in his journal reflected his character, echoing the brutally frank, cutting manner he cultivated in his wartime broadcasts. The entries expressed often contradictory attitudes towards personal aspects of his life, especially towards his wife. However, his real venom was reserved for his colleagues, Germany, Germans and the Nazi hierarchy, all of whom were subjected to withering contempt: all, that is, except his heroes Adolf Hitler and Josef Goebbels.

Joyce found time in his journal to ponder his future, or lack of it, in the postwar world. In this respect the journal reveals him both as a man of some personal courage and as a fatalist, philosophically accepting whatever the future might deliver – and he was under no illusions that for him this meant a traitor's death.

Although the entries ceased at the beginning of May 1945, Joyce's journal survived the end of the war and later fell into the hands of his British captors. It eventually came into the possession of MI5, where it formed part of the William Joyce files until they were released at the Public Record Office in April 2000. These extracts are no more than a representative sample. They are intended to show the many moods of the man who was Lord Haw Haw, at the most critical juncture of his life.

27ᵗʰ Feb. Sleeping badly. Foot hurts.
Feeling not so bad this
morning. Perhaps it does me good to be
without the awful cigarettes. Saw S——; my
He predicted real hunger. I agreed, but said
"Let the future look after itself." Twisted
ankle afresh in running to Wörtzleben.
    Churchill speaks today in House.
My blessed superiors, who do little or no
productive writing, don't or won't realize
that, after 5½ years, a steady writer
needs certain amenities. One might think
that writing was plumbing. If the time were
not one of crisis, I should ask for
much more consideration. But one must
not be petty at a time like this; still,
I am finding my work much harder;
    2.1th East and West, the situation
is undefined; but I believe that March
will bring definition. I make no prognoses. But I
think that if the Anglo-Russian alliance lasts
for 6 months longer, it will be a wonder. Frankly
I think the war must end this year. It may
last into 1946, but I doubt it. But those people
who think that peace will bring relief are mightily
mistaken. Austria, perhaps, re. U.S.A. If this diary
contains little reference to world events, it is
largely because I have enough to say about them
in public. On the other hand, I wish I had
time to describe my impressions of Berlin. I
shall not forget them. We are used to living
in ruins: but about the ruins of ——,
there is something almost funny. I remember
walking from Potsdamer Platz to Anhalter
Bahnhof with Margaret in twilight.

27 February, 28 February and 1 March (part) The first three entries in the journal cover the period when the couple were still living in Berlin. They reveal Joyce's oddly detached style of writing. At this stage he evidently did not believe the war to be a total loss, and speculated on its continuance into the autumn or even into 1946.

Translate Goebbels speech, which is really
good. Am not satisfied with translation
which would have been far better if I had had
a packet of cigarettes and, perhaps, a drink.
The speech suggests that we still have cards
up our sleeves. Schiborth & others off to Open.
Hear that Dombrowski was buried in
Schöneberger Rathskeller – but, got out.
Margery has run out of her marken.
No heating at home, my god damn.

Feb 2 8ᵗʰ/ Slept badly. Had a raid about
2.30 Nothing much. Feel quite fresh
this morning. Some trouble in getting
anymore. Succeeded at 10.50.
Rushed for time, unfortunately. Wonder
ruefully if I should ever have made
my reputation by my present standards. I
think not. However, I hope to do better.
What with scabies, enteritis, & burst ankle,
in succession, it is not strange that I
am not on top form. But drink, tobacco,
and food are the main desiderata.
Sorry Sharp – but there is some connexion between
physical satisfaction and mental effort.
Sam Worried by Churchill speech. Takes it at
its face value. I do not. The old devil
had his tongue in his cheek – and he
certainly does not think that Germany is beaten
already. But he is gambling on a very fine
margin. Today free.
Lunch at Club with Dombrowski.
Call on Drese in afternoon.

These entries show the inroads that shortages of food, tobacco and alcohol had made on Joyce: all three, he asserted, were essential if he was to continue working. The entry for 28 February concluded by noting yet another terrible row with Margaret after their usual alcohol-laden dinner at Berlin's International Club, while the 1 March entry began with the fall-out from the row. (KV 2/250/2)

Walk with M. in Tiergarten from Nollendorf Pl.
to Potsdamer Pl. ~~on the tree~~ lovely evening.
Swan on river — owl on tree. Dinner
at club. Discourse quite happily with V. Schimpff
on English literature. Bochow not interested.
Early alarm — and thus got only 1 schnapps after
dinner — more fool me. Ration cuts announced.
The fat Schustron will be desperate — for me at least.
The problem is that of less food in more time.
Unfortunately had a terrible row with M. when
we got home. I was helping her to make the
bed: and for some reason she infuriated me. I took
her. She wanted to leave the flat, but I would
not let her. She slept in front room - but at
about 3, I carried her into bedroom. Most
unpleasant!

1st March March at last! now things will begin to
hum, if I am not greatly mistaken. Had a
bath (home made) — wonderful. Margaret now threatens to
"punish" me for last night by going for a time
to Königin-E. str., I apologized to her, but I
resent the K.E. idea very greatly. After all,
she is not blameless — and she ought to learn
to control her temper. In the present circs., I
am not amenable to blackmail or matrimonial-
ize "reprisals" on her part.
Saw Peter. Called at flat for me this morning
and spoke very strongly of the general situation.
I think that he does not mean all that he says.
We went to Funehaus together and then I
took him across to Sammy's. He is going to
see Pf, but what good it may do, I cannot
tell. Precious little I imagine.

27 February, 28 February and 1 March (part)

4 March (part) and 6 March (part) These two short extracts show how Joyce was deeply attached to anniversaries, using them to recall past events and – a frequent occurrence in the journal – as an opportunity to revisit earlier phases of his life. (KV 2/250/2)

8th March / 15 years ago today - moved into
(Thursday) / 41, Cedars Rd. Battersea. memories
Had letter from ferda nebbe, went to
Ruth leben a los drent to shoot. never shot so
horribly in my life. I think that either the rifle - or
the markers were at fault we all did relatively
badly - even Georgen. There was something
fishy about it. Going again next thurs day.
Our temporary e.o. damned decent. But I
am sure that something was wrong. Felt quite
well - was, however, disturbed by so
many well-meant instructions which went
against all my experience. Clutching the heel
of the butt with the left hand is not my
idea of shooting. Margaret illish -
belly - heart - 2 head - I wonder why, at
intervals she is quite well! (tra! we shall
see. / Talk to Georgen, who wanted to know
why I took german nationality. He could not
understand. 5 years ago, I could not
have understood him. But I do today.
He has lived in England, and clearly he
shares my own private impressions of the
germans - I do not say of germany; He
thinks that when the Russians move towards
Berlin, we shall strike up from south and cut
them off. Says it is neck or nothing. I
reminded him of the pundits who before D-day
kept telling us that the British and the
americans must be allowed to land in large
numbers. Risky strategy, I said to g.,
is not what I like! but he said that
there is no alternative, since the
Russians will grow stronger with
time. He also expressed the

---

8 March and 9 March (part) These extended entries contain information about Joyce's Home Guard training: poor marksmanship is blamed on the rifle. They also refer to a conversation with a colleague on the future of the war, together with a note on the US bridgehead across the Rhine, which Joyce correctly predicted needed rebuffing if the Nazi state was to continue.

opinion, or rather categorically insisted
that the morale in the German
army is by no means what it used
to be. Well, I cannot judge, but
he, as an N.C.O. of the Groß Deutschland
Regiment ought to know what he is
talking about. He ~~is~~ doubtful if
we can hold out for 2 months. I hope
and believe that he is unduly pessimistic.
I told him that if we held out
till September, we might rely on a
diplomatic solution to our advantage.

• Went with Margaret to Club, walked
from Nollendorf Platz. Lunch at Club
Château neuf du Pape. Marvellous.
R.M. 6, per glass — but worth
far more at present rates. Bochow
joined us. Afternoon rested. T.×
Franz quite yowling for me nastily.
She wants to make trouble, the soured
conceited nincompoop. Of course she has lost
all sense of proportion and is definitely neurotic.
I call her attention to the actual amount of
my production work — but with the unwish to get rid
of it. Jersey Cathy is another nuisance. Also
Finn. well well. V₅₂ order that company
is to parade "ohne Rücksicht auf beruf dienst —

The entries illustrate Joyce's complex and often extreme attitudes towards women. He noted how he had been 'luckier in the marriages [he] did not contract than in those [he] did'. (KV 2/250/2)

Well, of course, this order means that we may be expected to go into action any time now — in the first instance, I suppose, against minor formations. Remember Geyer's warning about the preservation of civil order! I dare say there will be a number of false alarms to waste our time. I hope not — but fear there will. The toy is too attractive. Besides ~~penetrations are quite likely~~. It is stated this morning that the allied bridgehead across the Rhine (east) Remagen? is fully secured. If this claim be true, then, methinks, the outlook, both military and diplomatic, is almost as bad as it could be. Either that bridgehead must be removed OR, the game will soon be up. I am no pessimist and I am not worried personally: but there are limits, and we cannot afford to retreat further on two fronts at once. I should like to know what is the real cause of these failures. I may live to learn — or I may not. I must, however, admit that I am becoming more doubtful about the morale of the troops. Of course, much depends on their supplies and equipment — and the question of air cover doubtless plays a part.

If the west breaks, I do not trust the Volkgenossen to make a last stand. We think too fantastically and act too slowly. However, I shall soon know more!

Had to make Aufnahme in Bunker — STROMSPERR went to Bank and arranged for payment of RM.12.31 Income Tax due tomorrow. Fanny despondent but still clings to that useless S, which gives me a pain in the neck. Reflect on Gerda's letter. She seems so proud to have netted a husband. But has she? March 31st has yet to come, and

8 March and 9 March (part)

much may happen in the interval. - Very much.
I was well out of the Nebbe liaison, much
as I liked it at times & she still seem to bear a
slight resentment, probably, however, sub-conscious
we should never have been able to live together
(literally interpreted!) for even a week. I should
furiously resent being paraded as a "catch", and, on
most personal matters, her outlook is very
different from mine. I hope that if the marriage
does take place, it will be a success. So too,
Adami, who wrote to Sens̄bury about Margaret, she is
a louse of lice. not fit to be at large.
one of the most treacherous bitches I ever met
I think I am luckier in the marriages I
did not contract than in those I did. Exception
was Mary, with whom I am sure success
would have been certain. Too late now! -
Anyhow, Margaret & I pull together, if
not always in the same direction - aw usual is
usual. I am now (12·44) at Schöneberg
making my tardy and cordurous way to lunch. Have
left my cigarettes at home. The bloody train
is coming. This diary is disjointed. It is meant
to be. It is a pleasure not to have to preserve
order and sequence - but to be able to write down
what comes into my apology for a mind.
Financial position not as good as it should be in
relation to income Tax. But, does it matter?
Had letters from Timm & Hoffman pestering me for
articles. Konk wastes too much of my time.
A very light but quite good lunch
Fish, boiled. Better fried.

12 March and 13 March (part) Both of these entries start with Joyce complaining about his health, a fact he put down to the dreadful cigarettes he smoked. The disrupted journeys to and from home are also noted, and the entries peppered with angry comments about the inefficiencies of the Berliners both on the streets and in the Rundfunk. The loss of the cable links to several German transmitters and the general deterioration in the military situation caused Joyce's boss Dietz, referred to as D, to move the whole English-language operation to Apen near the Dutch border. Joyce's reaction to this was typical: first he angrily questioned Dietz's motives, and then he became regretful and melancholic at the thought of leaving Berlin, particularly the cellars of the International Club. Food and drink still dominated his thinking. In his 13 March entry he noted the deteriorating situation and wrote: 'Now we are going to reap the whirlwind, but, thank God, the Burgundy was very good today'.

had 2 divisions across the Rhine, well –
I'm thinking the prognosis not favourable,
How I am wrong. It's a damp sort of
morning and I don't feel very enthusiastic;
unpleasant going to town. Last night's raid
has interfered well S as well. Had a
lunch which, if not satisfactory, was well washed
down with good Burgundy. Am now at
Potsdamer Platz waiting for Ubrain. I don't
think I can come up tonight. The
traffic is in an unholy mess. If I ran
the same risk this evening, I should
probably be cut off. There is a so-called
Pendel verkehr and a vast crowd
waiting. Unpleasant sight. Usual mekerers.
We shall see how it is; but it looks bad
for tonight. A pity. // 17.35. Well,
perhaps March 1st was not so uneventful,
after all. Dretze rang to say that M 2 S
must set out for Often on Wednesday
night – as the cables are unlikely to be
mended for a fortnight. Well! Hell! Well!
Winkel intervened to reserve his decision,
As we have no liners, I decided to
come up to town to dinner. We are now
becalmed in the tunnel outside
Anhalter Bahnhof. Bad idea! However,
I suppose little harm will be done.
If I have to go to Often, I shall at least
welcome freedom from broken down
railways. Am beginning to wonder if
I shall get any dinner after all.
One can only call the present conditions
chaotic. And now I see, there
are preparations for an offensive on

the northern Rhine, nothing like really the enemy half way! It is now 3 minutes to see few people are the most accomplished time was Cersey I have ever known. Reach the Dine with M. And now even in quite a bloody mess. M. tells me that our 23 30 last night went over Hamburg, and of course that alters the whole situation. I have been working on the Poll drawer & both for about 15 minutes. Dare say I shall get through before dawn. Have not the least desire to leave the modest flesh pots of Berlin despite the fact that the loss of Kontk. would be a blessing. I am determined that neither I nor Margaret shall attempt to traverse D's orders, which may be his last, wie müssen dumm er scheinen. Actually, I want to hang on to the Club, and Margaret is almost heart broken. However, we shall see. It is now dark and I do not know the time, but I guess I shall get far more through to walk the rest.

12 March and 13 March (part)

just back, wrote V. vN. Seemed as if
we need not go to Apen, as we were on
all 4 stations and the municipality was
in order.

| 13th March Tuesday | slept badly. cigarettes have given me catarrh and generally affected my health. Horst rings |

up to say that Dietze insists on our
going to Apen as "anything may happen,"
I don't know what he expects to happen —
but still I suppose he has his
grounds. Sammy very perturbed; Rings
Kamm. But I don't think it will do
much good. Margaret does not want
to come — like me, she values the
club cellars — but they won't last
long anyhow.
    Today my programme is in chaos,
and the VSS has some sort of crazy
    alert to waste our time. well —
we shall see. I hate the idea of Apen —
but, there you are. I'd like to
know D's motives. Well, we lunched at the
club. Fish. Broke the bad news to S. von B., to
von Schnupp & to Heikies. Dismay amongst the
staff. Poor Margaret is crying, she could
not believe that it would ever come to
this. Poor Dorothy has worse surprises
in store for her. Now we are

going to reap the whirlwind. But,
thank god, the Burgundy was
very good today., Torten too.
Frankly, I regard Apen as the last
ditch. Its only merit is that our
tenancy of it will not last long.
I find it hard to write with complete
frankness, for, if I did, the diary
would not be very helpful if it fell
into the wrong hands. But I loathe to
think that these may be my last
hours in Berlin — a city which
I love, despite its swine, and despite
the heartaches it has brought me.
Berlin is a composite part of my
life, and I do not yield it up
gladly. I do not weep, like Margaret, but
I feel deeply. According to S.v.B.
the Küstrin position is not serious; but,
after Remagen, there is no ground
for complacency. // At the moment, am
held up at Gleisdreieck — same old
story. But I shall be lonely for
Berlin, even as I was for London,
perhaps more so. The lack of
alcohol in Apen will be AWFUL.

12 March and 13 March (part)

17 March By this date Joyce and his wife had moved to Apen. In contrast to their existence in Berlin the couple appeared to be enjoying an abundance of food. Joyce noted that they were starving in Berlin. Not in good health or spirits, Joyce questioned Dietz's motives at every turn, frustrated at the lack of information on which he could base his nightly broadcast commentary 'Views on the News'. Joyce turned in for the night noting regretfully: 'Not a drink on St Patrick's Day'. (KV 2/250/2)

feeling poorly! Hartmann & Wardon at
dinner. We are fortunate in our
personnel down here. A very good mess.
Normally I find people oppressive—
but not here. They keep distance and are
yet friendly. BBC Bericht pretty bloody.
In the evening, am wretchedly ill,
with a real grippe. Dietze, instead of
returning to Berlin, went to Dulag Nord
if you please! Alleges no D-Züge from
Bremen. I don't think he had the
least intention of returning directly to Berlin.
But what does he want in the camp?
What is the big idea? Why is he anxious
to keep away from Berlin? It is, of
course, ridiculous to expect me to write six
successive V.n.N. without knowing the news—i.e.
at 9 in the morning. Go to bed all
of a shiver. Feel deathly. Kidneys
hurt. Not a drink on St Patrick's Day.
Wrote a Jerry calling (IV)

17 March

20 March and 21 March Life in Apen clearly proved agreeable, and Joyce noted how he had come to love the place. His attitude towards Margaret is apparent in his comment concerning her monthly period: 'M still Mrs Thingish'. However other news brought home the reality of the war, which caused Joyce to retreat into a reverie about a lost love 15 years earlier. By this stage all he wanted was to: 'spend my last days in drinking, smoking and eating the best. I think I deserve it'. He noted how, even in Apen, the food situation was deteriorating and the war closing in, with a description of a massive daylight raid and of feeling bomb blast from distant explosions. But it is the lack of alcohol that bothered him, as he ironically noted: 'A week without drink. Hell, I'm in training for clink!'
(KV 2/250/2)

wrote to Peter this morning. Hope
to see him before the end. Margaret
is irritable, rude, and lazy. I
suppose she is not well;— doubtless she
feels rotten, and discouraged too —
we both need tobacco badly — but
alcohol *much* more — we must have
joy. Today's news makes it clear that the bloody
war is lost, unless a dozen miracles happen —
which they won't, I fear. Sad, but, true —
we have made a complete balls of it!
    I think much of Mary and 15 years
ago — that magic evening at
Prince's Risboro'! Ah! well, I am cut off
from that life anyhow; and as I told
M. on Sunday night, I have
nothing left to live for. If only I
could spend my last days in drinking,
smoking, and eating the best. I
think that I *deserve* it. My
employers are *mean*, undiscerning buggers.
They have *no* idea how to get good
work out of a man. They have the
proletarian mentality — poor things.
Anyhow, I suppose, it's only a matter
of weeks.

21

20 March and 21 March

At evening meal, food shows a marked
decline. I fear that we must live on
gas here as well. Everybody pessimistic.
Think of Mary — but how distant! I sleep
but little now. Belly full of gas (Katoji),
knee hurting like hell, bed hard and
cold; Margaret peevish and most unworthy —
so I have time to think; but no comfort
to sleep. Hear many bombers in
night.

21st March. Last day of winter. But
(Wedn). What will spring bring? Ho! Ho!
Think of Mary more than ever. I am
sure that she sometimes thinks of me
and watches me. Funny!
We witnessed the most spectacular daylight
raid I have yet seen — between 9. 30
and 10 a.m. Widespread. Some bombs
dropped between us and Oldenburg.
Tremendous blast effect. Distant explosions
shook the house and the old queer noise
was heard. I saw very many fortunes.
The fighter attacks were spectacular. The
sky looked as if it had been thrashed
with cat o' nine tails. Quite a
sight. Walked to Augustfehn —
Pleasant walk. Village long and

sleepy, but the natives would not part with their eggs. I must take drastic steps.

Lunch much too skimpy. A little meat fat, much cabbage — and too few spuds. Dinner worse. Only milk soup. Host poor devil Tony forgot to tell mine Host that we could not eat the muck. Went home and had an excellent supper of bread, butter, sausage, fried eggs, fried potatoes, and tea. The eggs were provided by our generous landlady — the best that I have struck for many years. After the raid, we were cut off again from the outside world. No Überspielung, either to or from and no courier. Blast him. I want my cigarettes. I am getting tired of Aspen — for I do need tobacco and alcohol — without them, my work is poor.

Margaret continues to be bad-tempered and most ungracious. She does not know how hurtful I find her attitude. However, it may make the awful separation a little easier. My thoughts of Dietze & Co. are most uncharitable. A week without drink

22

Hell, I'm in training for clink! It is a bastard! Get odds and ends - little U.S.W. from Bowlby & Heydebreck. Of course, no courier arrives. Quarrel with M. again & again. Poor solstice

20 March and 21 March

24th March. Well, the 23rd of March (23/24) (Saturday). did not prove to be devoid of significance. Today is one of Germany's blackest days in the war, great air activity all day. In the morning, 9.30 - 10, our shack was rattled and blasted by the battles, which we could see. Many formations of fortresses over us. Just before 10, see Schoberth, who tells me that the Yankees have crossed the Rhein at Oppenheim. In the afternoon comes the news of Wesel. Pop goes the weasel. We sha'n't be long now! Apparently the crossing was a success and is being reinforced by paratroops and airborne units. Churchill and Brooke at Montgomery's H.Q. Well! Well! If this move is not stopped, the war soon will be.

24 March and 25 March Joyce recorded what he described as two days of 'black news'. The air war continued over their heads, US forces crossed the Rhine at Oppenheim, and the British crossed the Wesel: as he put it 'Pop goes the weasel. We shan't be long now!' He also noted the death of David Lloyd George, the First World War British premier, and the crossing of the Rhine by Churchill.

Am furious, because after waiting
all these days for the courier, I
find that the confounded wretch
Guth has not sent my cigarettes,
nor has she said a word about them
in the Uberpruchung. She might at least
have sent a message — damn her. I
want very much to go back to
Berlin. As I write the enemy
planes are roaring about outside.
One seems now to be making for the
~~window!~~

— Today M. & I. walked to
Augustfen and back. The weather was
marvellous. Most of the people here
are wondering what will happen to
them. Perhaps I have the gravest
cause; but I feel quite serene,
not a bit worried. A life

25

24 March and 25 March Joyce also made periodic self-justifying claims about his idealistic attachment to Nazism and, curiously, to Britain. He admitted to his journal that he had never actually met Goebbels. In general the entries for these two days show Joyce resigned to his fate, although fighting on and complaining all the time. (KV 2/250/2)

without tobacco, alcohol, and moderately decent food has no interest for me. As for ideals, I respect them and intellectually support them. But enthusiasm! — well, I never could suffer fools gladly. 'Nuff said. The situation is so grave that I should hate to take it seriously. ..... Succobinism is a splendid doctrine; but if you ask me whether the Germans can capture the good-will of other nations and thus win them for the cause, I can only refer you to contemporary history. No — I am afraid that, against my will, I have become cynical. If I had been at F.H.Q. I could have

warned the old man against
most of his mistakes before he
made them. But I have not
even shaken hands with
Goebbels. This anomaly is known
as the "Führer-Prinzip" — God
save the mark!. If we lose this
war — the formula "Ja - mein
Führer!!!" is largely responsible.

Talk to Jerry H. and predict
that we shall get order to proceed to
Mergentheim : when we are cut off : then
we shall see.

_Arranging to send Margaret to Berlin for
a few days. I hope it is safe! I
shall be worried._

2 5ᵗʰ of March   Feast of Annunciation
(Sunday)   Churchill crosses Rhein and inspects
                    Wesel. No good news. Curious
proposal that Schörner should go to København. Why?
Am not being shown Marguelius report? to
Miss Hero - America. Did not go.
digging. I hate that way of spending

24 March and 25 March

a Sunday. Today I lay behind my
fox-belt. A pleasant refuge. Today
I have sad and haunting memories.
I yield nothing of my political opinions,
nor do I believe that I have acted
wrongly: but I hate the idea of dying
as England's enemy — or of being ~~despised~~
despised by those amongst whom I was
once regarded as an ardent patriot. A
damned nuisance.

        We can hear the noise of battle
now, all day and all night, growing
gradually clearer. Reported that
allied paratroops have landed near
Münster. We were wakened in night
by soldiers idiotically singing in the
moonlight. A silly C.O. Darmstadt
reported gone. Each day the
news is blacker. Well, well, it will
soon be over now. The west seems
to be crumbling. Arrange with Sch
for Margaret to go to Berlin on Tuesday.
        Schneider horrified to discover
that we have no false papers or currency.
Little does he know of official
ingratitude. He is decent.

29ᵗʰ March. — A healthy March
(Thursday) morning. Windy,
but not cold. Slightly misty. I am
writing now in the Apen arth wood,
which I have just found. Sitting on
a felled green tree trunk, thinking of
Margaret and the future. Piggy
is always uppermost in my thoughts.
I sent her a message this morning.
I do hope she has arrived in
Berlin, for tomorrow she should
set out on the return journey
I am counting the hours till

29 March With his wife Margaret in Berlin, Joyce spent the morning in a wood near Apen taking in the pleasures of nature. His journal entry for the day is filled with musings mainly written while in the wood. His comments about the lost war and his failure to meet or influence the 'old man' Goebbels, together with despair at being cast as a traitor in Britain, suggest that physical and nervous exhaustion were affecting him. He continued to worry about Margaret and her fate after the war, and usual blamed everyone and everything for the state of affairs Germany had fallen into: he also lamented the lack of alcohol and decent cigarettes. (KV 2/250/2)

Saturday. Fortunately she has Dietze to guide her. But even he cannot know everything, and there is

no doubt in my mind but that the general landslide has begun. What an ending to a grand enterprise.

I feel bitter because there was no need for this all-consuming tragedy. If only I had been near the old man, it would never have happened. The war would have been over 4 years ago. But the contemptible yes-men — the amateur psychologists, the portentous bunglers, and, above all, certain inherently German characteristics have lost it.

Those who wage a war without psychology are bound to lose it. I am worried for dear Peggy's sake — not for my own. I cannot bear to think of her suffering. However, we must be brave and trust in God, little as we have done to deserve His favour.

We are the victims of Hiartsia. For, sure as fate, England will have to fight Russia, and our principles will be vindicated in the end; but shall we

31

pursue to see their vindication. I still love England and hate to think that I am to be regarded as a traitor to her, which, in my own opinion, I am not. I am deeply sorry for Germany: but I can see how the whole ghastly situation has come about. Here amongst the dead leaves – with the gentle spring breeze blowing, as the sun fitfully struggles through the clouds, it is very peaceful: but for how long? I should like to be in the Grunewald this morning, or better still, in Richmond Park or walking down Buckingham Palace Road. Ah! well "Troja fuit, Troja est fuimus." I wish Margaret were with me. I have only the one great consolation that if she does not return, I need not live long. But I think she will come. Deep down, I am very hopeful – I do not know why. And I have no fear — only wonder. In any case,

before I could be of any real
use. I should need some months
of rest and proper food. When
I left Berlin, I was quite
exhausted. Gratitude? who
expects it? How! How!
Drew my Tages geld today.
Must now go back to lunch.

Had lunch and pleasant rest.

— Hear from Margaret in 2nd Überspielung,
she wants to stay till Saturday, as —
believe it or not, Friday is being
kept as a Holiday (Good Friday) in
Berlin. Can you beat it?
The R.R.G. has a Free Day!! No
cigarettes!!!! Well, from the viewpoint
of supplies, it would be better to let
her stay. I am very doubtful
about it — very. I ought to tell her to
leave tomorrow. But Dubin, bless his
soul is to ask Schweiter for alcohol
for me — and would like me to hear
the result. I suppose I shall have to
agree. But it is a long risk to
take. Apparently all is well with the mother
for the next fortnight. — Hik! Hik! We
shall see. Henk. promises a bottle! dear
old thing! Very difficult.

2 April and 3 April The return of Margaret with cigarettes and alcohol together with the appearance of decent food lifted Joyce out of his end of March depressed reverie. This entry begins: 'Continue our glorious drinking'. The madcap party mood continued into 3 April as the Third Reich crumbled around them. (KV 2/250/2)

~~West~~ and ~~Sth~~ and ~~South~~. I think the ~~East~~ ~~West~~ West more urgent. Nobody else does. It is now becoming clear that we must leave Open. Pity, I like the place very much. F.W. worried. Dützi tells us to keep control of our nerves as if that were necessary, but still remains secretive. Have wonderful birthday party with "Frau Krum" — a Dane — & Frau Brandt. The Dane and I see Frau Brunner home and the husband brandishes a bayonet at us. I fire off a round from my gun outside his house. Then back to fried eggs. Marvellous. It was a hellishly good party, with plenty of methyl Schnapps.

13 April By 13 April the Joyces had been moved from Apen to Hamburg. Lodged in the plush Atlantic Hotel they continued to broadcast and to dine well. The news of Roosevelt's death drew the comment 'Good, but it won't change the immediate military situation. Militarily the war is now lost'. (KV 2/250/2)

and a bottle of wine! Westy say the
Hamburgers see no sense in dying for a
lost cause. We shall see. This book
is nearing its end, and I wonder if there
will ever be any need for a second
volume.

OKW Bericht reports enemy at
Wittenberge on the railway line to Berlin.
Learn that at 8.25 Fernscheiber
and telephone stopped. Spoke to Dietze
this afternoon. Said he thought he had
"cut it fine". So do I, he expects to be
here tomorrow morning; but I
doubt if I shall see him then. We had
to work this afternoon under Bunker
conditions, but all went well. Fortunately
OKW Bericht arrived. Let Hansen go off to
Berlin. I wonder if he will ever come
back. Today's news has ceased to be
sensational. It is now merely catastrophic.
Rain on now. Am in our little dug-out
which is very practicable. Hear at

11 from BBC that the enemy are 20
miles from Oldenburg. I should think they
were nearer.

I am spending my money freely because
now it is only a matter of weeks, possibly
of days. The backbone of the German army
seems to be broken; and how the
forces will soon start again

44

We get home to Vierjahreszeiten and
find a bog bottle of delightful wine, which
we drink with appreciation. Then we
hear planes and a shot or two. M.
wonders what it is and sunsets. I think
it may be mosquitoes [...] the bombers [...]
I tell her to keep a firm hold on her
glass — and then the band played and the
balloon went up. I don't think I
have ever had so much to [...] in
my [...] before — certainly not in
an active state — Crash! Crash! crash!
But the culminating moment has a
wild thrill in it, like the [...]
peak of the crescendo in a great
piece of music. I looked after Margaret
and she was grateful. We lose part of
our vestibule wall, and of course most of
our windows — but otherwise all well.
Slept.

13 April

19 April to 22 April (part) Life in Hamburg continued. Joyce was still broadcasting live and recording his 'Views on the News', though the Bremen transmitter had gone off-air. The party air continued, as did the planning of the couples' escape. They visited the Hamburg Gestapo for fresh papers, there was talk of a U-boat evacuation, and Joyce pondered an escape to Ireland. Depression had set in again, and Joyce wondered, was it all worth it? (KV 2/250/2)

Me rings up and says she has
ordered wine. D. tells me that in
2 or 3 days we must be on the
move again! Towards H. Birthday is
going to be a problem. D. has little told;
Dosher wants to go home, D. goes further
oes frape writes us to have a Schnapps!
frölliches Wandertag food. Begin to feel
exhilaration. Much better. The others
getting worried.

———

20ª April (Friday)   Wake up early – 7 –
feeling unusually well – perhaps because
I smoked little. Anyhow still
exhilarated. Clock slow. expecty
to see D. at breakfast. We go to Gestapo
to get passports. Full alarm but no signs
of worry exant at Gestapo, where N.C.O. on
duty seems to be rattled. Cannot help
laughing at his bullying manner, when I
think that the Bolshel troops are about 5 miles
away – Quite plainly Hamburg is not
going to be defended. Evidently Kaufmann
cannot rely on his people. Well! Well!
We have some excellent gin with old
frappe. Cigarettes damned short.

48

19 April to 22 April (part)

Much gin and some talk, partly
related to flight from Eddy. At night
we have [?] bottle (!) of marvellous
wine sent up by 'Heinrich'! Pity it
could not be more! We hear the
shells falling on Harburg, but sleep
soundly for all that. D. was to
have gone today, but postponed.
Owing to the bloody old senators, did
not get V. or N. through still

23.30. D very anxiously. Neither he nor
v across was on duty. Quite a good day
Talk to S. about a U. boat
Get Schnaps from Busibar.

21st April (Saturday). So early to works to
write weekly review. Not much doing, weather
has changed. Back to lunch. M. gets
passes — but without visa. Dinner at
Stephensplatz. D. says good-bye at
Dinner Table. Seems very melancholy

Today the big news is the siege of
Berlin, into whose suburbs the Russians
have entered. Poor old Berlin! Goebbels
calls for a 'last ditch' defence. I am afraid
that Berlin will be rased to the ground. We
recover communication with area over
stade. Talk to Gadow re plans. He
seems pretty active, but don't know
how far he will go. Nearly quarrel with D.
over necessity of placating Eddie

22nd April.

Woke up thinking about Ireland and
wondering if escape is possible. In any case,
I shall be glad when this damned war is over.
No alcohol, no tobacco – not enough food – my
life is no better than penal servitude in
any case. How glad I shall be to get a
real rest from this mess and mental work,
even if only in the condemned cell. D
still hangs on here. I do not think he
wishes to go. I realize this morning so
clearly that, in the eyes of Englishmen, I
have forfeited all claim to live in
my land or to consider myself English. I
am very sorry; for I have now nothing
left. Long before Germany's defeat became certain,
I knew that I could never be at
home here. Hamburg is better than Berlin –
but still! Has it all been worth while?
I think not. National Socialism is a fine
cause, but most of the Germans, not all,
are bloody fools. Die haben's wirklich
versaut. My land means so much to me,
and I am old. Well, in that spirit, I
can take any punishment that is coming to me,
but I am sorry for Margret, whose outlook is
quite different. More quarrels with her
all day. At last Dietze goes. We have
our real last supper at ½ 8.
Much talk of submarines. J. too is very
worried. Say Hamburg has fallen!
Hear that Schwarzing and Intsche are
coming. Day of pouring rain

49

19 April to 22 April (part)

24 April to 2 May

This final collection of entries covers the last notebook pages and the period from Joyce's birthday on 24 April. The birthday entry recorded how colleagues spoke with Joyce about escape plans, but Joyce went to work and broadcast as usual. The following day he recounted the windfall acquisition of much-needed coffee, schnapps and cigars. The day after, Joyce received news concerning the siege of Berlin and speculated whether Adolf Hitler would go down in the fight. He remarked: 'I wonder! Sad, sad hours. We go home and drink Steinlager and think of our friends in Berlin'. On the following days Joyce mused over the rapidly advancing Allied armies, and wrote: 'Hamburg is next on the list'. His colleagues' naïve attitude towards the consequences of the impending surrender made him incredulous at the lack of insight as to their future: 'They think, poor dears, that they will be allowed to carry on as if nothing had happened'. On 30 April Joyce and his wife were entertained to a magnificent farewell lunch at which the alcohol flowed freely. During the evening they enjoyed a second dinner with Eddie [Schneider]. Joyce wrote: 'What a night – drink, drink, drink . . . I shed tears and left for the Funkhaus'. Very drunk, he made a recording for transmission that evening: it proved to be his final appearance at the microphone. He noted: 'Leave Hamburg between 3 and 4 in the morning'. His final entries record the death of Hitler and the transport chaos on the German–Danish border. The couple abandoned plans to escape through Denmark and returned to the German border town of Flensberg. The journal ended with comments about the release of not having to work. William Joyce was arrested by the British on 30 May 1945. (KV 2/250/2)

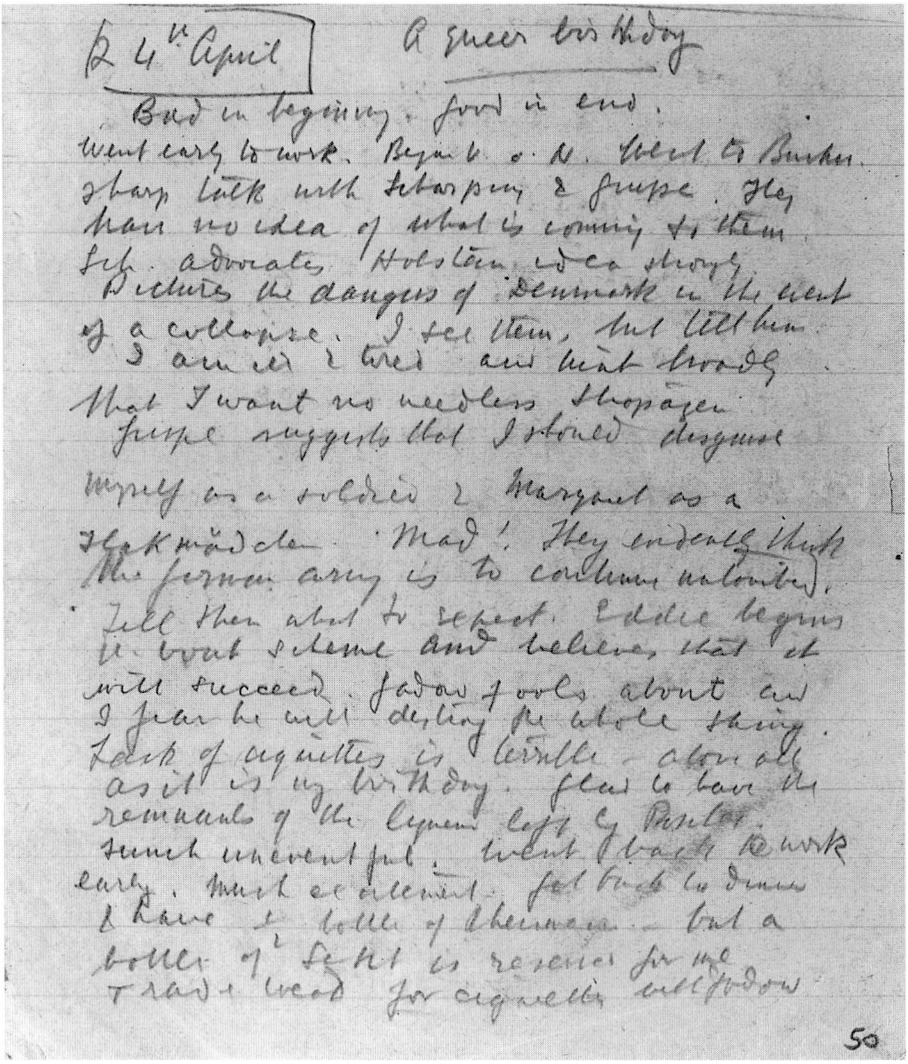
24th April   A queer birthday
Bad in beginning. Good in end.
Went early to work. Began [illegible]. Went to Bunker.
Sharp talk with [illegible] & [illegible]. They
have no idea of what is coming to them.
[illegible] advocates Holstein idea strongly
Pictures the dangers of Denmark in the event
of a collapse. I see them, but little [illegible]
I am ill & tired and [illegible] broadly
that I want no needless stoppages.
[illegible] suggests that I should disguise
myself as a soldier & Margaret as a
[illegible]mädchen. 'Mad'! They evidently think
the German army is to continue unbeaten.
Tell them what to expect. Eddie begins
the boat scheme and believes that it
will succeed. [illegible] fools about and
I fear he will destroy the whole thing.
Lack of cigarettes is terrible – above all
as it is my birthday. Glad to have the
remnants of the liqueur left by [illegible].
Lunch uneventful. Went back to work
early. Much excitement. Got back to dinner
& have ½ bottle of Rheinwein – but a
bottle of Sekt is reserved for me.
Trade bread for cigarettes will follow
50

24 April to 2 May

go to works – listen to news – return
with M. on beautiful moonlight evening.
The Alster looks marvellous.
Hear the seals and enjoy it greatly.
A little rain. Went to bed &
sleep well.

25th April.   Woke up feeling splendid.
Then had a cold bath. Took a
most agreeable walk down San Pauli
with Margaret. The dockside was
intensely and all work proceeds
as normal. Have not felt so well
for days. Drank beer in pub by
waterside. Lovely day. Jadow still
fooling about. Lunch peaceful. Went
off to Funk. Frl. Theiss gave me about
½ lb. coffee as present from Funpe.
Trade some of it to Jadow for cigarettes.
We may well need it soon. Eddie
comes along with the most magnificent present –
a bottle of Steinhäger. Hurrah! Later
in the day, I get two cigars. Ye gods!
Coffee, Schnapps & cigars all in one day.
Hip! Hip! Hooray! What a day!
Albrecht says there are just difficulties
over Division. There would be with
him – the silly old idiot. Super phone.
Banff & don't meanwhile feel tired
of the work. There is so little

material, and it is so bad that I cannot help feeling discouraged. Have let Eddie take the day off. Feel strain of waiting about nothing. Manage with trouble to get hold of a 23.30 figure to get a quilling from Bremen to show that Diddi has arrived in Apen or Norddeich. He knows a little too much. I think Bochow was right. Berlin surrounded. Last gap was between Zoo - Shenecke & Spandau. Selarpin & Vacum. Telephoned with Frutsch - who says - Kem Bernf mehr, nyr Panzerfaust. To judge by his spirit the Bolshevik are within a few hundred yards of the Reichskanzlei. Reports that A.H. will go down in the fight. I wonder! Sad, sad hours. We so home, drink Plentagen as think of our friend in Berlin. Discuss our plans, which are very nebulous. We have to depend on others.

Hark, in a way, I was in Berlin.

We wonder if Hamburg will be left to the Russians.

51

25th April/ Get up at 5.30, wakened
by artillery. Go & have a look round.
Rly Vaenen. Go back to bed and
sleep beautly. ——— find work in
26th April morning Olay Alster. See
Nabarro & Lt. Bird. Eddie has seen
many admirals. Have it all along
Must now enlist Vaenen & figure. Ellerbeck
Comes along with usual german "Nichts können
fuel. Thank Heaven. I am not at
all dependent on him. How hard it is
to get things done. But if I were a bloody
Kreisleiter — all would be well. Frankly
I am a bit tired of being treated as
an abstract phenomenon. Anybody else I
should at least have the cigarettes and
drink I require. Eddie has worked so
hard. I hope these people will not
disappoint him. I keep wavering at Herr B's
extraordinary statement of yesterday that I was
the main man and she the main woman.
Poor lad, how conceited some people are.
I have fresh plans now — but from it.
Reflect in evening on the complete
change in the relations between us and myself.
She does not know it, but she has quite lost her
hold on me, and once I have got her out and
safe, well — she can exercise her sex appeal
for what it is worth! I am sorry to be

better, but now that she is seriously useless,
it is possible for me to judge her character on its
merits. And it is not the sort of character that
suits me. She constantly over-bids her trumps
one day in Hamburg & then has been unhappy
mainly because she has developed all her worst
traits. However, if we do have to part, it will
be with less regret than formerly – which is, perhaps,
as well. Review news on the news at 22.30.

27th April

food week for Funktanis
(Paid back for first day for bottle
of Schnapps from Schürpiey) Feel well.
Pippo Guppi is to go to Plön.
work well. Have coffee with the
Hansen's
            Bremen falls. Hamburg is next
goal. But Russians also approaching! News
bad! Got cigarettes from Wachsom.
Drank excellent coffee at breakfast
grapes roasted! Short of butter now.
Met people from Königswusterhausen
work much easier. Fights in Berlin at
Bahnhof Heerstr! Fall of Bremen. Hamburg
named as next objective. Ha! Ha!
Fronts at Prenzlau and Rathenow! Gades
still submanning. Mussolini reported
captured Poldin arrested herewell! The
Mayor pieces on being taken. That doleful
hound Dittmar gives himself up
   food drink at hotel. Fine. Buy
fur jackets. Jan jorg.

52.

24 April to 2 May

28th April (Saturday)

An eventful day. Early to Funkhaus, to write Wochenschrift. Much trouble with Drüsen. Presumably the old ailment. Vaunen makes the intelligent suggestion that we get Swedish currency. Hope we do. Ullrich is buzzing about, and, of course, getting nowhere. I read O.K.W. Bericht. Germans on Elbe turn their backs on Americans and move eastwards to face the Russians. This is the bally limit. Reuters report Himmler with support of O.K.W. offers unconditional surrender to Western Allies but not to Russia and says the offer refused. Statement from I.O, downing street neither confirms nor denies, but stresses that any capitulation must be to all 3. Reuters allege that Hitler is not associated with the offer.

Dittmar, who has ratted, says that all will be over when Berlin falls, that the Southern Redoubt is a myth, and that the old man will either be killed or commit suicide. Goering, he says, may have been executed already. Always thought Dittmar was a Rat! Rimann has it that Goebbels has been killed. A few of us now care running the whole propaganda and information service in North Germany. The Gauleiter keeps ringing us up to ask

if we can tell him anything. Thanks to
the O.K.H. we are functioning well. It
is clear that Hamburg is next on
the list, and it may be a race between
the British and the Russians. But
the city will certainly surrender to the
British, if it can. I foresee no resistance
to Montgomery's troops. There is no sign
of any attempt to prepare a defence.
W. says: "Why should we? What good would it
do? We've had enough!" Well, I don't
blame them; but they have weird ideas
as to what will happen after the surrender.
They think, poor dears, that they will be
allowed to carry on, as if nothing had
happened. K. has been solemnly wondering
whether he should serve under the British.
Chance would be something! He's a good man,
but none of them can realize what is
coming to them! 'T is a pity.
D usw rings up from Apen. Thinks of transferring
the station to N. on Wednesday. Doubt if
he will have time. Looks as if A. and N.
should go simultaneously. We too, perhaps.
If the British cross the Elbe between here
and the sea, we may be dished! Nobody
seems to know where or what the
government is. Dittmar says that Brandhl,
Judenan & Rundstedt will probably offer
armistice on practically any terms.

53

a good dinner. Excellent steak. We
are enjoying all we can get now. The future
does not look promising. We have several plans,
but I doubt if any of them will work. However,
I am not worried, if I cannot dodge
the bill, I must pay it.

29th April (Monday) Up late. Long
breakfast. Cold, clammy, damp day. I
cannot feel dry. 100 guests in hotel — mostly
refugees, Hylda again for dinner.
Butter, worst, I bread for supper. Also
vaccine brings in a bottle of wine, food
slow! The hours are drawing in. The British
have crossed the Elbe near Lauenburg. The
Volkssturm have orders not to fight. We
can't be long now. Want my cigarettes on Wedn.
That ass Reinbeck has our passes, &
there are still no Divisey. 5 days &
nothing done. Padua annoys me very
much. That foul cissy Stewart Allman,
reads well just to the story of Mussolini's
body being spat upon in Milan. Ugh!
Filthy business. I have a cold.

Just 1 April 30th
went up to work. Gripe wants to see
us. We go to a marvellous lunch
with him and Scharping. A real
Deutsches Mahlzeit.

Ham & other meat. Schnapps & wine in plenty, cigarettes – everything. We dined at the Vier Jahreszeiten with Eddie & our driver. Kept & a special carafe. Paid up and enjoyed. No work in the evening. We soused with frisch. I was blind. By the way, we knocked down a number of the Germans. What a night – drunk. drunk. drunk – Jurgen was fine and so was Scharping. I shed tears as I left the Funkhaus. I fear I made a recording of an important speech. But what it was, Don't know. Well – perhaps it was best to finish thus. M. went with the car to the hotel and brought back baggage. All was ready & the driver waiting. Flirt with a girl I didn't know. Eddie Schneider came to the party and said good-bye to me. A good boy. ~~Then I~~ I read my last ~~talk~~ under the "influence" – Dietze rang up and M. said good-bye to him. I'm sure we shall meet again soon. Jurgen gave us a bottle of Aquavit & 1 of wine. Splendid. Leave Hamburg between 3 and 4 in the morning.

54

24 April to 2 May

May 1st Tuesday

On this tragic day, the death of Adolf Hitler was reported. Admiral Dönitz takes over as his nominated successor.

Reach Flensburg about 8. Have to drink wine for breakfast – as nothing else is available. see Finch ourselves would serious.

May 1 (Tuesday) 2nd day,

Here on the Danish border. Sunny. We have a good _____ pea field – we pass the border. Reach Apenrade about 3. Received by _____ of Haensch. No trains whatever! Eat at Deutsches Haus – Plenty of food – excellent – but too little to drink. Put up at Thorwald Petersen's. Simple plain room – but beds are good. Tired out so to bed at about 8.30.

We have no Lebensmittel Karten, but don't really need them. Feel lonely – though Margret is splendid. Think we shall have to go back. Bad reception in Both Danmark.

Wed (May 2nd)

Woke early on hear soldiers saying that the "Führer ist gefallen" and "der Admiral Dönitz hat übernommen." Eat our own stuff. Breakfast in hotel. See others drinking Schapps — but get none. Go to Haensch — who was unprepared for us and almost distracted with work. Asks us to come back tomorrow at 5. He cannot communicate with Berg. Two trains of 2 000 people have been stranded for 3 days. Doesn't he know if they are being fed. Apparently a complete muddle. However, we want to rest for a few days. If the Kronen don't come — we shall have to go back. — it is a difficult position — but we must face it. We went for a ... up the hill. Saw ... about ...

... coffee ... marvellous cake afterwards. Rested in afternoon or then met Riddle — who took us to his pals and gave us Schapps. I gave them cigarettes. We get a German paper & read the news. I miss the wireless very much indeed. This day of complete idleness seems unnatural. Perhaps it is well — for a change! but I feel I cannot stand it long. Well — we'll see. The more I rested — the more I am inclined to go back to Germany.

Further Reading

C. E. Bechhofer-Roberts (eds.), *The Trial of W. Joyce: Old Bailey Trial Series 5* (London, 1946).

Horst J. P. Bergmeier and Rainer E. Lotz, *Hitler's Airwaves: The Inside Story of Nazi Radio Broadcasting and Propaganda Swing* (New Haven and London, 1997).

Asa Briggs, *The History of Broadcasting in the United Kingdom,*
Volume I, *The Birth of Broadcasting* (London, 1961).
Volume II, *The Golden Age of Broadcasting* (London, 1965).
Volume III, *The War of Words* (London, 1969).

J. A. Cole, *Lord Haw-Haw and William Joyce: The Full Story* (London, 1964).

David Curry, *A History of the Security Service: 1909–1945* (London, 1998).

M. Doherty, 'Black Propaganda by Radio: the German Concordia Broadcasts to Britain 1940–1941', *Historical Journal of Film, Radio and Television*, Volume 14(2), 1994, pp. 167–97.

J. W. Hall (ed.), *Trial of W. Joyce* (London, 1946).

William Joyce, *Twilight Over England* (Berlin, 1940. Republished London, 1992).

Francis Selwyn, *Hitler's Englishmen: The Crime of Lord Haw Haw* (London, 1987).

Adrian Weale, *Renegades: Hitler's Englishmen* (London, 1987).

Rebecca West, *The Meaning of Treason* (London, 1949).

W. J. West, *Truth Betrayed* (London, 1987).

Index

Page references for documents and other illustrations are set in italic.